WITHDRAWN

The Economics of Conspicuous Consumption

To my parents and to
Marnie, Sarah and Christopher

The Economics of Conspicuous Consumption

Theory and Thought since 1700

Roger Mason

Professor of Consumer Theory, University of Salford, UK

Edward Elgar
Cheltenham, UK • Northampton, MA, USA

Published by
Edward Elgar Publishing Limited
8 Lansdown Place
Cheltenham
Glos GL50 2HU
UK

Edward Elgar Publishing, Inc.
6 Market Street
Northampton
Massachusetts 01060
USA

HB
801
.M328
1998
Sept-1999

A catalogue record for this book
is available from the British Library

Library of Congress Cataloguing in Publication Data
Mason, Roger, 1940–
        The economics of conspicuous consumption : theory and thought
    since 1700 / Roger Mason.
        1. Consumption (Economics)—History. I. Title.
    HB801.M328 1998
    339.4'7—dc21
                                                                      97-52042
                                                                           CIP

ISBN 1 85898 833 0

Printed and bound in Great Britain by Bookcraft (Bath) Ltd

Contents

Introduction

Today, considerations of status and prestige influence many decisions to buy. The modern pursuit of personal identity and style through consumption is now widely recognised and is actively encouraged by manufacturers, retailers and advertising agencies who promote many goods and services not only for their value in use but, often more effectively, for their social value as status symbols. Consuming for status has, in fact, become a defining element of the new consumer societies.

While conspicuous consumption is now commonplace, it is no recent phenomenon. Preoccupations with status-directed consumption on the part of the rich and powerful are found in the earliest societies, and the extravagances and excesses of ruling elites have been well documented. At the same time, these rulers feared the social and political consequences of allowing others to conspicuously consume for status and efforts were often made to suppress any tendencies towards ostentatious display in those whose rank was not seen to merit such behaviour. At the time of the Roman Empire, the authorities became so concerned about the level of ostentatious consumption that sumptuary laws were introduced to suppress it. Similar laws were in force throughout medieval and early modern Europe and in the later feudal economies of China and Japan.

European sumptuary legislation peaked in the seventeenth century but fell away sharply thereafter as social, economic and political realities changed. In effect, legislation had never been successful – it was always difficult to enforce and did little in real terms to suppress status-motivated consumption. A legislative record extending over several hundred years, however, bears witness to the fact that the existence and the significance of conspicuous consumption was widely recognised, and that those enjoying political and economic power were determined to preserve their exclusive rights to indulge in such ostentatious display.

By 1700, attempts in Europe to control conspicuous consumption by law had been largely abandoned, for by then a newly prosperous merchant class was insisting on a wider distribution of wealth and privilege and was prepared to use their economic strength to bring about change. At the same time, political economists were beginning to question the value of restricting luxury consumption and expenditure, arguing instead that any productive manufacturing activity, supplying whatever needs, added to a nation's economic and commercial strength. As the first consumer societies began to emerge, conspicuous consumption was increasingly tolerated and later encouraged by the commercial interest at all social and economic levels. In this sense, modern day status consumption, available to all, has its origins in the late seventeenth and early eighteenth centuries.

The growing importance of conspicuous consumption could have been expected to generate a new and necessary interest in the phenomenon on the part of economists who had traditionally taken a very limited view of such behaviour as an indulgence of the rich and privileged, a sometimes distasteful yet understandable expression of social, economic and political power. Any tendencies towards ostentatious consumption by the 'less deserving' in society were frequently attacked on moral and religious grounds, but the nature of such consumption, with few exceptions, was not explored in any detail. This neglect continued at a time when conspicuous, status-motivated expenditures were increasing exponentially in all social and economic groups, particularly in the period after 1850 when mass markets for consumer goods were being rapidly established in Europe and the United States.

The reluctance of economists generally to explore the nature and consequences of conspicuous consumption is not difficult to understand. First, the phenomenon was, for many years, considered to be so trivial in overall macroeconomic terms that, as the contemporary literature shows, it was not seen to merit any serious discussion or analysis. Implicit in this view was the belief that, for the most part, conspicuous consumers represented a small, affluent and often self-indulgent minority, and that consuming for status would not be seen, or tolerated, as a necessary activity by right-minded people within the wider community. Others outside economics protested that the use of consumption to secure and enhance status, far from being the concern only of a small privileged group, was a central preoccupation of people at all social and economic levels, and while a few, more heterodox, economists shared this belief, they were often branded, pejoratively, as 'sociologists' by their contemporaries and their arguments either ignored or pushed to the margins of debate.

A second reason for economists' discomfort with conspicuous consumption was that it generated a demand for goods and services which was motivated by social considerations of status and prestige rather than by any classical or neoclassical notions of value and utility. To many economists, then and now, any social motives underpinning consumer choice are the proper business of other behavioural scientists; such motives could, perhaps, inform economic debate, but it was on outcomes rather than on any social processes determining these outcomes that the economist had to focus. While the argument of economists that social theorising is best left to others can be sensibly defended, however, it is not then legitimate to ignore or discount purely economic effects on demand which are subsequently identified by others but which are social in origin. In reality, the degree to which social issues and the sociology of consumption have, over time, 'informed economic debate' on consumer preference formation has been trivial and has made no significant contribution towards integrating the social and economic dimensions of consumer demand within economic theory.

Finally, the neglect of conspicuous consumption within economics has resulted from the persistent attempts by the discipline to secure recognition as an exact science, capable of providing precise economic systems, models and measurements. As a form of status-inspired consumption which, by its very nature, can appear to be both economically 'irrational' and socially complex, conspicuous consumption does not easily lend itself either to quantification or to mathematical precision. Although economists do not deny that such behaviour exists, it has, for the most part, been either marginalised (often as a footnote) or entirely ignored in describing and modelling the nature of consumer demand. Socially-motivated consumption and econometric analysis, by their very nature, still sit uneasily apart.

The reluctance of economists to address the issue would not be important if the consequences of conspicuous economic display could be safely ignored, but the nature and true extent of status-led consumption is such that its neglect, over time, has called many economic assumptions, and much economic analysis, into serious question. At the theoretical level, for example, a basic tenet of neoclassical demand theory and of much subsequent economic reasoning was that individual preference formation was independent of the opinions or preferences of others. On this assumption, conspicuous consumption could then be properly included within a catch-all 'tastes and preferences' variable which, in part, was seen to determine individual choice and which allowed for variations in demand between individuals. Aggregate demand could then be cardinally measured by summing these independent, individual demand schedules In reality, conspicuous consumption cannot be so easily accommodated for it is the tastes and preferences *of others* which play such a large part in deciding the purchases and consumption of any status-seeking consumer. Given these interdependent preferences, any notions of demand 'additivity' in markets where consumer considerations of status and prestige were important were plainly not valid: aggregate demand could not be calculated by simple summation, nor could it be disaggregated into its component parts. In truth, neoclassicists were well aware of these shortcomings in consumer theory but chose to ignore them and to retain the additive utility function in order to make possible the cardinal measurement of utility.

Later, when neoclassical doctrines were challenged, and when analysis moved from cardinal to ordinal measurement, these preoccupations with additivity were effectively ended. However, the new consumer theories which were developed between 1930 and 1960 were highly mathematical and made a virtue out of the fact that what little 'psychology' there had been in marginal utility theory had now been removed. Conspicuous consumption, with its emphasis on interpersonal effects and interdependent preference formation, continued to be neglected at a time when consumers themselves were becoming more and more preoccupied with image, status and prestige. And while some greater interest has necessarily been given to socially-derived consumption in more recent years, the subject still lacks recognition and gravitas within the economics mainstream; much economic theory still succeeds in circumventing the 'nuisance' of trying to explain and accommodate interpersonal effects on demand.

Away from theory, the long-standing failure to explore the nature and extent of consumption motivated by considerations of social status and prestige has also weakened much market analysis and demand forecasting. It is still easy (and often suspiciously convenient) to assert that status goods are relatively small in number, always expensive, purchased only by the rich and wanted exclusively for reasons of social prestige. The reality is that consumer goods of all types are today purchased not only for their practical use but also because of a real or imagined status which 'visible consumption' subsequently bestows on the buyer. This is as true of food, drink and washing machines as it is of fashion clothes, furniture and automobiles. Certainly, the significance of the status component of demand can and does vary within and across product categories, but it is rarely so insignificant that it can be entirely ignored, and often so significant that its exclusion from demand analysis makes subsequent interpretations of market behaviour either meaningless or, at best, inaccurate.

This unwillingness to address consumer preoccupations with symbolism, status and prestige has, in fact, not only weakened macroeconomic analysis and forecasting, but, at a more commercial level, has led to tensions between economists and a business community which, while professing no interest in theoretical issues, has always recognised and exploited the sales and profits potential of status-seeking consumer behaviour and has played no little part in encouraging and institutionalising all forms of conspicuous consumption. As early as the 1920s and 1930s, business leaders, already working closely with psychologists and others to improve the advertising and retailing of status-linked consumer goods and services, voiced their concerns that, while other disciplines were contributing substantially to a better understanding of socially-motivated consumer demand, economists seemed remote from the process and showed no great wish to become involved. Certainly, issues of commercial 'demand management' have never appealed to conventional economists, and there has been little enthusiasm to move in this direction, particularly with regard to what is often seen as the exploitation of seemingly 'irrational' consumer preoccupations with status and prestige. These tensions between economists and business practitioners persist to this day and explain, in part, the continuing reluctance of many academics to explore the economics of conspicuous consumption in greater detail.

Finally, the lack of recognition that external social effects can and do significantly influence consumer demand has had consequences at the level of economic policy and policy making, for without due consideration of those consumer motives which, though largely social in origin, nevertheless affect patterns of demand and decisions to buy, macroeconomic demand management, particularly in relation to pricing, taxation and tariff policies, becomes more uncertain and can, at the extreme, produce unintended distortions of supply and demand which can themselves have far-reaching consequences. For the most part, however, macroeconomic policy making has paid little serious attention to status-motivated consumption – an understandable omission, perhaps, given the lack of theoretical treatment of a difficult subject and the largely mathematical priorities of much conventional economic analysis.

With the exception of welfare economics, where issues of perceived relative deprivation have been explored in some depth, the neglect of interpersonal comparisons and interdependent preferences in consumption theory is, in one sense, puzzling, for economists have always recognised and acknowledged that considerations of social standing and prestige play a part in deciding patterns of consumption under certain market conditions. For the most part, however, they have always resisted appeals to integrate what has been described (or dismissed) as 'the sociology of consumption' into mainstream economic theory. Persistent attempts by more heterodox economists over many years to broaden the treatment of consumer theory have been largely unsuccessful, but there is now some evidence that modern-day concerns with image, identity and status and the clear links which are now established between these social aspirations and consumption are beginning to generate a greater interest in the subject and some reconsideration of consumer theory within economics.

The following pages look at the development of conspicuous consumption from its origins as the indulgence of a privileged few to its position today as a major determinant of consumer demand in mass consumption societies. They chart also the attempts of economists to come to terms with a form of consumer behaviour which increasingly could no longer be dismissed as trivial but with which they felt instinctively uneasy. Above all, perhaps, they highlight the conflicts and tensions which have beset economics in seeking to accommodate a 'problem' which has refused to go away.

1   The New Consumer Society

Economic writers of the seventeenth century saw a clear connection between thrift and prosperity. To the Mercantilists, who had dominated economic thought since 1500, high levels of savings, properly invested in domestic and international trade, secured future wealth and economic progress. Production, not consumption, lay at the heart of Mercantilist belief and was seen to advance a nation's wealth at the expense of others. Only by forgoing consumption at home could international competitive advantage be secured.

Just as saving and investment were considered central to economic success and national prosperity, any tendency towards unproductive, luxury consumption on the part of the developing merchant classes was roundly condemned. Such condemnation contained elements of hypocrisy, for the Mercantilists were well aware that ruling élites and privileged social groups had indulged for centuries in what were often outrageous levels of ostentatious economic display and conspicuous waste, yet such behaviour had, for the most part, been tacitly or explicitly condoned. The conspicuous consumption of European aristocracies in the early modern period had been tolerated and understood as a necessary part of the marriage between ascribed status and economic power. However, this tolerance was afforded only to the few. Luxury consumption on the part of merchants and traders had, in contrast, always been condemned as an unnecessary and harmful indulgence which worked against national interests. The Mercantilists now echoed these sentiments, arguing that personal indulgence could not be reconciled with future economic success.

Mercantilist warnings against the evils of luxury expenditure were never really effective, and levels of conspicuous consumption soon began to rise significantly. In England, by 1540, the streets of central London 'had been turned into a Carnaby Street of the sixteenth century' as money circulated more freely and generated demand for (mostly imported) luxury goods (Thirsk, 1978). And as fashions arrived in London and were taken up by Londoners, so they subsequently spread to the provinces, creating a demand for emulative consumption throughout the economy.

These increasing propensities to conspicuously consume were condemned by the Mercantilists, who continued to argue that such frivolous consumption could only direct money away from investment and production and so ultimately weaken the nation-state both domestically and internationally. They emphasised again that high levels of personal consumption and sustainable economic development were incompatible, and that it was the duty of the business community to meet its responsibilities to the state by controlling any tendency to profit from conspicuous consumption. For their part, individuals were expected to show constraint and to moderate purchases of superficial luxuries. However, such exhortations went largely unheeded and the markets for fashion and luxury goods continued to prosper.

These tensions between market realities and Mercantilist thought were to persist through the sixteenth and seventeenth centuries. By 1690, however, the Mercantilist emphasis on thrift and austerity began to be questioned for the first time by other political economists. First, 'the economic advantages of competition, envy, emulation, vanity and fashion' were more and more explicitly stated, for it was now becoming evident that the experience of countries which suppressed luxury consumption did not support any link between thrift and prosperity (McKendrick, Brewer and Plumb, 1982). Sir Dudley North observed in 1691:

> Countries which have sumptuary Laws, are generally poor; for when Men by those Laws are confin'd to narrow Expence than otherwise they would be, they are at the same time discouraged from the Industry and Ingenuity which they would have imployed in obtaining wherewithal to support them, in the full latitude of Expence they desire (1691: 14–15).

Too great an emphasis on saving, argued North, had the effect of withdrawing money from circulation and so caused unemployment. Far from suppressing luxury consumption among the rich, the State should allow and even encourage it as a means of increasing the circulation of money and the general prosperity of the community at large.

Doubts as to the desirability of frugality in economic affairs were being raised by others (Barbon, 1690; Locke, 1692), but criticism tended to be piecemeal and disjointed. At the turn of the century, however, a reasoned and highly controversial defence of luxury and of luxury consumption was published in London, and was to provoke a much wider economic debate.

Bernard Mandeville, born de Mandeville, was a Dutch émigré who had settled in London in the 1690s. He studied medicine at the University of Leiden before moving to England where, in 1705, he published a poem *The Grumbling Hive: or, Knaves Turn'd Honest*. In 1714, the poem reappeared in a book *The Fable of the Bees: or, Private Vices, Publick Benefits*, together with a prose commentary, *An Enquiry into the Origin of Moral Virtue*, and some twenty *Remarks* relating to the poem.

The book attracted immediate attention. In essence, it proposed a theory of the division of labour, argued for laissez-faire economic organisation (an argument which was to have a significant influence on Adam Smith later in the century) and offered a passionate defence of luxury consumption. The defence of luxury was both well argued and convincing, for Mandeville was able to draw on personal observation in constructing his case – observations made not in London but in his native Holland, where Mercantilist arguments in favour of frugality in consumption had effectively failed. To understand why, it is necessary to look in some detail at developments in the Dutch Republic at that time.

The economic success of The Netherlands during the seventeenth century produced what has been referred to as a Golden Age. Prosperity was based initially on productive efficiency, later on commerce and trade. It had become a world empire in two generations and its power extended across the globe. And 'all that power and stupendous wealth was, in the end, sucked into the cramped space between the Scheldt and the Ems' (Schama, 1987).

Mercantilist doctrine attributed the Dutch success to hard work and to conservative economic behaviour. Calvinist religious beliefs reinforced the view that modest habits underpinned prosperity, and church leaders liked to claim that the Dutch had been rewarded for rejecting conspicuous consumption in all its forms. The reality, however, was that the merchant class, far from submitting to the teachings of the Church, were prodigious spenders and had indulged a taste for luxury consumption and ostentatious display not seen elsewhere in Europe. Moreover, this propensity to consume luxury goods and services had coexisted happily with continuing prosperity in commerce and trade.

In *The Fable of the Bees*, Mandeville set out to expose the myth that austerity was a prerequisite of economic success, and was able to use the Dutch experience to great effect. In particular, he argued, conspicuous consumption was not confined to the ruling élites of more traditional societies (a well-documented phenomenon) but could be observed wherever a successful merchant class competed for social recognition and position in a 'modern', more egalitarian society:

> In other Countries you may meet with stately Courts and Palaces of great Extent that belong to Princes, which no body can expect in a Commonwealth, where so much equality is observ'd as there is in this; but in all Europe you shall find no private Buildings so sumptuously magnificent, as a great many of the Merchants and other Gentlemen's Houses are in Amsterdam, and some other Cities of that small Province; and the generality of those that build there, lay out a greater proportion of their Estates on the Houses they dwell in than any People upon the Earth (1714, I: 188–9).

There could be no doubting the levels of luxury consumption indulged in by those Dutch merchants who had profited from the Golden Age. Some chose to move away from the major cities and were building elegant country mansions as early as 1630. Others invested in elegant villas and houses closer to town which sprang up 'in dense and elegant competition'. And in

Amsterdam, where consumption was taken to greatest excess, sumptuous canal houses appeared, furnished and decorated to the highest standards.

Property, then, was used to demonstrate material wealth and those with money vied with each other to build and furnish the most distinctive and expensive homes. These expenditures were made not only for utilitarian purposes but also, without question, for ostentatious display; success or otherwise was measured in part in terms of the impact on others, that is, by the extent to which others were impressed with the wealth and taste displayed. Consumption was, therefore, driven by interpersonal effects as well as by utilitarian considerations, and the more conspicuously wasteful the expenditure, then the greater the 'external effects' became.

Mandeville claimed that the Dutch merchant classes were conspicuous consumers on a grand scale, and that this consumption was competitive and intended to impress others through the ostentatious display of wealth. As Schama points out, 'in matters of grandiose conspicuous waste, Amsterdam needed no tuition from aristocracies', and it is true that a part of the ostentatious display was to 'rub home the lesson of the new parity' as well as to impress fellow merchants. Mandeville went further, arguing, as Veblen was to do nearly two hundred years later, that conspicuous consumption was not the preserve of the very rich but could be found at all levels of society.

Society, Mandeville argued, judged individuals by their possessions, and, more particularly, by those possessions which were socially visible. For the very rich, the ostentatious display of wealth through land, property, conspicuous leisure and conspicuous waste, was easily available, while those less fortunate had to look to alternative, less demanding, ways of achieving status in the eyes of others. Nonetheless, to Mandeville, the propensity to conspicuously consume at all levels of society was not in doubt. Identification with, and emulation of, the consumption of higher social and economic groups could be observed right across the spectrum. Clothes, in particular, lent themselves to ostentatious display:

> The Druggist, Mercer, Draper and other creditable Shopkeepers can find no difference between themselves and Merchants, and therefore dress and live like them. The Merchant's Lady, who cannot bear the Assurance of those Mechanicks, flies for refuge to the other End of Town, and scorns to follow any Fashion but what she takes from thence. This Haughtiness alarms the Court, the Women of Quality are frightened to see Merchants Wives and Daughters dress'd like themselves: this Impudence of the City, they cry, is intolerable; Mantua-makers are sent for, and the contrivance of Fashions becomes all their Study, that they may have always new Modes ready to take up, as soon as those saucy Cits. shall begin to imitate those in being (1714: 129).

This wish of people to be judged 'not as what they are, but what they appear to be' extended across the social spectrum, and the need for respect and acceptance, argued Mandeville, was so strong that it often encouraged the very poor to go without food in order to be 'properly' dressed. These external effects on consumption, therefore, had a significant influence at all social and economic levels. And they were in no way limited to fashion, but could be observed in consumer behaviour towards many other goods and services where social visibility was high.

In Mandeville's view, this pursuit of luxury and status, long condemned by moralists and theologians, had to be seen as positive. Emulation encouraged people to work harder, and could be harnessed as a means to greater productivity and wealth. The belief that luxury corrupted a people and wasted resources was, in reality, economically dangerous. On the contrary, it was not only inseparable from great states, but necessary to make them great.

Mandeville's defence of luxury was timely, for it was becoming increasingly obvious that, as trade and commerce increased in the later seventeenth century, so wealth and luxury were companions. Until Mandeville, however, the contradiction between the pursuit of wealth and the condemnation of vanity and the luxury it engendered remained:

> Mandeville gained his effect by consciousness of a contradiction in current opinion which had escaped his contemporaries. And by playing on this contradiction, by confronting, in his usual manner, the ideal with the actual, he secured a greater effect on his contemporaries than the modern reader may suspect. Since to Mandeville's public, luxury was morally evil, when Mandeville demonstrated that it was inseparable from flourishing states, he was not only challenging orthodox economic theory, but forcibly achieving once more the moral paradox of *Private Vices, Publick Benefits* (Kaye, 1924, I: xcviii).

Mandeville's defence of luxury gave meaning and legitimacy to seventeenth century luxury consumption. More important for economic theory, however, was his argument that such consumption could be seen at all social and economic levels and could profitably be encouraged. While a few earlier detractors from Mercantilist theory had sometimes argued for greater luxury consumption, they had assumed that such consumer behaviour was the reserve and preserve of the very rich; in essence, they argued for luxury consumption among the newly-rich merchant classes in order that others could benefit from the 'trickle down' employment effects of such ostentatious economic display. In France, greater consumption of French silk by the rich was encouraged on the grounds that such demand created work for the poor. Similarly, in England, expenditure on 'entertainments, magnificent shews and triumphal arches' was seen as a means of putting money into the pockets of brewers, bakers and tailors (Petty, 1662). Mandeville went further by showing that perceptions of luxury and status were relative concepts, and that, while absolute and relative wealth always acted as constraints on consumption, the Dutch experience showed that individuals, Calvinist doctrine notwithstanding, could and did conspicuously consume within these constraints. In so doing, they generated demand for a wide range of goods and services which worked to the benefit of all.

Mandeville attempted to drive luxury consumption and conspicuous economic display into the mainstream of economic thought by arguing that it could no longer be dismissed as an indulgence only of the very rich but had to be considered a significant factor in determining the economic behaviour of all consumers and in promoting national prosperity. In the event, it did not generate any immediate revision of consumer theory and the influence of interpersonal effects on consumption was for the most part ignored. Indeed, so violently did some within the economic (and clerical) establishment react to his work that *The Fable of The Bees* was declared 'a public nuisance' by a grand jury in Middlesex in 1723. As Keynes (1936) later observed:

> No wonder that such wicked sentiments called down the opprobrium of two centuries of moralists and economists who felt much more virtuous in possession of their austere doctrine that no sound remedy was discoverable except in the utmost of thrift and economy both by the individual and the state (1936: 362).

Mandeville's work, then, was more criticised than acclaimed, not least because it was seen as an attack on contemporary moral and economic doctrine. At the beginning of the eighteenth century, such views were not acceptable, for any move to encourage the acquisitive instincts of all social classes still posed too great a threat to the overall class system. Any formal approval of emulation would have suggested that class distinctions were based on little more than purchasing power; and it would also have legitimised an ethic of consumption based on little more than a calculating hedonism (Appleby, 1978).

Pressures to protect existing values and social structures led some to concede that Mandeville's observations concerning the incidence of conspicuous consumption and luxury expenditure were well-founded, yet at the same time to reject his argument that such activity, regardless of circumstance or personal motives, was a force for good which could be encouraged at all social levels. Hume (1739) agreed with Mandeville that the rich, by living well and ostentatiously, conferred benefits on the poor, but he saw the motives for such behaviour as being those of pride in ownership and possession. Interpersonal effects were acknowledged, but, unlike Mandeville, Hume believed that, among the rich, these effects were unsought and secondary rather than the primary motive for consumption. Morally, pride in ownership was at the heart of such 'innocent display' and luxury consumption. In contrast, when excessive display was intended only to indulge personal vanity it was to be condemned:

> Wherein, then, consists Vanity, which is so justly regarded as a fault or imperfection? It seems to consist chiefly in such an intemperate display of our advantages, honours and accomplishments; in such an importunate and open demand of praise and admiration, as is offensive to others. It is besides a sure symptom of the want of true dignity and elevation of mind, which is so great an ornament in any character (1751: 265–6).

Hume drew a clear distinction, therefore, between innocent and vicious luxury, the latter being defined as that consumption which 'engrosses all a man's expence, and leaves no ability for such acts of duty and generosity as are required by his situation and fortune'. Such vicious luxury was morally wrong, and Mandeville's view that moral arguments against such behaviour could be safely ignored was directly challenged:

> Is it not very inconsistent for an author to assert in one page that moral distinctions are inventions of politicians for public interest; and in the next page maintain, that vice is advantageous to the public? And indeed it seems upon any system of morality, little less than a contradiction in terms, to talk of a vice, which is in general beneficial to society (1752: 31).

Hume was not alone in holding to the view that human vices could never be considered beneficial to social and economic development, and through the mid-eighteenth century, Mandeville's views were generally thought, in England at least, to be ill-considered and mischievous. This was not the case, however, in France, where the Physiocrats were taking a far more pragmatic view of luxury consumption. Any income needed to be immediately recirculated to ensure economic growth, and the nature of this recirculation was of no real consequence. Far from condemning ostentation, Coyer (1756) believed that the nobility needed to increase their luxury expenditure and consumption in order to sustain production at high levels, while Mirabeau (1763), Butel-Dumont (1771), Condillac (1789) and others predicted national ruin if such 'productive' spending was halted. To the Physiocrats, the connection between consumption and the circulation of money and wealth was central to prosperous economic activity, and philosophical debates as to whether certain forms of consumption were ethically acceptable played little or no part in their considerations. This view was predictable, for France was a leading manufacturer of luxury products, and had actively encouraged investment in such goods since the days of Louis XIV and his Finance Minister, Jean-Baptiste Colbert (1619–1683). To have moved against luxury expenditure would have had serious consequences for the French economy in general, a fact of which French economists were only too aware.

While consumer spending was encouraged, the Physiocrats, through the work of Quesnay and Turgot, were essentially economic system builders. It was at this time, also, that the ground work was being laid for the classical period of economics most closely associated with Adam Smith. Smith himself had a more sympathetic interest in the economics of consumption than many of his counterparts in Britain, and models of economic growth were now beginning to emerge which recognised the importance of the propensity to consume to economic development and prosperity. The concept of the elasticity of demand and its relation to productive activity was looked at in far greater detail. Smith put consumption at the centre of his own work, arguing, famously, that consumption was 'the sole end and purpose of all production, and the interest of the producer ought to be attended to, only so far as it may be necessary for promoting that of the consumer'. At the same time, his attitude to the rights and wrongs of luxury consumption was ambivalent.

In *The Theory of Moral Sentiments*, published in 1759, Smith had attacked Mandeville's defence of luxury, arguing that his persuasive skills had wrongly convinced readers of an association between private vices and public benefits:

> Though the notions of this author [Mandeville] are in almost every respect erroneous, there are, however, some appearances in human nature, which, when viewed in a certain manner, seem at first sight to favour them. These, described and exaggerated by the lively and humorous, though coarse and rustic eloquence of Dr. Mandeville, have thrown upon his doctrines an air of truth and probability which is very apt to impose upon the unskilful (1759: 308).

While Smith was hostile to Mandeville's views of vice, consumption and the public good, he recognised that vanity could have a significant effect on consumption by encouraging high levels of ostentatious display which could not be justified. The vain man, argued Smith:

> sees the respect which is paid to rank and fortune, and wishes to usurp this respect, as well as that for talent and virtues. His dress, his equipage, his way of living, accordingly, all announce both a higher rank and a greater fortune than really belong to him (1759: 256).

Vanity, argued Smith, produced an obsessive desire for the esteem and admiration of others and encouraged unnecessary levels of ostentation in an effort to secure this esteem. In this sense, he conceded that Mandeville's 'private vices' were observable; at the same time, he rejected any further extension of the argument which suggested that this conspicuous consumption could and did work for the public good.

To Smith, those vain enough to want to emulate their betters were never rewarded for 'they assume the equipage and splendid way of living of his superiors, without considering that whatever may be praise-worthy in any of these, derives its whole merit and propriety from its suitableness to that situation and fortune which both require and can easily support the expense'. Those of real social status, the rich and the great, could legitimately conspicuously consume as a statement of their social and economic superiority; and while vanity might induce men of lower social status to imitate such behaviour, it could not be sustained nor would it be rewarded.

Although condemning all conspicuous consumption motivated only by ambition and envy, Smith accepted also that the opinion of others could, in certain circumstances, weigh more heavily than utility on consumption and consumer behaviour – circumstances closely associated with social respect and standing. Concern for the opinion of others was something more than vanity, and could be seen as a necessary consideration at all social and economic levels. In *The Wealth of Nations* (1776), he argued that the possession of certain commodities 'renders it indecent for creditable people, even of the lowest order, to be without', and these goods could be considered to be the necessaries rather than the luxuries of life. Labourers 'would be ashamed to appear in public without a linen shirt' and the ownership of leather shoes was seen as an essential expression of social standing.

To Smith, therefore, necessaries were properly described as 'not only those things which nature, but those things which the established rules of decency have rendered necessary to the lowest rank of people'. In essence, while continuing to condemn luxury consumption which was motivated only by vanity and by the wish to emulate social superiors, Smith was prepared to concede the importance and legitimacy of purchasing which was intended to protect an individual's status among his peers, but hostility to the conspicuous consumption of 'the vain man' was rooted in his belief that, for society to progress, the ostentatious consumption of the rich should act as a spur to hard work rather than to conspicuous emulation. Over time this hard work would then generate the wealth by which deserving individuals could join the ranks of the rich and successful, and could then legitimately display their new social status through personal consumption.

Smith's view of social progress and material consumption fitted well with the orthodox moral and religious sentiments of the day, but his prescriptions were clearly at odds with market realities. Levels of luxury consumption and ostentatious display in the new consumer societies of the eighteenth century suggested that conspicuous consumption was now established at all social levels and could no longer be regarded as economically trivial. At the top of the social pyramid, the rich continued to indulge themselves. The wealth enjoyed by the English aristocracy between 1700 and 1800 was as great as any class had hitherto enjoyed, finding expression in the construction of palatial country houses, landscaped estates, Gothic lodges and Ionic arches – all statements of economic and social supremacy. At the same time, developments in manufacturing, communications and transport were opening up wider economic opportunities for the less privileged and creating new markets which were being effectively exploited. 'Fashion' in goods and services was increasingly manipulated and products given a social cachet which had not hitherto existed. In France, for example, a substantial demand existed among lower-class Parisians for 'populuxe' goods, products which were in reality no more than cheap copies of aristocratic luxury items. These products were desired not for their utility but for their value as symbols of an aristocratic lifestyle, and the percentage of lower-class household inventories containing these populuxe items increased dramatically between 1725 and 1785 (Fairchilds, 1993). By 1800, the importance of interpersonal effects on consumption was well established at all social and economic levels in the capitals and major cities of Europe and was being actively promoted by increasingly sophisticated production and marketing systems.

The emergence of commercially organised sponsorship of product symbolism and conspicuous consumption should have fed through to the developing economic theories of consumer demand. In the event, little attention was given to these new realities, which were seen to be of cultural rather than economic interest. Bentham (1789) found no place for them in developing the pleasure–pain principles of Utilitarianism, taking the view that, for the most part, satisfactions came from 'within'. He did concede that qualitative measures of satisfaction, not measurable in money terms, could and did play a part in consumer preference formation, but disagreed with Adam Smith's attempt to distinguish between necessaries and superfluous luxuries, arguing that both could have very real value to the consumer. Smith was wrong, in Bentham's view, to argue that diamonds, for example, had great value with a view to exchange but none with a view to use. Any woman, argued Bentham, could have told him 'that in society, or at a ball, she who is most richly covered with diamonds overshadows the brilliance of all her rivals' (1801:87).

In using this reference to 'rivals' and to the implied satisfaction gained from the reaction of others to any possession or socially visible consumption, Bentham was acknowledging that utility or value in use could have a social dimension and that the opinions of others could often be a part of the pleasure of consumption. At the same time, he agreed with Smith that, while conspicuous consumption within any social class was natural and could be safely encouraged, it was less acceptable to see men striving to emulate their betters through overt displays of ostentation which could not easily be funded. More importantly, his observations on socially-founded, qualitative measures of 'pleasure' were in no way incorporated into Utilitarian thought.

This relative neglect of interpersonal effects on consumer demand continued through the early part of the nineteenth century. Ricardo (1817) gave little thought to the subject, although he was generally hostile to the production and consumption of luxuries. Taxation of these goods could be safely encouraged, he argued, because such taxes fell directly and exclusively on those who consumed luxury products and therefore had no wider repercussions on the poorer sections of society. In the longer term, he believed that nations should work to ensure that all productive resources be given over to the manufacture and supply only of necessaries, but this view was more controversial. In a letter to Ricardo, Malthus (1821) disagreed, arguing that a certain proportion of seemingly unproductive consumption was always necessary 'to call forth the resources of a country'.

Neither Ricardo nor Malthus considered that the consumption of luxury goods for status purposes was central to the economic concerns of the day. The first industrial revolution, rapidly changing international market conditions and large scale increases in population were directing interests elsewhere, and it was understandable that macroeconomic rather than microeconomic issues came to the fore. Not until the 1830s, in fact, was further work of any significance done on the influence and economic importance of luxury expenditure and status-motivated consumption on individual tastes and preferences and on patterns of consumer demand.

References

Appleby, Joyce (1978), *Economic Thought and Ideology in Seventeenth Century England*, Princeton, NJ: Princeton University Press.

Barbon, Nicholas (1690), *A Discourse of Trade*, London.

Bentham, Jeremy (1789), *An Introduction to the Principles of Morals and Legislation*, reprinted (1879), Oxford: Clarendon Press.

Bentham, Jeremy (1801), *The True Alarm*, book 1, ch. 5, reprinted in W. Stark (ed.) (1954), *Jeremy Bentham's Economic Writings*, vol. 3, London: George Allen & Unwin.

Butel-Dumont, G.M. (1771), *Théorie du Luxe: ou traité dans lequel on entreprend d'établir que le luxe est un ressort non seulement utile, mais même indispensablement nécessaire à la prospérité des états*, London & Paris.

Condillac, Etienne Bonnot de (1789), *Le Commerce et le Gouvernement, Oeuvres IV*, Paris.

Coyer, G.F. (1756), *La Noblesse Commercante*, Paris.

Fairchilds, Cissy (1993), 'The Production and Marketing of Populuxe Goods in Eighteenth-Century Paris', in J. Brewer and R. Porter (eds) (1993), *Consumption and the World of Goods*, London: Routledge, pp. 228–48.

Hume, David (1739), *A Treatise of Human Nature*, reprinted in L.A. Selby-Bigge (ed.) (1888, reprinted 1967), Oxford: Clarendon Press

Hume, David (1751), *Enquiries Concerning the Human Understanding and Concerning the Principles of Morals*, vol. 2 (posthumous edition, 1777), reprinted in L.A. Selby-Bigge (ed.) (1894, third revised edition 1975), Oxford: Clarendon Press.

Hume, David (1752), *Of Refinement in the Arts*, reprinted in E. Rotwein (ed.) (1955), *David Hume: Writings on Economics*, Edinburgh: Thomas Nelson & Sons, pp. 19–32.

Kaye, F.B. (ed.) (1924), *Mandeville's Fable of the Bees: or, Private Vices, Publick Benefits*, Oxford: Clarendon Press, 1966.

Keynes, John Maynard (1936), *The General Theory of Employment, Interest and Money*, reprinted by The Royal Economic Society (1973), *The Collected Writings of John Maynard Keynes* vol.VII, London: Macmillan.

Locke, John (1692), *Some Considerations of the Lowering of Interest*, London.

McKendrick, Neil, John Brewer and J.H. Plumb (1982), *The Birth of a Consumer Society: The Commercialization of Eighteenth-century England*, London: Europa Publications Ltd.

Malthus, Thomas (1821), Letter to David Ricardo, July 16, reprinted in P.Sraffa (ed.) (1955), *The Works and Correspondence of David Ricardo*, vol. IX, Letters 1821–1823, Royal Economic Society, Cambridge University Press.

Mandeville, Bernard (1705), *The Grumbling Hive: or, Knaves Turn'd Honest*, London.

Mandeville, Bernard (1714), *The Fable of the Bees: or, Private Vices, Publick Benefits*, Oxford: Clarendon Press. Further editions appeared after 1714 and a two-volume edition was subsequently published in 1733, reprinted in F.B. Kaye (ed.) (op. cit.).

Mirabeau, Marquis de (1763), *Philosophie Rurale, ou Economie Générale et Politique de l'Agriculture*, Amsterdam.

North, Sir Dudley (1691), *Discourses Upon Trade*, London: Thos. Basset at the George in Fleet Street.

Petty, Sir William (1662), *A Treatise of Taxes and Contributions*, London.

Ricardo, David (1817), *On The Principles of Political Economy and Taxation*, London: John Murray.

Schama, Simon (1987), *The Embarrassment of Riches: An Interpretation of Dutch Culture in the Golden Age*, London: Collins.

Smith, Adam (1759), *Theory of Moral Sentiments*, reprinted in D.D. Raphael and A.L. Macfie (eds) (1976), *Adam Smith: The Theory of Moral Sentiments*. Oxford: Clarendon Press.

Smith, Adam (1776), *An Inquiry into the Nature and Causes of the Wealth of Nations*, reprinted in R.H. Campbell and A.S. Skinner (eds) (1976), *Adam Smith: The Wealth of Nations*, Oxford: Clarendon Press.

Thirsk, Joan (1978), *Economic Policy and Projects: The Development of a Consumer Society in Early Modern England*, Oxford: Clarendon Press.

2 John Rae and 'The Passion of Vanity'

John Rae was born in Aberdeen, Scotland, in 1796. He graduated from the University of Aberdeen in 1815 and subsequently enrolled as a medical student at Edinburgh University, but had to abandon his studies when the family business failed in 1817. In due course, he continued his medical education in France, but eventually emigrated to Canada in 1822 where he earned his living both as a doctor and as a schoolteacher. He later moved to the United States, living and working first in Boston, then in New York and California. Subsequently, he spent some twenty years on the Hawaiian island of Maui, earning his living by farming, teaching and providing medical services to the local community. He finally returned to the United States, dying in New York in 1872.

During his time in Canada in the 1820s and early 1830s, Rae became deeply involved with the economic and political debate over the country's colonial status. His sympathies lay with those émigré Scottish merchants who argued that Canada's best interests lay in retaining the link with Britain. Rae's views were heavily influenced by the fact that, by 1830, he had become a leading member of the Scottish Kirk in Canada and saw a continuing association with the mother country as the best means of securing a continuation of the Presbyterian tradition. However, he realised that for any argument in favour of colonialism to be more widely accepted and to provide a counter to the radicalism of the French Canadians, who were increasingly attracted by the republicanism of the United States, the economic case for colonial status had to be made. To this end, he set about producing a comprehensive economic and statistical survey of Canada.

Rae's research led in 1834 to the publication of his only book *Statement of Some New Principles on the Subject of Political Economy, Exposing the Fallacies of the System of Free Trade and of Some Other Doctrines maintained in the 'Wealth of Nations'*. To Rae, the book offered a reasoned defence of the benefits of colonial status, but the title suggested that it was a polemic against free trade in general and Adam Smith in particular. It enjoyed brief popularity among those who were anxious to promote the protectionist cause in the United States, but soon faded into relative obscurity.

Rae's *New Principles* was for the most part concerned with the nature of capital accumulation and with the importance of what he termed the 'inventive faculty' as a means of securing long-term economic progress. More importantly for this study, however, Rae explored in some detail the sociological influences on capital accumulation and on consumer behaviour and attempted to assimilate these into current economic thought. In effect, although he rejected Mandeville's defence of 'private vices for the public good', he, too, attempted to move discussion of interpersonal effects on consumer demand into the economic mainstream.

Rae argued that, together, capital accumulation and society's inventive faculty were capable of generating increasing levels of economic development and prosperity. At the same time, he recognised that there were other forces, or 'contrary principles', at work which could slow down or even reverse this positive process. Among these forces was the tendency of individuals to indulge in high levels of luxury consumption. To Rae, a religious man strongly influenced by the Protestant work ethic, Mandeville's contention that luxury expenditures added to national wealth was not in any way convincing. He also took issue with Adam Smith in rejecting any proposition that individual self interest and the national interest were one and the same.

Rae defined luxury, very selectively, as 'the expenditure occasioned by the passion of vanity'. Vanity he defined in turn as:

> The mere desire of superiority over others ... A purely selfish feeling; its pleasures centre on the individual; and if it does not endeavour to diminish the enjoyment of others, it is never directly its object to increase them ... Its aim in all cases that concern our subject, is to have what others cannot have (1834: 265–6).

He recognised such consumption by the degree to which it was conspicuous to others, whether by dint of its scarcity, its high price, or its wastefulness. Goods and services which offered a high degree of utility or value in use and which lacked 'social visibility' were, regardless of their cost, of little or no value to the vain man, for they served a practical purpose, gave value for money at whatever purchase price, and offered no opportunity for ostentatious display.

Conspicuous luxury consumption was seen to be at its most effective, therefore, when it successfully displayed wealth either through demonstrating an ability to pay prices for goods and services which others could not afford to pay, or when it represented a high degree of conspicuous waste. As illustration, Rae cited examples of the excesses and extravagances of earlier civilisations – from Babylon and the Roman Empire to the 'Asiatic Monarchies'. Such excesses were well documented, but they served his purpose in establishing that luxury consumption, as he had chosen to define it, needed always to be socially visible and wasteful. He pointed also to the frequent attempts of privileged minorities to suppress the luxury consumption of others through the introduction of sumptuary laws. Why should such laws have been considered necessary? Because, he argued, a propensity to conspicuously consume existed at all social and economic levels, and the only preconditions to ostentatious economic display were vanity and the ability to pay. Under free market conditions, Rae believed that man's vanity would ensure that many who could find the resources to indulge themselves would seek to conspicuously consume to the detriment of society at large.

While opposed in principle to all acts of conspicuous display, Rae agreed with Adam Smith that the need for people to maintain a respectable social status within their own communities was self-evident and tended to generate significant amounts of socially visible conspicuous consumption which was perceived as necessary rather than extravagant expenditure by the individuals concerned. Given these social pressures, such expenditures were seen by Rae as, at the least, understandable:

> No blame can attach to individuals, for compliances with follies to which the passion of vanity prompts. It were a great mistake to imagine that even its absurdities are easily avoidable. It is in vain for any one man to oppose general opinions and practices, however ridiculous. If he does so, he is sure to encounter greater evils than a compliance with the customs of society would inflict. It is the business of the poor to stand well with the world, else he will scarcely make his way through it. It is his business, too, to avoid a display of poverty (1834: 281).

In those less than ideal societies where conspicuous display had been made socially important, therefore, Rae conceded that no blame could attach to individuals who felt a need to conspicuously consume in order to protect their position in society. Such expenditures had to be seen as necessaries rather than as luxuries; only when luxury consumption was driven by personal vanity could it be considered to have no justification and to be damaging to the community at large.

While Rae recognised this need to conform, he saw it as a failure of society that such needs had been created. Adam Smith had implied that such socially necessary conspicuous consumption would continue to be a part of the modern world; Rae, in contrast, saw it as wasteful and unnecessary, and as something which had to be actively resisted. In this, his views were undoubtedly influenced by his active involvement with, and commitment to, the Presbyterian Church, which had always taken a strong stand against any forms of conspicuous display at whatever social and economic level.

The degree to which the more pernicious forms of luxury consumption were present in any society, argued Rae, was determined by the relative strengths of two 'benevolent' factors which were present in any civilised society. First, man's 'intellectual powers', properly developed, condemned all forms of vulgarity and tastelessness associated with conspicuous consumption. Second, the 'social and benevolent affections' heightened the social conscience of man and rejected any self-centred displays of supposed superiority. In the ideal society, these two benevolent factors would both be strong, keeping conspicuous consumption to a minimum. At the same time, the effective desire for accumulation would be high and material and spiritual progress sustained. There was, in short, a clear, inverse relationship between levels of conspicuous consumption and national prosperity and well-being, a claim which Mandeville would have rejected out of hand.

While the establishment of such vanity-free social and economic systems should always be a long-term objective of nations, Rae was realist enough to know that the two benevolent influences on consumption could never be sufficiently strong to entirely eliminate the status-driven propensity to conspicuously consume, and that some degree of luxury consumption would always be present in even the most well-managed societies. In all cases, however, he believed that the nature and direction of conspicuous economic display within any society was determined by the relative strengths of the two benevolent influences. When intellectual powers were stronger, conspicuous consumption tended to be channelled into objects of 'permanent excellence' which were perceived by the consumer and by others, to have real intellectual merit; when the social affections dominated, in contrast, the intention was to demonstrate wealth and social standing by inviting others to share in the consumption of status-conferring goods and services.

To Rae, the conspicuous excesses of Mandeville's Dutch merchants reflected a desire for improvement in social status in a cultural setting where the intellectual powers were strong. This had channelled conspicuous consumption into items of so-called permanent excellence, whether fine houses, paintings, or furniture. Similarly, Rae could see the same intellectual powers influencing luxury consumption among the rich merchants and traders of nineteenth-century North America, again reflected in expenditures on fine houses and, lower down the social order, on gold watches of enduring value. In contrast, he saw Britain as a country where the intellectual powers were weaker, but where the social and benevolent affections came to the fore. Here, shows of vanity were consequently focused more on luxuries associated with hospitality, with rare wines, and with extravagances associated with the 'dainties of the table'.

The virtuous powers were seen as equal partners working to keep conspicuous consumption within manageable levels. At the same time, Rae saw other factors at work which either raised or lowered levels of luxury consumption. In particular, he believed there was a demographic and geographic dimension to such behaviour, for it had long been recognised that the propensity to conspicuously consume varied significantly between urban and rural areas. The inhabitants of major towns, and especially of capital cities, Montesquieu had noted, 'are filled with notions of vanity, and actuated by an ambition of distinguishing themselves by trifles'. This owed much to population size and to the fact that people were, for the most part, strangers to one another. This impersonal, competitive environment encouraged conspicuous display as 'marks of a superior condition'. In contrast, rural areas, particularly in the 'new countries', placed no such demands upon vanity. To Rae, 'the very scattered state of the population effectually keeps down vanity ...There is hence no better school for the dissolute European than the back woods. After a dozen years' residence in them, he comes out a completely altered man' (1834: 281).

John Rae's condemnation of any luxury consumption intended to satisfy some inner vanity went far beyond the individual, for he was convinced that such behaviour had the most serious economic consequences for any nation. The manufacture of luxury goods to satisfy a desire for ostentatious display was in itself a loss to society. To Rae, it satisfied no tangible needs and the goods and services produced indulged one man's vanity only at the expense of other, less fortunate, individuals. It was, in essence, a misuse of wealth, adding nothing to the overall public good and dissipating resources on a substantial scale.

He was prepared to concede that, exceptionally, society could benefit from investment in luxury goods production, but only when the luxury good in question had 'a substratum of utility under it'. In such circumstances, manufacturers, attracted initially by the high prices associated with luxury products, would subsequently recognise a potentially lucrative mass market for the product if it could be manufactured in greater quantities and produced at far lower cost. As those improvements were made and market prices fell, the status value of the product would fall correspondingly and it would, in due course, be abandoned by status-seeking consumers. Demand then came from a new consumer group interested in purchasing the product for its genuine utility rather than for any supposed status value. What had then started out as a manufacturing investment in luxury goods ultimately came to provide products of real value to the general public.

As examples of such positive market effects, Rae pointed to the development of products as diverse as soap, silk, cotton fabrics and glass, all of which had originally been considered luxuries but which, over time, had become commonplace and had served an entirely utilitarian purpose. However, he was at pains to stress that these developments were the 'accidental effects of luxury' and emphasised that, as a general rule, luxury goods manufacture worked only to dissipate a part of the national wealth and served no substantial purpose.

Rae's analysis extended also to a consideration of the economics of luxury goods demand and supply in international trade. Demand for the importation of such goods, he argued, was governed solely by the product's scarcity and consequent status value. Foreign luxuries become quickly established 'if half a dozen people of rank adopt the use of the article as a sign of their superiority'. Others quickly wish to emulate these market leaders, and demand for the product increases significantly over time. Under free market conditions, this demand then attracts increasing numbers of suppliers and the price is subsequently driven down. 'People of rank' once again consider the product to have lost its status value and leave the market – to be followed in due course by those whose original motives were essentially imitative and who, in turn, lose interest in the product. Opinion leaders then move on to new, scarcer products and, in Rae's view:

> At the end of the process the whole difference observable, if the article be completely a luxury, is a change of fashion. The principle of accumulation has not been led to grasp a greater compass of materials, nor has any addition been made to the general stock of the society, a new set of marks of distinction has merely been introduced (1834: 307–8).

The desire of individuals to emulate their social superiors leads to an eventual fall in price for any product initially introduced to the market as a luxury good. To the exporter, such markets held no long-term attraction under free market conditions. However, Rae argued, luxury goods markets could, in certain circumstances, sustain high prices over the longer term. First, when free market conditions did not prevail, access to the market became severely restricted and premium pricing could be sustained. Second, demand might be sufficiently strong to ensure that producers did not have to lower their prices significantly as market supplies increased. Under such conditions, the effects of increased demand upon price would be considerably reduced and could sustain high market-clearing prices over the longer term.

Rae drew clear distinctions between what were, to him, the real benefits of free market competition in utilitarian goods and the more questionable gains arising from international trade in luxury goods. Even allowing for the special conditions which could sustain profitability in luxury goods markets, Rae argued, real gains to the community were hard to secure. Although any gains were for the most part largely illusory, however, some benefits could flow. Merchants, manufacturers and workers in the luxury goods industries naturally profited from sustained trade, and provided that profits and salaries were themselves not 'dissipated in luxuries', society at large stood to benefit from their subsequent expenditures on other goods and services. Also, the 'overcharge' on luxury goods gave merchants the opportunity to make quasi-monopolistic profits which might then be invested in other economic activities which ultimately worked to the benefit of the wider population. To Rae, however, these gains could never justify any policy directed towards maximising investment in the luxury goods sectors of any economy.

Any international trade benefits accruing from luxury goods production and consumption required restricted access to markets. Under free market conditions, Rae could see no justification whatsoever for encouraging the manufacture and trade of pure luxuries, believing instead that nations had a responsibility to shape the nature and direction of their international trade by encouraging and rewarding investment in utilitarian products and by minimising any involvement with luxury goods and luxury consumption. If the wrong product mix was allowed to develop, then adverse social and economic consequences would soon become apparent. As an example, British trade with continental Europe following the end of the Napoleonic Wars and the subsequent removal of wartime restrictions on trade, had provided an opportunity for Britain to restructure its pattern of international trade in the country's best long-term interests. Instead, Rae argued, British manufacturers had been preoccupied with luxuries and had 'applied themselves largely to objects, the direct effects of the attainment of which are worse than useless to society'. This, in turn, had led to general poverty and distress; the country had still to learn that it was upon the manufacture and trade of products which satisfied 'real' wants that the long-term prosperity of nations depended.

Rae emphasised the need, therefore, to encourage trade in utilitarian goods and services, a trade which prospered best, in his opinion, under conditions of free trade. At the same time, he gave some comfort to protectionists by arguing that past (wartime) restrictions on trade had often proved to be beneficial. At war with France in the eighteenth century, Britain had seen significant investment in the manufacture of basic commodities such as glass, paper, silk, copper and brass products which had formerly been imported from France in considerable quantities. These investments, argued Rae, had worked very much to the public good, and he suggested that, in certain special circumstances, protectionism could be a force for good in redirecting manufacturing investment into more productive channels.

While both Rae and Adam Smith recognised that unfettered conspicuous consumption was morally reprehensible and often economically inefficient, Rae went further than Smith, arguing that, left unchecked, it must inevitably lead to national economic decline. In well-ordered economies where the virtuous powers were strong, community values came to the fore and ostentatious economic behaviour within the family was seen as a matter of no interest and of little real value. While some limited, socially necessary conspicuous display would always be undertaken as a means of securing improvements in a family's social standing and to protect the interests of future generations, such spending would be kept within reasonable bounds and certainly within the limits necessary to ensure that the effective desire for accumulation remained strong enough to see the economy as a whole prosper. Society remained stratified and social mobility was restricted, but this again only served to ensure that the distance between social groups was kept stable over time.

This social and economic stability was threatened, in Rae's view, when those forces which worked against too great a level of conspicuous consumption were weakened and made ineffective. Then the capitalist class which, to Rae, had the greatest propensity to conspicuously consume, would begin to indulge more freely and openly in ostentatious consumption. This extravagance would eventually deteriorate into acts of conspicuous expenditure fuelled only by personal vanity. Over time, the social and economic distance between classes would then widen and a necessary degree of social cohesion would be lost.

This breakdown, in Rae's view, had major economic implications, for the working man, soon faced with what he would see as an unbridgeable gap between himself and higher social groups, would abandon all hopes of gradual upward mobility over time, turn away from saving and accumulation, and seek to gain status among his peers through 'wasteful expenditures on the purchase of fineries, in treating his companions at the ale-house, and in similar extravagances'. Predictably, the family was then neglected and kept short of necessaries; the labourer himself became workshy and ultimately dishonest; little or no attempt was made to save in good time to make provision for future possible hardship, so exaggerating swings between prosperity and poverty; the inventive faculty was diminished; in short, the moral and economic well-being of society was seriously undermined.

It was the vanity of the capitalist class which, in Rae's opinion, led directly to the social and economic degeneration of society, with all its consequences for economic growth and renewal. When the middle and higher classes of society indulged in excessive conspicuous consumption, they were unknowingly destroying the industry and ambitions of the lower class on which they rested; and 'when decay affects the foundations, then the structure must fall'. Vanity and its attendant evils were, therefore, a root cause of national decline and had to be rejected on both moral and economic grounds.

Rae's belief that vanity-driven ostentatious and conspicuous consumption needed to be held in check and subsequently eradicated led him to propose a set of policies to counteract any tendencies towards luxury consumption. Taxes on 'pure' luxuries, with no inherent utilitarian value, should be steeply increased – this would not of itself discourage conspicuous spenders, who would still be attracted by high prices, but would certainly raise substantial funds for the Exchequer which could then be put to more productive uses. Second, new domestic investment in luxury goods production should be heavily discouraged, prohibitive protectionist tariffs placed on imported luxuries, and attempts at import substitution prevented. Third, for those luxury goods which did contain recognisable and significant utilitarian value, competition should be actively promoted, with a view to driving prices down and making such products more widely available to the general public. All these policies, argued Rae, would work to diminish any interest in the luxury goods market on the part of existing and intending suppliers.

While Rae, therefore, had policies and prescriptions to ameliorate what he saw as the twin threats of luxury production and conspicuous consumption, he was, at heart, more concerned to tackle the root cause of the problem – that of vanity itself. If vanity could be eradicated, then wasteful luxury consumption would, in turn, disappear over time. Rae believed that man's behaviour, and in particular much of his economic behaviour, was conditioned by prevailing social attitudes, and that these attitudes were by no means fixed or immutable. They could be changed, he argued, by two forces which, taken together, worked to ensure that a society's values were both positive and productive.

First, strong religious beliefs led individuals to be more concerned with furthering the well-being and prosperity of the community rather than with self-indulgence. Without this necessary religious foundation, 'vanity, vice and folly' came to exert a pernicious influence on the individual and on the capital accumulation and inventiveness of any society. With 'the Church in the house', however, the proper moral and ethical foundations were laid.

Religious education, and the moral values it secured, was seen then as an essential element in the proper ordering of society. However, it was a necessary but not sufficient condition, for societies also needed to achieve the highest standards of general education in order to succeed. 'The power of knowledge', he wrote to the Montreal Gazette, 'is irresistible in advancing the best interests of the human race'. Working together, religion and education would effectively remove vanity and conspicuous consumption and secure the proper ordering of society.

John Rae's *New Principles* was written, first and foremost, to counter the proposition that individual self-interest and the national interest could be one and the same. The study of luxury consumption allowed him to demonstrate that, while individuals could improve their social and economic status by increasing their relative share of existing national wealth, nations themselves had to secure increases in absolute wealth before they could become richer. Moreover, greater national wealth was not necessarily assured by increases in commercial activity. It was only certain when higher levels of capital accumulation and productive investment were secured and when the society fostered an inventive faculty to underpin technological advances and improvements in manufacturing systems.

Luxury consumption, to Rae, could not add significantly to this national prosperity. There was some slight prospect that it might stimulate invention, particularly when the luxury good in question had the sub stratum of utility which could be developed to the wider public good. For the most part, however, investment in luxury goods manufacture had to be seen as a misdirection of resources.

In essence, Rae, the committed Presbyterian, was concerned above all with the moral dimensions of conspicuous consumption. He was a defender of the 'intelligent and moral community' which, to him, formed the necessary bedrock of civilised society. At the same time, he realised that moral arguments would carry little real weight unless it could be demonstrated that it made sense, in economic terms, to reject luxury, extravagance, and their attendant evils. In constructing an economic case against conspicuous consumption, he, in fact, offered a counterweight to the views of Mandeville.

Rae's treatise on luxury consumption and on the need to sustain the moral foundations of the state attracted little immediate attention after the publication of *New Principles* in 1834. John Stuart Mill subsequently showed some interest (q.v.), but, for the most part, the book's treatment of consumption and consumer behaviour made little impact on the economic community in the middle years of the nineteenth century. A part of the problem was undoubtedly Rae's belief that a large part of economic activity had to be seen from a cultural and sociological viewpoint. This had the effect of moving *New Principles* out of the mainstream of economics and did nothing to encourage recognition or debate among economists. (The problem was later compounded when, in 1905, Mixter published a revised edition of *New Principles* under the title *A Sociological Theory of Capital* – a title which, as Mair (1990) has pointed out, was 'likely to be the kiss of death for any book on economics wishing to be taken seriously').

Rae's work has not gone entirely without recognition. Nassau Senior, John Stuart Mill, and, later, Bohm-Bawerk, Fisher and Schumpeter, all paid generous tribute to his contribution to the development of a theory of capital accumulation. And his analysis of conspicuous consumption and ostentatious display is now believed to have had a significant impact on the Institutional School of economics and, in particular, on the work of Thorstein Veblen and his *The Theory of the Leisure Class*, written in 1899 and now a standard reference work on the phenomenon of conspicuous consumption and pecuniary emulation.

Although the term 'conspicuous consumption' was never used verbatim by Rae, he talks in *New Principles* of consumption which 'is conspicuous', and emphasises the importance of social visibility in status-motivated purchase and display. The precise phrase 'conspicuous consumption' is rightly attributed to Veblen, but the concept, role and status value of 'conspicuousness' in consumption should, perhaps, be more properly attributed to Rae.

Veblen never acknowledged any debt to Rae, and made few references to him or to his work. In his only published reference (1909), he paid mild tribute to him as 'a good and authentic utilitarian theorist', but certainly never associated Rae's ideas with his own work. There are sufficient points of similarity between *New Principles* and *The Theory of the Leisure Class*, however, to suggest that Rae's work on luxury consumption was not unknown to Veblen, and had, consciously or subconsciously, informed Veblen's treatment of the subject.

Veblen was, in later years, certainly made aware of John Rae, and of others' suspicions that Rae had indeed been a major influence on his own work. Joseph Dorfman, Veblen's biographer, recalls:

> There is an amusing story on Veblen's handling of the Rae issue, which was told to Professor J.M. Clark around 1924 by a student. The student had attended a party at the home of a colleague of Clark, and Veblen had been present. The colleague steered the talk around to John Rae. Veblen and the others could feel something coming ... Then [the colleague] asked Veblen 'Are you familiar with the work of John Rae?' 'Yes', Veblen drawled in his deliberate way, and then: 'Some people have accused me of stealing my ideas from him' (1973: 31).

There is no evidence as to who these accusers were, but Veblen clearly felt ill at ease with what Dorfman refers to as 'the Rae issue'. In the event, while Rae had, without question, made a significant contribution to work on luxury expenditure and status-seeking consumption, no clear connection to Veblen can be established, and his work has always been overshadowed by Veblen's later explorations of conspicuous consumption and the formation of tastes.

There is a sense in which John Rae's analysis of luxury consumption and the economics of interpersonal effects looked backward rather than forward. Before 1600, the case against ostentatious economic behaviour had been based largely on spiritual considerations; it had been considered sinful in the eyes of God to indulge in excessive consumption. After 1600, the issue was transposed from the moral to the social and economic spheres. Lack of frugality was then condemned firstly because it was seen to threaten the fabric of ordered society, and secondly because it weakened the productive ability of a nation.

Rae's rejection of luxury consumption bridged these two earlier traditions, arguing that 'dissolute' economic behaviour not only threatened social order but also undermined the spiritual and moral values on which society itself was built. It was a conservative thesis, opposed to Mandeville's more radical interpretation of the relative benefits of conspicuous consumption, and to

Smith's implicit recognition that such behaviour was, however regrettably, a natural expression of consumer choice in any free market system. Seen at the time as part of a wider (and generally discredited) polemic against Adam Smith and *The Wealth of Nations*, however, it made little immediate impact on the economic thinking of the day For all that, it represented the most comprehensive analysis of luxury expenditure and conspicuous consumption since Mandeville.

References

Dorfman, Joseph (1973), *Thorstein Veblen: Essays, Reviews and Reports*, Clifton, NJ: Augustus M. Kelley.

Mair, Douglas (1990), 'John Rae: Ugly Duckling or Black Swan?', *Scottish Journal of Political Economy*, **37** (3), 275–87.

Mixter, C.W. (ed.) (1905), *John Rae: The Sociological Theory of Capital*, New York: Macmillan.

Rae, John (1834), *Statement of Some New Principles on the Subject of Political Economy, Exposing the Fallacies of the System of Free Trade and of Some Other Doctrines maintained in the 'Wealth of Nations'*, Boston: Hilliard, Gray & Co, reprinted in R. Warren James (1965), *John Rae, Political Economist*, vol.2 (text), Toronto: University of Toronto Press.

Veblen, Thorstein (1899), *The Theory of the Leisure Class*, New York: Macmillan.

Veblen, Thorstein (1909), 'Fisher's Rate of Interest', *Political Science Quarterly*, **24** (June), reprinted in L. Ardzrooni (ed.) (1934), *Essays in our Changing Order*, New York: Augustus M. Kelley, pp. 137–47.

3   A Confusion of Ideas

John Rae's *New Principles* went largely unnoticed by economists at the time of its publication in 1834. There were several reasons for this neglect although, as James has pointed out, Rae 'was merely a colonial in a period when colonies were associated with savages of various hues, with transported felons, and with primitive and picturesque living conditions. The notion that a mere colonial could make any significant contribution to political economy was far-fetched enough and it was more absurd to consider seriously any work which challenged the entrenched and authoritative views of Adam Smith' (1965, I: 171).

Shortly after Rae's *New Principles* appeared, Nassau Senior, Professor of Political Economy at Oxford, published his *Outline of the Science of Political Economy* (1836). Like Smith, Senior understood and condoned the ostentatious display of the very rich. 'The duties of those who fill the higher ranks in society', he argued, 'can seldom be well performed unless they conciliate the respect of the vulgar by a certain display of opulence' (1836: 56). At the same time, he fully recognised the desire of people at all social and economic levels to conspicuously consume:

> Strong as is the desire for variety, it is weak compared with the desire for distinction: a feeling which, if we consider its universality and its constancy, that it affects all men and at all times, that it comes with us from the cradle, and never leaves us till we go into the grave, may be pronounced to be the most powerful of human passions.

> The most obvious source of distinction is the possession of superior wealth. It is the one which excites most the admiration of the bulk of mankind, and the only one which they feel capable of attaining. To seem more rich, or, to use a common expression, to keep up a better appearance, than those within their own sphere of comparison, is, with almost all men who are placed beyond the fear of actual want, the ruling principle of conduct. For this object they undergo toil which no pain or pleasure addressed to the senses would lead them to encounter; into which no slave could be lashed or bribed (1836: 12).

Senior saw the need for distinction (which he did not condemn) as being directed by men only towards those 'within their own sphere of comparison'; he made no comment about those who might seek to emulate their social superiors, although it must be assumed that, like Smith, he did not condone such behaviour. Second, he implicitly acknowledged that Bentham's felicific calculus of pleasure and pain was not able to accommodate this search for social distinction.

Senior, again like Smith, recognised three particular categories of good – necessaries and luxuries, certainly, but also 'decencies' which individuals were required to purchase and consume in order to preserve their position and status in society. As individuals prospered and moved upwards both socially and economically, so the nature of these decencies changed, but they had to be seen as essential purchases which ensured the well-being of the family group.

Senior's 1836 book makes no reference to John Rae, but there is evidence that he had certainly read his work before 1847 (Bowley, 1937: 161n). However, it appears to have been Rae's work on capital accumulation rather than on luxury consumption and related issues which had attracted Senior's attention. Certainly, John Stuart Mill knew of Rae's work and paid tribute to him in his *Principles of Political Economy* published in 1848. Again, it was Rae's work on capital accumulation which had particularly impressed Mill, but he was also aware of his treatment of luxury consumption, in particular as it related to taxation policy.

Mill agreed with Rae that luxury expenditure and conspicuous consumption was often driven only by vanity and a desire to 'buy' social superiority. When vanity alone was the motive for such behaviour, Mill, too, could see nothing of merit. He was ready to concede that when luxury goods were purchased only for their utility in use and for personal satisfaction, then such behaviour could not sensibly be condemned. But when expenditure was intended solely to display wealth to others in an attempt to gain in social status, it could not be defended. At the same time, Mill argued, such indulgence could be made to serve the public interest through the taxation system.

Rae had argued in 1834 that any increases in price caused by the taxation of goods which were being purchased only to display wealth would not have a negative effect on demand, for the high price of such products was the real measure of value in the eyes of conspicuous consumers. Furthermore, if the production and distribution costs of such goods were to fall, their status value would be retained if taxes were levied on them which had the effect of preserving their high purchase price, so ensuring their continuing social value. Mill agreed with this analysis and with Rae's view that the taxation of luxury goods used for the purpose of conspicuous display was an ideal way of raising public revenues to nobody's disadvantage. At the same time, luxury taxes were capable of acting as 'an useful, and the only useful, kind of sumptuary law':

> I disclaim all asceticism, and by no means wish to see discouraged, either by law or opinion, any indulgence (consistent with the means and obligations of the person using it) which is sought for a genuine inclination for, and enjoyment of,

the thing itself; but a great portion of the expenses of the higher and middle classes in most countries, and the greatest in this, is not incurred for the sake of the pleasure afforded by the things on which the money is spent, but from regard to opinion, and an idea that certain expenses are expected from them, as an appendage of station; and I cannot but think that expenditure of this sort is a most desirable subject of taxation. If taxation discourages it, some good is done, and if not, no harm; for in so far as taxes are levied on things which are desired and possessed from motives of this description, nobody is the worse for them. When a thing is bought not for its use but for its costliness, cheapness is no recommendation. As Sismondi remarks, the consequence of cheapening articles of vanity, is not that less is expended on such things, but that the buyers substitute for the cheapened article some other which is more costly, or a more elaborate quality of the same thing; and as the inferior quality answered the purpose of vanity equally well when it was equally expensive, a tax on the article is really paid by nobody: it is a creation of public revenue by which nobody loses (1848, V vi: 869).

(Mill's reference to the Swiss historian and economist Sismondi is interesting, for the two men shared little in common. Sismondi was strongly opposed to the classical laissez-faire economics of Smith, Ricardo and Mill, and was, in many ways, a forerunner of the socialist school of economists which emerged in the middle years of the nineteenth century to promote the belief that state intervention in economic affairs was essential for successful economic management. However, Sismondi and Mill were agreed that, though morally wrong, conspicuous consumption was an inevitable consequence of capitalist society and could be usefully exploited in the public interest through appropriate taxation policies. In this, at least, classical and socialist economic thinking came together.)

While the moral argument against luxury consumption and status-driven economic display still enjoyed support for religious and social reasons in the 1830s and 1840s, events in Britain, Continental Europe and America were transforming patterns of economic organisation and were at the same time beginning to have significant effects on economic and social thinking. The rise of industrialisation and the factory system brought with it not only the nascent socialism of Saint-Simon and Sismondi but also encouraged a greater emphasis on the industrial interest in economic affairs. While this early form of industrial economics never took firm hold in England, it found a stronger voice in Germany and in other countries which felt themselves to be at a comparative disadvantage in trade terms.

Foremost among these new industrial economists was Friedrich List (1789–1846), whose most significant contribution to economic theory, *The National System of Political Economy*, was published in 1841. Active in German politics, and leader of the General Association of German Manufacturers and Merchants, List was concerned above all with protecting and furthering the interests of German manufacturing industry, and tailored his economics to this purpose. An ardent supporter of tariff reform, he argued that Germany was not then a fully industrialised nation and so needed protection from British and other imports.

While busy promoting the protectionist cause, List was also conscious of the need to stimulate and nurture consumer goods markets. Unlike Rae, Mill and Sismondi, he saw luxury consumption and the emulation it generated in others lower down the social and economic order as an engine for economic growth and was not at all prepared to condemn it:

> Jewels and plate are not more convenient in gold and silver than in steel and tin; but the distinction attached to their possession provokes the exertion of both mind and body, encourages order and economy, and society is indebted to this stimulant for a considerable proportion of its productive power (1841: 381).

To List, the 'independent gentleman', dedicated to purchasing and consuming luxury goods and to high levels of ostentatious display, was a force for good. He 'excites by his luxury the emulation of all classes' and so stimulates others to hard work in the hope that they too would become rich. This benign influence disappeared, however, when wealth could not be possessed and openly enjoyed by the fortunate few.

Luxury consumption, in short, stimulated manufacturing productivity, and this productivity increased again as emulation grew and as more shared in the overall prosperity. Moreover, consumption of goods for public display was important in the lives of individual consumers themselves, argued List, quoting the German proverb 'People see my cravat but not my stomach'. He was convinced that conspicuous consumption needed no defending and should not be resisted either in the public or in the commercial interest. Sumptuary laws 'have effected nothing but to extinguish emulation among the mass of the inhabitants, and have encouraged only laziness and routine'. List was, in fact, at one with Mandeville in seeing such consumption as a positive asset and a significant contributor to the public good. At the same time, his lack of objectivity has to be recognised – given the interests of German manufacturing industry, moral objections to luxury goods consumption were never likely to carry weight.

List's defence of conspicuous consumption highlighted the ambivalent attitudes to such consumer behaviour which were developing in the 1840s. On the one hand, traditional moral and religious objections to ostentatious display were still in place, and these had not been seriously challenged by Adam Smith and the classical school of economists who had for the most part joined in the condemnation of 'vanity' and its consequences. At the same time, by 1840, economic and social conditions had been in turmoil for some fifty years, and it was becoming increasingly difficult to accommodate the moral certainties of the past in the new world. Greater industrialisation and growing competition for world markets were effectively relegating moral issues to a subordinate role in economic affairs. Luxury consumption and the 'trickle down' effects which created the desire to emulate such consumption at all social and economic levels were together capable of creating large, highly profitable markets for those who could supply the products in demand. As a consequence, by 1850, values and attitudes were beginning to change in response to the new economic realities.

The emerging tensions between the morality and the economics of luxury goods consumption were well illustrated by Wilhelm Roscher (1854). Roscher, a founding member of the German Historical School of economics, looked at luxury consumption from both ethical and commercial viewpoints. On the moral issue, he considered past debates on the phenomenon to have been largely sterile, observing that 'when a political economist declares for or against luxury in general, he resembles a doctor who should declare for or against the nerves in general' (1854: 223n). Mandeville, he protested, had 'called anything a luxury which exceeds the baldest necessities of life'. And while Voltaire and Hume had been defenders of such consumption, Pliny, Rousseau and others had been violent opponents. For the most part, the debate had centred on whether such consumption was salutary or reprehensible but had, to Roscher's mind, been of little real value.

Like many before him, Roscher associated luxury consumption and ostentatious display with the very rich and politically powerful. However, he drew a clear distinction between such consumption in what he termed less civilised societies, where the excesses of the privileged few had no redeeming social features and were both morally and economically indefensible, and that in modern, 'civilised' communities, where the effects of such behaviour were very different.

In these civilised societies, he argued, greater affluence and the more equitable distribution of wealth and income allowed a far larger percentage of the population to enjoy significant levels of discretionary income. The luxury consumption of the rich then served as a spur to emulation and so promoted the production of goods and services in the wider public interest. This emulation was both understandable and constructive, producing what Roscher described as an equalising tendency in the consumption of luxuries which was defensible on both moral and economic grounds. Only when nations declined, and the distribution of income became once again inequitable, did luxury consumption become unacceptable:

In declining nations, luxury assumes an imprudent and immoral character. Enormous sums are expended for insignificant enjoyments. It may even be said that costly consumption is carried on there for its own sake. The beautiful and true enjoyment of life makes place for the monstrous and the effeminate (1854: 241).

Roscher's view that luxury consumption and ostentatious display could not be defended when the social and economic conditions of the mass of the people allowed them no opportunity to rise above subsistence, found echoes in the work of Karl Marx. Working to a political agenda, Marx condemned all conspicuous consumption as a privilege afforded to a very few on the basis of a morally indefensible accumulation of capital. Modern industrial society displayed an appallingly unequal distribution of opportunity, wealth and income, thanks to the inequities and unfairness of the capitalist system of business enterprise. In such societies, the poor were concerned only with survival, and any suggestion that they could sensibly seek to emulate the behaviour and consumption of the rich was a nonsense. Marx, moreover, rejected Roscher's view that, within a capitalist system, national wealth could be radically redistributed and emulatory consumption could and would then emerge as a force for good; any permanent redistribution of wealth required revolutionary political and cultural change which itself would remove any desire or incentive to conspicuously consume for status. Indeed, under socialism, acts of ostentatious economic display would come to be condemned rather than admired, and it would become necessary to demonstrate hostility to such behaviour in order to secure status within the community.

While conspicuous consumption was being used to some extent in the middle years of the nineteenth century to further both commercial and political agendas, the attention given to it within economic theory was derisory. Apart from some consideration by Roscher, Historical School economists generally showed no interest in external effects on consumer demand, although their preoccupation with the development of cultural and socioeconomic laws relating to economics should, perhaps, have generated more interest in an essentially sociological interpretation of consumer behaviour. Elsewhere in Europe, in France and Britain particularly, conspicuous consumption, with all its cultural and behavioural overtones, was neglected because, within the mainstream of economics, there was now a growing belief that the way forward for economics was through a more scientific, mathematical treatment of the subject. Cournot, whose *Researches into the Mathematical Principles of the Theory of Wealth* (1838) laid much of the groundwork for this mathematical approach, was prepared to concede that some products were, in fact, purchased only for the purpose of ostentatious display. This, in turn, could create perverse demand/price relationships in that, as the prices of such status goods fell, a corresponding fall in demand could be generated. However, he discounted the significance of such market behaviour, arguing that 'objects of this nature play so unimportant a role in social economy that it is not necessary to bear in mind the restriction of which we speak' (1838: 46).

Cournot's dismissal of conspicuous consumption and of its market consequences was important because it influenced later generations of economists who adopted a more mathematical approach to the subject. His views became doubly significant because he was later widely credited with 'discovering' the law of demand – that quantity demanded is a function of price – and with proposing a theoretical specification of demand as negatively sloped and continuous. His treatment of conspicuous consumption as trivial was understandable, as such perverse behaviour did not sit happily within the microeconomic models he was developing. Cournot, in a sense, legitimised the neglect of status-driven consumption which was evident in the work of other nineteenth century mathematical economists, notably Dupuit in France, Gossen in Germany and Jevons in Britain.

A few of the early mathematical economists had been prepared to acknowledge elements of conspicuous consumption in the demand for goods and services, and had attempted some accommodation. William Whewell (1850) distinguished between goods which were necessaries and those which were 'popular luxuries' where demand was to some extent influenced by considerations of status and display. For the most part, however, such contributions to the economic debate were minimal and largely ignored. Whewell's work was later derided by Jevons, who dismissed his mathematical treatments as 'nonsense' and 'built upon sand'. In reality, the new mathematical school accepted Cournot's recommendation that examples of seemingly perverse demand formation were rare enough to be safely ignored and could, for this reason, be excluded from microeconomic analysis and theoretical expositions.

William Stanley Jevons, in his *Theory of Political Economy* published in 1871, was convinced that a mathematical approach to economics afforded the only positive way forward. 'I write', he said, 'as an economist wishing to convince other economists that their science can only be satisfactorily treated on an explicitly mathematical basis' (1871: xiv). At the same time, he was aware that others were promoting inductive, empirical work in the subject and believed that this was contributing to its present 'chaotic state'. He believed that, eventually, economics would have to subdivide into economics and economic sociology.

Economic sociology was certainly not the path chosen by Jevons. A great admirer of Cournot and Gossen, he promoted a mathematical interpretation of utility theory. Together with Menger (1871) and Walras (1874), who was then developing his general equilibrium analysis, Jevons laid the foundations of a new utility theory. All three economists, however, treated the utility function as additive and did not discuss the possibility that interpersonal effects could have a significant influence on patterns of consumer demand. Jevons was, in fact, not unaware of such effects, once acknowledging that people go to places of recreation, music or art 'because people of a class just superior to themselves are likely to be there'. However, he never attempted to incorporate such considerations into his economic work.

While the mathematical school was a dominant force in nineteenth century economic theory and thought, there were parallel non-mathematical developments in economics which also contributed to neoclassical theory. Towards the end of the nineteenth century, the Historicists had come to dominate economics in Germany, where theoretical analysis had never taken strong root. At the same time, analytical economics shifted to Austria, where a Viennese or Austrian School of writers, led by Carl Menger (1840–1921), emerged after 1870.

Although Menger had worked upon, and developed, a marginal utility theory of value at the same time as Jevons and Walras, his approach was markedly different in that his use of mathematical analysis was minimal. Indeed, in the later nineteenth century, the principal members of the Austrian School – Menger, Friedrich Wieser and Eugen Bohm-Bawerk – all opposed the use of mathematics on methodological grounds. This non-mathematical bias provided a theoretically happier home for the treatment of more 'behavioural' aspects of consumer demand, but, in the event, the Austrian approach to consumption and to consumer behaviour generally was no less orthodox than that of the mathematical economists. If Menger's notion of subjective value could have been placed in a wider analytical context, ideally within Walras's general equilibrium analysis, then there may have been some greater interest in status-directed consumption as a subject for serious discussion. In the event, the mathematical and non-mathematical schools both contributed to the development of neoclassical demand theory without recognising, or offering any explanation for, the fact that millions of people in Europe and the United States were by this time consuming for status on a daily basis.

By 1890, the several strands of neoclassical thought were beginning to form around related issues of utility and value, demand and supply, production and productivity and the distribution of national income across land, labour and capital. This work was now for the first time drawn together into a comprehensive economic theory by Alfred Marshall, whose *Principles of Economics* appeared for the first time in 1890. *Principles*, as it became known, was to become a seminal contribution to economic theory and was to dominate the agenda for many years to come; at the same time, it continued an orthodox tradition of largely disregarding events which seemed only to illustrate the perversity of human behaviour.

References

Bowley, Marian (1937), *Nassau Senior and Classical Economics*, reprinted (1967), London: George Allen and Unwin.

Cournot, Augustin (1838), *Researches into the Mathematical Principles of the Theory of Wealth*, reprinted (1960, N.T. Bacon (trans.)), London: Hafner Publishing Co.

James, R. Warren (1965), *John Rae: Political Economist*, vols. 1 and 2, Toronto: University of Toronto Press.

Jevons, William Stanley (1871), *The Theory of Political Economy*, reprinted (fifth edition) (1965), New York: Augustus M. Kelley.

List, Friedrich (1841), *The National System of Political Economy*, reprinted (1974), New York: Garland Publishing Co.

Marshall, Alfred (1890), *Principles of Economics*, London: Macmillan.

Marx, Karl (1867), *Capital: A Critique of Political Economy*, vol. I, book 1 'The Process of Production', third German edition (Friedrich Engels (ed.)), reprinted (1954, S. Moore and E. Aveling (trans.)), London: Lawrence & Wishart.

Menger, Carl (1871), *Principles of Economics*, reprinted (1950, J. Dingwall and B.F. Hoselitz (trans.)), Glencoe, Ill.: Free Press.

Mill, John Stuart (1848), *Principles of Political Economy*, reprinted in J.F. Robson (ed.) (1965), Toronto: Routledge and Kegan Paul.

Rae, John (1834), *Statement of Some New Principles on the Subject of Political Economy, Exposing the Fallacies of the System of Free Trade and of Some Other Doctrines maintained in the 'Wealth of Nations'*. Boston: Hilliard, Gray & Co, reprinted in R. Warren James (1965), *John Rae: Political Economist*, vols.1 and 2. Toronto: University of Toronto Press.

Roscher, Wilhelm (1854), *Principles of Political Economy*, vols. 1 and 2, thirteenth (1877) edition reprinted (1878, J.J. Lalor (trans.)), New York: Henry Holt and Co.

Senior, Nassau William (1836), *Outline of the Science of Political Economy*, fifth edition (1863), London: Charles Griffin and Co.

Walras, Leon (1874), *Elements of Pure Economics,* reprinted (1954, W. Jaffe (trans.)), Homewood Ill.: Irwin.

Whewell, William (1850), *Mathematical Expositions of Some Doctrines of Political Economy, Second Memoir*, Cambridge Philosophical Society Transactions.

4   The Neoclassical View

The first edition of Alfred Marshall's *Principles of Economics*, published in 1890, gave little consideration to the influence of interpersonal effects on consumer demand. What little discussion there was examined such effects in relation both to the consumption of necessaries and of luxury goods, but Marshall made a clear distinction between what he saw as two very different forms of economic activity.

With regard to necessaries, he took a liberal view, agreeing with Adam Smith that there was a social as well as a physiological dimension to such consumption. Smith, he noted, 'recognised that ... differences of custom make things necessary in some cases, which are superfluous in others' and this Marshall could accept. Expenditure on dress and personal appearance, as an example, could be deemed to be conventionally necessary if it could not be dispensed with without carrying a serious risk of losing social standing and influence at the workplace. Such needs depended on the nature of a man's calling but could be considered entirely legitimate expenditures. Necessaries could also extend into leisure time, where it remained important to project a social status consistent with rank and profession:

> In England now a well-to-do labourer is expected to appear on Sunday in a black coat and, in some places, in a silk hat; though these would have subjected him to ridicule but a short time ago. There is a constant increase both in that variety and expensiveness which custom requires as a minimum, and in that which it tolerates as a maximum; and the efforts to obtain distinction by dress are extending themselves throughout the lower grades of English society (1890: 87).

Marshall accepted this need for recognition as a major factor in determining patterns of consumption, agreeing with Senior that the desire for social distinction had always been, and would always be, strong. At the same time, he was careful to distinguish between those acceptable forms of conspicuous consumption which were intended to confirm and reinforce achieved social standing and those expenditures, driven only by vanity, which were purely ostentatious and self-indulgently status-seeking. Luxury expenditure that was intended purely for the sake of display was, in Marshall's eyes, an abuse of wealth and a denial of the satisfaction of real wants. At the same time, he acknowledged that is was on the increase:

> Even among the artisans in England, and perhaps still more in new countries, there are signs of the growth of that unwholesome desire for wealth as a means of display which has been the chief bane of the well-to-do classes in every civilized country. Laws against luxury have been futile, but it would be a gain if

the moral sentiment of the community could induce people to avoid all sorts of display of individual wealth. (1890: 136–7).

Luxury expenditures, thought Marshall, were justified when they were free from any taint of personal vanity on the one side and envy on the other. Expenditures on the fine arts, on improved craftsmanship, on cultural events and on public collections could all be considered worthwhile, and contrasted strongly with the ostentatious waste which was at that time becoming increasingly apparent. Like John Rae before him, he thought that preoccupation with status-seeking conspicuous consumption was not only tasteless but, more importantly, eroded the moral values and well-being both of communities and nations.

Marshall was clearly concerned with the increasing levels of display expenditure. Perhaps more than half of the consumption of the upper classes of society in England was wholly unnecessary, he argued. His references also to conspicuous consumption in 'new countries' was certainly a reference to the United States, where the Gilded Age consumption of the nouveaux riches was reaching epidemic proportions. At the same time, although he was fully aware of the economic and social significance of such behaviour, he took discussion no further. The subject, he argued 'exceeds the proper scope of the present Book' (Book III), but promised that 'the mode in which each individual spends his income is one of the more important of those applications of economic science to the art of living which will find their place at the end of this treatise'. In the event, no further discussion appeared and was not to appear in subsequent editions of *Principles*.

While Marshall recognised the growing importance of status consumption both in England and in the United States, he was clearly uneasy with these market realities. He acknowledged that social considerations could and did play a significant part in determining demand preferences and that these considerations had to be recognised:

> Comte's doctrine that all the aspects of social life are so closely connected that they ought to be studied together was one side of a great truth. But no serious attempt has yet been made to construct a social science that should do the same work for social life as a whole which has been done for one side of it by economics, young and full of imperfections as that is ... As Mill urges, Comte only proves what no thoughtful person would deny that 'A person is not likely to be a good economist who is nothing else'. Social phenomena acting and reacting on one another, they cannot rightly be understood apart (1890: 770–71).

However, he expressed serious reservations about the degree to which these social factors could sensibly be incorporated within economics. His concern was that, if economic analysis was to become too all-embracing, then it would necessarily begin to lose much of its scientific precision in order to make dubious gains in 'reality' and philosophic completeness. Better in his view to live with some loss of reality in order to further economics as a valuable method of enquiry. For explanations of consumer demand and market behaviour, therefore, the precision of partial equilibrium analysis offered Marshall more than other approaches which might perhaps have been more socially comprehensive yet would inevitably have been less exact in their scientific treatment of the subject.

The first edition of *Principles* does acknowledge some empirical evidence of interpersonal preference formation, and the fact that social considerations, as Comte and others had pointed out, could and did influence consumer choice. At the same time, Marshall made no attempt to accommodate such market behaviour. In developing his theories of consumer demand, he made full use of ceteris paribus assumptions in order to facilitate analysis, and these assumptions relegated any recognition of interpersonal effects to the margins of his work. Socially-motivated consumption was, for all practical purposes, ignored in developing his theories of consumer demand, for no consideration was given to the fact that an individual consumer, in certain status-sensitive areas of consumption, could and would be influenced by the consumption patterns of others. Total market demand was, other things being equal, decided only by a commodity's price and was defined as 'the sum of the demands of all the individuals there'. By measuring total demand at a given time and under given conditions, with all other factors held constant, Marshall was able to avoid the complications which external social effects on consumer choice would have brought to the analysis.

Marshall's decision to discount social influences on patterns of consumer demand in the interests of a greater scientific precision was not immediately seen as a matter of any consequence, but in 1892, after publication of the second edition of *Principles* some wider implications of this decision were raised in the *Economic Journal* by Sir Henry Cunynghame. Developing on an earlier privately published paper which had proposed an alternative approach to the derivation and diagrammatic representation of demand curves, Cunynghame accused Marshall of wrongly ignoring interpersonal effects on consumption in developing his theory of consumer's rent.

Marshall's definition of rent, argued Cunynghame, would only be true 'on the assumption that to each purchaser the money value of the article he got was quite independent of whether or no other persons also possessed the article'. This could well be true when basic necessaries were being purchased but the argument could not be sustained in some other circumstances:

> Almost the whole value of strawberries in March, to those who like this tasteless mode of ostentation, is the fact that others cannot get them ... The demand for

diamonds, rubies and sapphires is another example of this. As the number increases, not only does the price go down, but the very pleasure of those who already have them is decreased by their becoming common (1892: 37).

Cunynghame's view was that a part of the money value of any article varied in direct proportion to its supply and its availability to others. A product's worth, or money value, to an individual was therefore determined to some extent by changes in market supply which made it more or less accessible to others. He then attempted to translate these interpersonal effects on utility into a diagrammatic reinterpretation of consumer's rent, disputing the claim that changes in supply associated with a socially sensitive good caused shifts over time in the demand curve for that product rather than moves along the existing demand curve. Time, he claimed, was not a relevant phenomenon in this case:

> Generally speaking, it is desirable so to draw (demand) curves that they show in one glance all changes of price and consumer's rent which would be caused by a mere alteration in quantity supplied without the intervention of other causes (1892: 39).

Cunynghame's concept of successive demand curves, identifiable at any period of time, interested Professor F.Y. Edgeworth, then editor of the *Economic Journal*. Edgeworth, in developing his own earlier concept of a generalised utility function (1881), had already acknowledged that the quantities consumed by other people could influence the utility function of the individual. He now discussed Cunynghame's arguments privately with Marshall. Marshall had written directly to Cunynghame for clarification of certain points but had remained unconvinced by his arguments, and in April, 1892, he wrote to Edgeworth, attacking Cunynghame's analysis and calling his abilities as an economist into question:

> When I read his article, I knew I did not understand [certain phrases in the text] and thought he did not. I then wrote to him, and I have now no doubt in my own mind that he does not. He is quick, but impetuous; and all through his life has constantly supposed himself to know what he means when he does not (Guillebaud, 1961: 809).

Marshall was, above all, not prepared to concede that any possible perverse reaction of demand to quantities supplied, based on the argument that demand could and would vary in inverse proportion to the number of people possessing a socially significant product and/or to its general availability, was anything other than trivial in terms of general theory construction. Even if consumers were to behave in this way, he argued, it would represent a change in tastes and preferences over time and would be reflected in a shift in the demand curve rather than in a move along the original demand schedule.

Marshall took issue with Cunynghame over the correct interpretation of the 'short period' in economics, claiming that, regardless of the length of time involved, changed perceptions concerning product worth and the money value of commodities necessarily take place over time, whether measured in minutes or years. Marshall's view was widely accepted, and Cunynghame's case for so-called successive demand curves was never considered convincing. However, in trying unsuccessfully to reinterpret Marshall's treatment of consumer's rent, he had indirectly succeeded in drawing attention to the influences of interpersonal effects on utility, and had raised questions as to whether it was sensible or acceptable to remove them from economic theories of consumer demand.

Cunynghame's intervention had posed little real threat to Marshall, but the issue of status-seeking market behaviour was raised again one year later when Caroline Foley, writing in the *Economic Journal*, pointed to the importance of fashion in determining demand for many consumer goods. Noting the almost total neglect of the role of fashion in shaping consumption within the emerging theories of demand, she claimed that Marshall and others 'graze the fearful subject with hasty comment'.

Foley defined fashion as a 'want in wants' which not only shaped demand for luxuries but which could also be seen to influence the demand for necessaries such as bread. The desire for fashion goods was driven, she argued, by a nexus of social factors including the love of distinction, imitation and 'the effort after equalisation', and was important enough to demand a place within any emerging theory of consumption. It represented a law of variety in wants and was present in every society or social epoch, influencing the kind and quality of goods consumed, the quantities demanded and the rapidity of consumption. Although the importance of fashion in determining patterns of demand and consumption had been widely recognised by eighteenth and nineteenth century sociologists and philosophers, it had been largely ignored by economists, whether by accident or design, in constructing their theories of demand towards the end of the nineteenth century. Her criticisms, however, raised little real interest and were, in effect, ignored by economic theorists.

The third and fourth editions of Marshall's *Principles*, published in 1895 and 1898 respectively, made no concession to the reservations of Cunynghame or Foley, and interpersonal preference formation continued to be seen as a largely trivial issue. In 1903, however, the subject was raised again by a more eminent economist whose criticisms could not be so easily dismissed. Writing in the *Economic Journal* in March of that year, Professor A.C. Pigou, a former pupil and close friend of Marshall's, supported both

Cunynghame and Foley in arguing that the utility of many status-linked products was clearly influenced in the consumer's eyes by the quantities possessed or consumed by other socially relevant groups and that it was unacceptable for this fact to be ignored in the construction of any new consumer theory. Demand for diamonds, in Pigou's eyes, was often stimulated only by a 'desire for the uncommon'. Similarly, the demand for top hats referred to by Cunynghame reflected a desire to be 'in the swim'. Pigou, however, elaborated on Cunynghame's argument by pointing out that demand for socially conspicuous articles was not only a function of the quantities owned by others but of the specific distribution of the commodity:

> If a million extra diamonds or top-hats were miraculously created and entailed, without the power to lease, upon a single individual for ever, the effect on my utility curve for these two articles would be of a degree of smallness that even in this study of small quantities it would be pedantic not to neglect. Similarly, if the million extra top-hats went to the normally top-hatted class and merely allowed them to have three each instead of two, my utility curve would not be appreciably affected, while it might be if the miracle resulted in the so-called lower classes adopting this head gear. Again, if there were a second miracle destroying two-thirds of all existing top hats, the curve would not be affected if one were left to all accustomed to wear them, but it would be affected if the destructive forces were concentrated upon those belonging to people in my immediate neighbourhood (1903: 60).

Pigou argued that social distinction was never gained by simply being generally fashionable, but through 'a combination of resemblance to certain persons and of difference from certain other persons'. Consequently, the nature and direction of conspicuous consumption linked to an individual's desire for distinction was decided by his or her particular social and economic circumstances. The search for distinction led individuals to desire commodities which were consumed by groups which were seen as socially acceptable and to reject those goods and services which were widely identified with social groups with which he or she did not wish to be associated. If consumption of a particular product increased among a favoured social or economic group, then purchase and consumption of that product became more desirable. Conversely, if consumption increased among groups from which the individual wished to distance himself or herself, then the product's appeal was correspondingly diminished. Demand, claimed Pigou, was also significantly influenced by the views of 'distinguished persons' who were seen to set standards of taste and quality: as an example, he quoted the case of a housekeeper who had once observed to him that when a family ate little meat, the servants came to think that it was no longer a luxury and ate less of it themselves (1903: 61).

Marshall's marginal utility theories were, for the most part, accepted by Pigou, who agreed that it was highly improbable that a slight change in the consumption of anything would have an appreciable influence upon the utility of earlier increments. However, the validity of Marshall's treatment of utility was seen to be more suspect when larger changes in consumption caused individuals to be more aware that a change in what he termed 'commonness' had taken place. Marshall replied to Pigou in a letter dated 19th March 1903:

> I have just been reading your article in E.J. March 1903 ... Well! Am I right in supposing that your main argument is this: Though we may pass from the utility curve of an individual to the demand curve of a nation (or other group) as regards bread and milk or any other commodity which is valued only for its direct benefit to us, yet we cannot do that for commodities which we value partly because they impart social distinction. For a large change in the supply all round of such a commodity alters the conditions which we have assumed to be practically constant when making out the curve for an individual.
>
> So far as I can see I concur in this: and think something ought to have been said by me. But of course I have always insisted that the demand price of a group is not any approximate measure of satisfaction, save on the assumption that people of different incomes and also of different sensibilities are evenly distributed throughout the group. And next it may be said that the continued references to the effect of changes in fashion include in the purview such changes as alter the distinction-giving power of a thing (Pigou, 1925: 433).

Pigou's 1903 paper led Marshall to qualify his definition of utility in the fifth edition of *Principles*, published in 1907. However, the concession he made was limited and designed to pose no threat to emerging theories of value and utility. Total utility was defined more broadly as 'the total pleasure or other benefit it yields [the individual]' but, in a footnote, he made it clear that he felt discussion and analysis of any interpersonal effects on demand which were rooted in the desire for social esteem and recognition lay well outside mainstream economics:

> It cannot be too much insisted that to measure directly, or *per se*, either desires or the satisfaction which results from their fulfilment is impossible, if not inconceivable. If we could, we should have two accounts to make up, one of desires, and the other of realized satisfactions. And the two might differ considerably. For, to say nothing of higher aspirations, some of those desires with which economics is chiefly concerned, and especially those connected with emulation, are impulsive; many result from the force of habit; some are morbid and lead only to hurt; and many are based on expectations that are never fulfilled. Of course many satisfactions are not common pleasures, but belong to the development of man's higher nature, or to use a good old word, to his

beatification; and some may even partly result from self-abnegation. The two direct measurements might then differ. But as neither of them is possible, we fall back on the measurement which economics supplies, of the motive or moving force to action: and we make it serve, with all its faults, *both* for the desires which prompt activities and for the satisfactions that result from them (1907: 92–3n).

Marshall's comments on the difficulties associated with any attempts to measure the effects of socially-directed consumption would not have been disputed by Cunynghame, Foley or Pigou. However, the disagreement between Marshall and Pigou had been followed by Edgeworth, who then (1907) decided to conduct what appears to be the earliest statistical investigation into the claim that any one individual's demand may be affected by the amount demanded and consumed by other people. The 'investigation', however, was hardly rigorous. Edgeworth, a Fellow of All Souls, Oxford, decided to collect statistics from 'a certain Oxford College':

> The conception may be illustrated by the common supposition that at social gatherings which are cheered by alcoholic beverages the consumption of liquor per head is likely to be greater the more numerous the company. An opportunity of testing this belief is afforded by the varying size of the dinners at a certain Oxford college, whose members are thought to be susceptible to the influences of good fellowship. The dinners on the Sundays during that part of the terms which is described as 'full' seem well suited for the purpose of verification, the number varying considerably – from seven to forty-two in the course of the period which I have observed – while the character of the entertainment is not otherwise materially altered. The amount of wine (of different kinds) drunk on each occasion, and the cost thereof, have been recorded. I have utilised the records for four years, 1903–1906 inclusive, employing the following assumptions. I take the cost of the wine consumed as the measure of the quantity; and I take the variations in the quantities consumed per head as an index of variation in effective demand (1907: 223n).

Edgeworth then calculated whether the size of the 'party' had had any influence on the consumption of wine. In the event, he concluded from his analysis that 'no constant or considerable excess of consumption is shown by the larger as compared with the smaller parties' and that, for this particular study, the influence of the amount demanded by all on the average demand of each was inappreciable. Marshall, it seemed, had been vindicated.

Edgeworth's experiment was, in reality, so crude as to be effectively worthless, and no real value could be placed on its conclusions. Pigou, especially, ignored Edgeworth's supposed contribution to the debate, and continued to be unhappy with Marshall's grudging concessions over an issue which, to Pigou's mind, had serious implications for the development of demand theory. He returned twice more to the subject over the next ten years.

In 1910, writing on the money measurement of producers' and consumers' surplus, Pigou claimed that economists were still choosing to ignore the fact that when a change in the consumption of one consumer had the effect of indirectly altering the satisfaction associated with a given level of consumption by others, then individual and collective marginal demand curves could not be the same. This was particularly true in those cases where commodities were partly desired because they were rare or had special status value, or where they were desired partly because they were commonly consumed by others. This always had implications for any calculation of consumers' surplus when measured in money terms, and inevitably affected any demand/supply relationship.

In 1913, he returned again to the issue he had first raised some twenty years earlier. It was still usual to assume, he wrote, 'for purposes of elementary discussion', that an aggregated demand schedule was always made up by the simple addition of a number of independent demand schedules. Beyond elementary discussion, however, this assumption would not do. It posed no problem with regard to commodities which were desired wholly for the direct satisfaction they offered but could not be justified at all in relation to products wanted 'for the indirect satisfaction which their possession contributes through our thirst for reputation or distinction'.

Pigou, again, did not dispute that, for small changes in demand, such external effects could be safely discounted. However, when larger changes occurred, this inevitably altered perceptions of a product's rarity, status value, or 'commonness', and was bound to influence that part of consumer demand which turned upon the reputation-value of a commodity. Many goods and services were demanded not merely for their own sake but also because they were able to confer reputation or distinction on the owner. The consequence of this, argued Pigou, was obvious – demand for any distinction-giving article depended not only on its price but also on the extent to which it was seen to be fashionable and thus, indirectly, upon the purchase and consumption of others. When, he wondered, would economists recognise this fact and act upon it?

At the heart of Pigou's argument was his insistence that status-seeking consumer behaviour, far from being marginal and insignificant, could be commonly observed at all social and economic levels. If this were true, then Marshall's earlier admission that an individual's consumption could well depend on the consumption of others carried far greater implications than had hitherto been accepted. First, the derivation of demand curves became infinitely more complex than had been assumed. Demand theories which removed all consideration of social standing and prestige from consumer preference formation were now certainly flawed, for if consumer demand for certain products was heavily influenced by interpersonal effects, then aggregate demand for these products could not be derived from the simple compounding or summing of individual demand schedules. Conversely, aggregate demand, if known, could not with any accuracy be disaggregated into its component parts. Pigou's case was that the social influences on demand were there for all to see, and that demand schedules were, therefore, far too complex to be represented diagrammatically as Marshall had proposed. He believed that appropriate schedules could be sensibly constructed, but that a more sophisticated approach would be needed:

> When the conditions are such that the demand schedule of the separate sources in a market must be represented by formulae of this complex kind, problems, for the investigation of which it is necessary to go behind the demand schedule of the market as a whole, are still, theoretically, soluble; there are a sufficient number of equations to determine the unknowns. The solution, however, must needs be an algebraic solution, and no translation into the language of plane diagrams is possible (Pigou, 1913: 24).

In truth, Marshall's attitude towards interpersonal effects on demand had always been schizophrenic, for while he acknowledged that consumers were often motivated by a desire to impress others or to retain social standing and prestige, in his theoretical work he associated such behaviour only with a very rich, privileged minority and was then able to argue that it was of no relevance to general theories of consumer demand formation. He held to this view and was subsequently not persuaded of any need to make substantive revisions to later editions of *Principles*.

Marshall had certainly never denied that ostentatious display was often the motive behind the consumption of the rich, and he had come to believe that such behaviour, while trivial at the theoretical level, was a significant force acting against the general improvement of society at large. In a paper given to the Royal Economic Society in January 1907, he addressed the issue directly. 'The well-to-do classes', he observed, 'expend vast sums on things that add little to their happiness and very little to their higher well-being, but which they regard as necessary for their social position'. This conferred no real benefits on the spenders 'beyond the honour, the position, and the influence which it buys for them in society'. The answer to this conspicuous waste, he argued, was to change attitudes – to have society condemn such activity and to confer social status only on those who chose to display their wealth and success in ways which could be seen to be of direct benefit to society at large. In essence, he was restating the argument he had first used in the first edition of *Principles* in 1890:

> So long as wealth is applied to provide for every family the necessaries of life and culture, and an abundance of the higher forms of enjoyment for collective use, so

long the pursuit of wealth is a noble aim; and the pleasures which it brings are likely to increase with the growth of those higher activities which it is used to promote (1890: 137).

By 1907, Marshall was still arguing for more 'chivalry' in the individual's use of wealth. 'Gradually, it may be hoped, public opinion may be worked up to the point at which a rich man who lives idly will be despised ... and expenditure for the sake of display, however disguised by an aesthetic atmosphere, would be thought vulgar'. Real status would then be properly conferred on those who used wealth to invest in public goods which were seen to benefit society at large.

The rich, thought Marshall, had it in their power to improve the social and cultural environment of the community at large and had a key role to play in this respect. This they would only do, however, if society were to openly confer status on those whose philanthropy was widely recognised while at the same time condemning expenditures driven only by personal vanity. Not only was it ethically and morally right to change the nature and direction of conspicuous consumption, but the rich had a vested interest in so doing in order to diminish the growing political appeal of socialism and collectivism.

There is no doubt that Alfred Marshall fully recognised the existence and importance of status-led conspicuous consumption at the end of the nineteenth century, and knew that the most casual observation of market behaviour quickly established that it existed at all social and economic levels. Like Smith, he also acknowledged that expenditure on dress and personal appearance was often driven not by vanity but by a desire to retain social standing and position in the community, and that such socially-motivated consumption could be seen as necessary rather than as ostentatious expenditure. At the same time, he was never prepared to incorporate these commonplace expenditures into economic analysis and theory construction.

Marshall was never at ease with the concept and existence of status-directed consumption, and was always happy to distance himself and his work from such activity. The strong social character of expenditure for display allowed him to argue that it was no part of the economist's brief to examine such behaviour, and that any detailed exploration of motives and objectives was best left to anthropologists, sociologists and others far better equipped to carry out such work. Many economists would agree today with this viewpoint, and it has never been controversial to claim that detailed examination of the non-economic motives underpinning consumer behaviour is the proper province of other social sciences. However, Marshall went further than this when he chose to marginalise and dismiss the economic consequences of such behaviour, and to then derive demand schedules which, for status-sensitive products at least, were conveniently 'cleansed' of any suggestion that interpersonal effects could and did influence consumer choice and the marginal utility of products. His motives for so doing are not difficult to understand, for by limiting discussion in this way, theory construction was made less complicated, and demand measurement more feasible. Any attacks on the concept of demand additivity, which lay at the heart of much of Marshall's economic analysis, could also be more easily deflected.

It was this refusal to address the economic consequences of consumption intended for social distinction, consumption which Marshall himself had acknowledged as widespread and extending across society, that Pigou could not accept. In the event, however, few chose to join with Pigou, and the level of protest among economists was insignificant. At the turn of the century, any serious consideration of status-directed consumption, within European economic theory at least, was entirely missing. The subject, however, was by now receiving far greater attention across the Atlantic.

References

Cunynghame, Henry (1892), 'Some Improvements in Simple Geometrical Methods of Treating Exchange Value, Monopoly and Rent', *Economic Journal*, **2** (March), 35–52.

Edgeworth, F.Y. (1881), *Mathematical Psychics: An Essay on the Application of Mathematics to the Moral Sciences*, London: Kegan Paul.

Edgeworth, F.Y. (1907), 'Appreciations of Mathematical Theories I', *Economic Journal*, **17** (June), 221–31.

Foley, Caroline A. (1893), 'Fashion', *Economic Journal*, **3** (September), 458–74.

Guillebaud, C.W. (ed.) (1961), *Alfred Marshall's Principles of Economics*, ninth variorum edition, vols.1 and 2 (text and notes), London: Macmillan.

Marshall, Alfred (1890), *Principles of Economics*, London: Macmillan. References to this and to subsequent editions of *Principles* are in C.W. Guillebaud (ed.) (1961), ninth variorum edition, (op. cit.)

Marshall, Alfred (1907), 'The Social Possibilities of Economic Chivalry', paper given to the Royal Economic Society, 9th January, reprinted with additions in the *Economic Journal*, **17** (March), 7–29.

Pigou, A.C. (1903), 'Some Remarks on Utility', *Economic Journal*, **13** (March), 58–68.

Pigou, A.C. (1910), 'Producers' and Consumers' Surplus', *Economic Journal*, **20** (September), 358–70.

Pigou, A.C. (1913), 'The Interdependence of Different Sources of Demand and Supply in a Market', *Economic Journal*, **23** (March), 19–24.

Pigou, A.C. (1925), *Memorials of Alfred Marshall*, London: Macmillan.

5   Thorstein Veblen and the Gilded Age

In an address to the Cambridge Economic Club in October 1896, Alfred Marshall had looked at the progress made in the development of economic theory and thought in the nineteenth century and identified what he considered to be the work facing the new generation of twentieth century economists if this progress were to be sustained.

Marshall argued that sound foundations had been laid by the classical and neoclassical economists, and challenged those critics of *Principles* who had found his treatment of economic behaviour too limiting and restrictive. He conceded that economists had to recognise the wider social setting of economic activities, but any attempt to embrace 'the whole man' within economic theory and thought was too ambitious; economics could not concern itself too much with anthropological, psychological and sociological considerations, but had to focus on those aspects of man's behaviour which were clearly economic in nature. At the same time, he was prepared to concede that, even within this narrower focus, economics had, on occasion, pursued taxonomic solutions at the expense of realism:

> We must not picture to ourselves an unreal world as it might, or ought to be; and make schemes for it. That way lies social madness, leading to a failure of hot aspirations and thence to cold reaction. Our first duty as economists is to make a reasoned catalogue of the world as it is ... and to make that estimate ... somewhat less badly than it has been made hitherto (1897: 125).

Marshall's warning that economics had always to reflect market realities was hardly controversial. However, a small but increasingly vociferous group of American economists had come to believe that the discipline had failed to respond at all to the great changes which had occurred in the industrialising economies since 1850, not least in matters relating to consumption. Nowhere was change more evident than in the United States, an economy which was now largely unrecognisable from the one which would have been familiar to John Rae. From the 1830s onwards, value systems had changed substantially as movements towards individualism and the pursuit of wealth took hold. By the end of the Civil War, a self-help doctrine was being established, and the cult of the self-made man was becoming a central part of American social thought.

The commercialism which took root after 1860 allowed the new business class to compete with the country's traditional élites for status and social prestige, for while the former lacked 'pedigree', their increasing wealth gave them the means to engage in conspicuous competition with the old aristocracy. The period from 1840 to 1860 saw a marked increase in ostentatious expenditure, but it was after 1860 that conspicuous consumption rose to often outrageous levels as the country entered a Gilded Age which was to endure for some fifty years.

Riding on the back of Samuel Smiles's self-help philosophy, the new business élite used its wealth in ways which totally broke with tradition. So intense did competition for status become that the period after 1880 became known as the era of the status revolution. These high levels of conspicuous consumption were nurtured and sustained by the concentration of wealth among a privileged few, and by a 'soft' tax system which secured the highest levels of discretionary income for those fortunate enough to be members of the new industrial aristocracy.

By 1890, levels of ostentatious luxury expenditure had reached new heights. Many expenditures had become so conspicuously wasteful that the direct physiological or physical utility of the goods and services consumed often approached zero. In truth, the new rich were trying to establish a code of behaviour in which belonging to 'Society' was simply determined by wealth rather than by any considerations of inherited position or breeding (Mason, 1981).

To some more radical American economists of the late 1890s, the significance of Gilded Age patterns of consumption, and the emulation it generated in others, convinced them that Marshall's seeming complacency over the past record and continuing relevance of neoclassical economic theory could not be justified. These dissenters, many of whom identified with the Historical School of economic thought, were more sympathetic to the potential contributions of other social sciences, and could not accept that economic theory had been moving in the right directions over the last half of the nineteenth century.

One of the few economists with a particular interest in the study of consumption at the time was Simon Patten, an economics professor at the University of Pennsylvania. In 1889, he had published a small book, *The Consumption of Wealth*, which had explored the social psychology of consumption from the particular viewpoint of an economist. Patten had insisted that, far from occasionally taking note of certain aspects of man's behaviour, as Marshall was suggesting, consumer economics was dependent on psychology to provide, through deductive reasoning, a theory of human nature relating to consumption which would properly explain the conduct of people when faced with the necessity of making choices.

Patten returned to this theme again in 1892, this time berating the classical Mill for excluding consumption almost totally from economic discussion, and the neoclassical Jevons for using a theory of consumption which often bore no relation to observed market behaviour. With antecedents such as these, Patten argued, it was little wonder that consumption theory was both neglected and inadequate; not until the subject was taken more seriously and was opened up to more plausible explanations of human behaviour, would a credible theory of consumption begin to emerge.

While Patten is today seen by some as the first economist to point to the shortcomings of consumption theory within economics, his work made little impression at the time. However, a far greater impact was to be made by another dissenting voice. Between 1898 and 1900, Thorstein Veblen, then a relatively obscure lecturer in economics at the University of Chicago, published a series of articles in the *Quarterly Journal of Economics* in which he attacked the neoclassical approach to consumer theory with a greater rigour and sophistication.

Veblen did not believe that economics had made the advances claimed for it by Alfred Marshall and was not at all sure that Marshall himself really believed it:

> Probably no economist today has either the hardihood or the inclination to say that the science has now reached a definitive formulation, either in the detail of results or as regards the fundamental features of theory. The nearest recent approach to such a position on the part of an economist of accredited standing is perhaps to be found in Professor Marshall's Cambridge address of a year and a half ago. But these utterances are so far from the jaunty confidence shown by the classical economists of half a century ago that what most forcibly strikes the reader of Professor Marshall's address is the exceeding modesty and the uncalled-for humility of the spokesman for the 'old generation' (1898a: 374).

Marshall's seeming reticence was understandable, argued Veblen, because economics was demonstrably not an evolutionary science, rooted as it was in the inflexible body of natural laws and fundamental truths of the classical period. Adam Smith, claiming that men were led by the invisible hand of the Creator to establish a natural order to serve the ends of human welfare, had believed that human events were ultimately controlled by the 'design of God', and Veblen was able to sympathise to some extent with this naive eighteenth century view of the world. However, he believed that, after Smith, economics had fallen into 'profane hands'(1899b: 411), and he showed little sympathy for Benthamite Utilitarianism, and the hedonistic calculus based on twin principles of pleasure and pain. To Veblen, the Utilitarians had rejected the immutability of the divine hand of God, but had tried to hold to, and develop, many of the natural laws and universal truths which underpinned earlier classical doctrine in an attempt to construct a scientific taxonomy. Political economy and economic theory had, consequently, become obsessed with sequences of pecuniary events and with wholly pecuniary motives which assumed nothing more sophisticated than a search for the greatest economic gain at the least economic sacrifice:

> This perfect competitive system, with its untainted 'economic man', is a feat of the scientific imagination and is not intended as a competent expression of fact. It is an expedient of abstract reasoning; and its avowed competency extends only to the abstract principles, the fundamental laws of the science, which hold only so far as the abstraction holds. But, as happens in such cases, having once been accepted and assimilated as real, though perhaps not as actual, it becomes an effective constituent in the inquirer's habits of thought, and goes to shape his knowledge of facts. It comes to serve as a norm of substantiality or legitimacy; and facts in some degree fall under its constraint, as is exemplified by many allegations regarding the 'tendency' of things (1899b: 422).

This lack of realism was attributed to the fact that economists were, for many years, determined to emulate the physical sciences and to develop a body of natural laws and universal truths. The assumed truths of classical economics, argued Veblen, might, at best, explain the economic behaviour of individuals in primitive, small-scale communities in which man's needs were dominated by the need to survive and by little else. However, in larger, more prosperous and sophisticated societies, choices increased, behaviour became far more complex, and could not then be accommodated within an inflexible set of taxonomic solutions.

In the latter part of the nineteenth century, this search for scientific taxonomy led both neoclassicists and Austrian School economists to acknowledge and adjust, in part, to a rapidly changing world, while at the same time clinging to concepts of 'normal' behaviour, and treating any causal sequences which did not conform to these norms only as disturbing factors of little real relevance. Economics, to Veblen, still showed 'too many reminiscences of the "natural" and the "normal", of "verities" and "tendencies", of "controlling principles" and "disturbing causes" to be classed as an evolutionary science' (1898a: 381).

As a result of this inability to accept and explain the complexities of economic life in modern societies, Veblen believed that economics had lost the support of the wider population who could not reconcile economic theory with what they saw around them. Economics was, quite simply, out of touch, and 'only for those who by the fortunate accident of birth or education have been able to conserve the taxonomic animus has the science during the last third of a century continued to be of absorbing interest' (1898a: 386).

Preoccupation with taxonomic schemes had, in Veblen's view, stifled progress in economics. For progress to be made, the discipline had to be more concerned with the economic life process and with a more realistic interpretation of man in society. In particular, economics had to stop believing that man was passive within his economic and social environment, that he was 'a lightning calculator of pleasures and pains, who oscillates like a homogeneous globule of desire of happiness under the impulse of stimuli that shift him about the area, but leave him intact' (1898a: 389). Such assumptions were, claimed Veblen, based on a belief in hedonistic man not as a prime mover, but as an individual not in control of life and subject to a series of events forced upon him by circumstances beyond his control.

This interpretation of man as a passive respondent to events found no place within current psychological and sociological thought, argued Veblen. On the contrary, it was now clear that man was active within his environment, and had aims and objectives which themselves determined behaviour both in terms of production and consumption. Activity, in short, was typically directed to an objective end, as men always and everywhere sought to do something with their lives. Furthermore, it was no part of economics to impute moral or ethical values to these objectives. Whether the desired end was considered to be worthy or unworthy was irrelevant; it was sufficient that it generated a causal sequence which could be observed and which was therefore a part of economic activity.

Veblen's views on the relative sterility of economic theory were conditioned not only by his personal observation of late nineteenth-century institutions and society, but also by his conviction that economics could not be treated in isolation from other social sciences, in particular from sociology and psychology. Born in 1857 in Wisconsin, the son of Norwegian immigrant farmers, he had graduated from Carleton College Academy in Minnesota in 1880. After further periods of study at Johns Hopkins and Yale, where he read philosophy and economics, his health deteriorated and he spent the years from 1884 to 1891 living in considerable poverty in Stacyville, Iowa. In 1891, however, he succeeded in obtaining a teaching fellowship at Cornell University, moving in 1892 to a teaching post at the University of Chicago, where he spent the next ten years developing his radical economic ideas.

Veblen's attack on economic orthodoxy was wide-ranging: he was unhappy with many of the assumptions and values of American finance capitalism, with theories of capital, labour and wage determination, and with industrial production and productivity. Most of all, he was unable to accept classical and neoclassical theories of utility and value and the theories of consumer demand which they underpinned. Observation of Gilded Age consumption in late nineteenth-century America, he argued, quickly established that conventional economic explanations of consumer behaviour and consumer choice could not be defended.

To Veblen, existing consumer theory failed because it refused to recognise that a large part of an individual's consumption of goods and services was shaped by social relationships and by the need to secure status within society. He first rehearsed these views in an 1892 article which was primarily concerned not with consumer theory per se, but with the relative strengths and weaknesses of the new theories of socialism which were attracting considerable attention after 1880.

Socialists were wrong, argued Veblen, to claim that the poor had suffered in absolute terms under capitalist industrial systems based on private ownership and free competition. On the contrary, under capitalism, individual wealth had been gradually improved. At the same time, he did acknowledge that the gap between rich and poor was widening and producing demands for a fairer distribution of wealth. And it was this wealth and income gap, rather than absolute poverty, which was generating demands for social and economic change.

Controversially, Veblen argued that protest was coming not from those who were suffering intense physical privation, but from the relatively disadvantaged who were finding it increasingly difficult to maintain their status in society – those for whom the cost of maintaining a decent appearance was becoming so high that it was diverting more and more resources away from expenditure on necessaries in order to preserve some outward show of social respectability. He was in no doubt that expenditure on securing social rank and position was seen by consumers as indispensable and would not be neglected, even at the cost of physical well-being. A substantial part of the privation suffered by many poorer Americans, he argued, was not physically necessary, but was caused by the poor diverting a significant part of their income towards maintaining outward appearances. Moreover, this self-inflicted privation could not be wished away, for the need for social esteem was an ever-present characteristic of man.

In the increasingly impersonal modern societies of the nineteenth century, Veblen believed, wealth served as the principal indicator of economic success, and was used to secure personal status with people who were not immediate neighbours. However, it was never sufficient simply to possess wealth, the wealth itself had to be displayed through the purchase of goods and services which were expensive enough to impress others and so preserve, or improve, social standing. In short, the appearance of success had become more important than the substance. and 'it becomes indispensable to afford whatever expenditures other people with whom we class ourselves can afford, and desirable to afford a little more than others' (1892: 394).

Capitalist society could not be held guilty of creating cravings of human vanity, argued Veblen, for concern with personal status and social standing was evident in the most primitive societies. However, in these earlier societies, esteem was measured not only by wealth but by other non-pecuniary virtues and characteristics. It was capitalism and the process of increasing industrialisation which had raised one form of emulation above all others by promoting admiration only for economic success and by narrowing the scope of emulation to this one line. And as industrial societies grew and became increasingly impersonal, so the display of wealth became the only effective means of winning respect from others who were effectively strangers in a cosmopolitan and geographically dispersed community.

Under such conditions, the struggle for existence had been transformed into a determination to keep up appearances. This change had, for the most part, been created by the institution of private property, and socialism seemed to offer a way of avoiding what he saw as a significant misdirection of funds into unnecessary expenditure:

> Under a regime which should allow no inequality of acquisition or of income, this form of emulation, which is due to the possibility of such inequality, would also tend to become obsolete. With the abolition of private property, the characteristic of human nature which now finds its exercise in this form of emulation, should logically find exercise in other, perhaps nobler and socially more serviceable activities; it is at any rate not easy to imagine it running into any line of action more futile or less worthy of human effort (1892: 399).

Veblen saw socialism as having the potential to produce an economic system and culture similar to those earlier, primitive societies which had been able to channel the desire for social esteem into less harmful, non-pecuniary activities. However, his interest in status-driven ownership and consumption extended well beyond socialist theory. Through the 1890s he returned to the subject on several occasions (1894; 1898b; 1899c), exploring the relationship between cultural values, economic and social change, and the evolving nature of status-seeking within society.

In *The Theory of the Leisure Class*, published in 1899, he drew his work together and developed a theory of status-led consumption. Although the book was intended primarily as an attack on business ethics and on the value systems of American finance capitalism (and was often mistakenly seen only as a satire on the aristocratic classes and business élites), a large part of the book was concerned with the motives and nature of conspicuous economic display. It remains today one of the major theoretical works on the subject.

The existence of a 'leisure class', argued Veblen, could be traced back to the most primitive barbarian cultures, albeit not in a fully developed form. While distinctions between people in the earliest communal societies were necessarily blurred, once differences in role and occupation became more clearly defined, the resulting division of labour allowed distinctions to be drawn between the working and leisure classes within society, in essence between those involved in industrial as opposed to non-industrial employment. Man's ability to demonstrate membership of the leisure class brought with it a social standing and personal prestige within the community, and this membership was demonstrated through ownership and possession. In the most primitive societies, the ownership of women had conferred status, but as societies had evolved, leisure class membership was more effectively achieved through the ostentatious display of wealth. In essence, the physical aggression of early societies was replaced by an industrial aggression based on wealth.

As men competed with each other to secure the status which came with the ability to display wealth, so this competition encouraged high levels of acquisition and ownership. Veblen believed that while physical consumption was often assumed by economists to be the legitimate end of acquisition, it was social motives which often explained the desire for consumption and ownership: acquisition was, in fact, used to display wealth, and this, in turn, conferred status on the owner. 'The possession of wealth confers honour: it is an invidious comparison' (1899d: 26).

The ownership of property, goods and services, therefore, inevitably led to such 'invidious comparisons'. In earlier tribal societies these comparisons were based on the group (or tribe) rather than on the individual, but when the custom of individual, rather than communal, ownership grew, then invidious comparisons began to be made between individuals even within the same group.

As status competition increased, the possession of wealth, intended originally as recognition of an individual's enterprise and industrial efficiency, became meritorious in its own right. And as comparisons of individual wealth became the norm, so respectability in society came to depend on being able to demonstrate a certain standard of living. As the need for social esteem fed through into self-respect, conspicuous consumption came to be seen not as an option but as a social necessity. Furthermore, levels of consumption were never static for, as prevailing norms of reputable ownership were widely achieved, the more affluent in society then raised standards to once more distance themselves socially from others. This in turn encouraged a general revision of standards at all social and economic levels, and had the effect of raising expectations and consumption across the socioeconomic scale. In this way, status competition became an ongoing, dynamic process for individuals at all levels of society, placing increasing demands on their standards of purchase, ownership and consumption.

Veblen argued that the ostentatious display of wealth was achieved in two principal ways. First, the relatively well-to-do in society were able to demonstrate their superiority through 'conspicuous leisure', or the conspicuous abstention from labour – an indicator of wealth as it demonstrated that the individual or family had no need to work. However, while productive work was seen as demeaning, this conspicuous leisure had, in its own way, to be put to good use if it was to secure maximum social recognition. To this end, men of rank and status were expected to spend time on scholarly and artistic pursuits which added to their cultural and literary accomplishments and to their overall manners and breeding (in this way, 'old money' had always sought to distance itself from the pretensions of the nouveaux riches).

Despite this need to use leisure time creatively, Veblen argued that, in the final analysis, there was an overriding requirement on the part of such consumers to demonstrate a substantial and patent ability to waste the time which could otherwise have been used for productive work. This conspicuous waste also had to extend to a rich man's wife and even to household servants who themselves needed to be seen to be underemployed. In this sense, the leisure of the servant was not seen as his or her own free time but as a reflection of the employer's wealth and status.

Veblen acknowledged that the excesses of conspicuous leisure once seen in society were, by the late nineteenth century, becoming rarer. Employers (in essence, the new business élites) were increasingly involved in productive activity and were not preoccupied with their own ability to consume substantial amounts of leisure time. In reality, however, conspicuous leisure had not disappeared, but had changed in nature. Now greater emphasis was being placed by the rich man on the conspicuous waste of the household unit and on the vicarious (or delegated) leisure of wife and servants, who were then also made responsible for securing the family's social reputation within the community.

A second and often equally effective means for the rich to display their wealth and social standing was through the conspicuous consumption of expensive and often superfluous goods and services. The utility of consumption as an evidence of wealth was a derivative growth, a characteristic which traditionally had also been seen as the preserve of the wealthy, leisured class. Taboos and other restrictions on the consumption of luxury goods had been used to limit consumption only to ruling élites, and the later use of sumptuary laws in more developed societies served the same purpose. Through such devices, the conspicuous consumption both of non-productive leisure and of high-status commodities had been reserved for the wealthy.

It was recognised in the earliest societies that status-directed consumption could only be successful if it was truly conspicuous and commanded attention as an ostentatious display of wealth. This often led to inordinate expenditures on socially visible goods and services and on banquets and other entertainments which served as ideal vehicles for ostentatious waste. In Veblen's time also, the excesses of Gilded Age conspicuous consumption served to demonstrate the perceived importance of putting wasteful consumption in evidence. Wealth, in short, was not enough: status was secured only when such wealth, and the ability to pay, were on open view.

For the very rich, the goods and services favoured for conspicuous consumption were those which commanded prices which put them beyond the financial reach of the less well off. At the extreme, when the individual was motivated only by a wish or need to display purchasing power, the direct utility of the commodity being purchased, that is, its utility in use, was of no real interest. Indeed, if the product was not only expensive, but had a perceived utility value approaching zero, this only served to underline the degree of conspicuous waste associated with the purchase and consequently added to its status value. To the buyer, satisfaction was derived from a given audience reaction not to any positive attributes of the good or service in question but to the social status which was secured by demonstrating an ability to pay for what was often a superfluous, conspicuously wasteful product. And, as with conspicuous leisure, many business leaders of the nineteenth century did not conspicuously consume for themselves as individuals, but passed responsibility for vicarious consumption to the household unit and, more particularly, to their wives.

This consumption of conspicuous leisure and of expensive, superfluous goods and services, therefore, became the hallmark of the very rich. At the same time, while such consumption had traditionally been associated with the wealthy at the top of the social and economic pyramid, Veblen was in no doubt that the need to secure social standing and prestige was evident at all levels of modern society, making it possible to observe status-motivated consumption at all levels of society. While the rich indulged in conspicuous consumption intended to generate 'invidious comparisons' with others less fortunate than themselves, so the poorer sections of society turned to 'pecuniary emulation' in order to be thought of as members of a higher class or social group. At the same time, opportunities to conspicuously consume were far more limited further down the social scale, and status-seeking consequently took different forms.

First, opportunities to enjoy significant amounts of leisure time were not available to a man whose limited means required him to work in order to support his family. Only the vicarious leisure of his wife offered an opportunity for status-seeking. When the family was so poor that the wife herself needed to work, then all attempts at conspicuous leisure had to be abandoned and status sought only through the conspicuous consumption of goods and services. Even the poorest in society, argued Veblen, found the resources, at whatever cost, to attempt to sustain and protect the family's social reputation and pecuniary decency:

> No class of society, not even the most abjectly poor, foregoes all customary conspicuous consumption. The last items of this category of consumption are not given up except under stress of the direst necessity. Very much of squalor or discomfort will be endured before the last trinket or the last pretence of pecuniary decency is put away. There is no class and no country so abjectly before the pressure of physical want as to deny themselves all gratification of this higher or spiritual need (1899d: 85).

At the very lowest levels, Veblen believed that individuals and families could, at best, strive only to protect their existing status within society. Among those who could command greater resources, however, he believed that conspicuous consumption was used in an attempt to join the social class immediately above them. 'The members of each stratum', he claimed, 'accept as their ideal of decency the scheme of life in vogue in the next highest stratum, and bend their energies to live up to that ideal'. These ambitions to join higher social and economic groups inevitably placed significant demands on available resources, demands which individuals were prepared to meet, even at the price of reducing consumption of the most basic necessaries.

Modern industrial society, argued Veblen, had seen a general improvement in the living standards of vast numbers of people who, as a consequence, had far more discretionary income at their disposal. Whilst consumption of basic foodstuffs and other necessaries had undoubtedly increased, a proportion of these increased discretionary funds had also been channelled into consumption which was intended not to improve personal well-being in physiological terms, but to secure social status in societies where the display of wealth had become honorific and added to an individual's prestige and reputation within the community.

Modern society, and the increased opportunities for status-seeking at all levels, argued Veblen, had seen a marked swing away from conspicuous leisure and towards conspicuous consumption as the principal means of securing status in the community. This greater reliance on consumption rather than leisure had been further promoted by the movement of people out of rural areas, where social groups were small, tightly-knit, but relatively impoverished, into towns and cities where consumption rather than leisure served more effectively as a means of repute. Additionally, conspicuous consumption gained in respectability, because, unlike conspicuous leisure, it was seen by an increasingly industrial society to encourage what Veblen described as man's innate instinct of workmanship by promoting excellence in the design and manufacture of goods. Conspicuous leisure, in contrast, was considered to be non-productive and a more reprehensible waste of time.

To Veblen, the propensity to conspicuously consume was now self-evident within society, and was of primary importance. 'With the exception of the instinct of self-preservation', he claimed, 'the propensity for emulation is probably the strongest and most alert and persistent of the economic motives proper' (1899d: 110). And in any capitalist, industrial society, it could only express itself in pecuniary emulation and as some form of conspicuous waste. Such emulation was, moreover, a dynamic force, and was infinitely expansible, with opportunities to consume for status increasing as industrial efficiency itself increased. It would endure because it was incorporated into individual perceptions of decency, and so became a part of each person's standard of living – a standard measured not only in terms of personal, utilitarian consumption but also in terms of achieved social standing and position within society.

Veblen believed that, at all levels of consumption, purchases typically possessed both utilitarian (productive) and status (non-productive) value. Even in those articles which, at first sight, appeared to be wholly wasteful, there was often some trace of useful purpose. Similarly, there was an element of conspicuous display in the more mundane, utilitarian purchases made at all levels of society. While the poor were compelled to spend their more limited incomes on goods and services which had a high practical value, they would pay some premium on price for even the most basic necessaries in order to secure social status – seen, for example, in the strong preference of the nineteenth-century poor for more expensive white bread rather than for the equally nutritious, yet socially inferior, black variety.

Demand for consumer goods and services was, therefore, driven by a desire to purchase both productive utility and status value. To the consumer, the status attributes of any given product were not seen as waste but as an integral part of the overall utility of the product. It was this failure to properly integrate status-seeking elements into the total utility function and into associated theories of value which, in Veblen's view, discredited classical and neoclassical demand theory. The challenge facing economists was, therefore, to develop ideas of utility and value which more properly described the patterns of purchase and consumption which were readily observable in the real world.

Although *The Theory of the Leisure Class* made a considerable impact at the time of its publication, Veblen was, for the most part, disappointed with its reception, primarily because it was liked by those for whom he had little time, and was disliked or, even worse, ignored, by those whom he most wanted to influence.

He was particularly disappointed at the popular view of the book as a satire upon the aristocratic classes, and thought that a majority of the people who were most lavish in their praise were of little real consequence. As Dorfman (1934) pointed out, 'Veblen became the god of all the radicals, although he despised them', and was seen to be promoting a socialist, even Marxist, agenda. Some declared the work to be of real value; Ward (1900), reviewing the book in the *American Journal of Sociology*, felt that it was 'likely to become a classic'. At the same time, conservative opinion was extremely hostile. In *The Yale Review* of August, 1899, D. Collin Wells wrote that the book had been written by a 'dilettante', and brought both sociology and economics into disrepute. The book, he argued, was often ill-considered, vicious and full of ex-cathedra propositions which had no basis in fact. Veblen's style was a 'scientific jargon from which no clear meaning can be extracted'.

Most significantly for Veblen, *The Theory of the Leisure Class* gained little immediate respect from economists, and was largely ignored. John Cummings of Harvard University, in a review article for the *Journal of Political Economy* (1899), was critical of many of Veblen's views. In reply, Veblen (1899e) suggested that Cummings had, in effect, misunderstood much of the argument set out in the book – misunderstandings for which Veblen was (tongue in cheek, perhaps) prepared to take the blame:

> Had I the good fortune to say what I intended, and no more, my critic would, I believe, have been saved a good share of the corrections which he is good enough to offer, as well as much of the annoyance which he is at pains to conceal. Indeed, to such an extent does this appear to be true that the greater portion and the weightier of Mr. Cumming's criticisms appears to proceed on misapprehension that might have been obviated by a more facile use of language (1899e: 17).

Veblen was, nonetheless, depressed by the generally adverse reaction to the book within the academic world, and hurt by the way in which it was largely ignored by economic theorists of the day. In truth, the series of articles which had appeared between 1898 and 1900 in the *Quarterly Journal of Economics* and the appearance of *The Theory of the Leisure Class* in 1899, failed to make any immediate impact on mainstream consumption theory, and contributed little or nothing to the development of economic thought at the turn of the century. Given that Veblen's views on the nature of status-directed consumption were not called into serious question at the time (most conceded that the influence of status considerations on patterns of consumption was easily observable on a day-to-day basis in the United States), this failure to influence economic thought might seem puzzling. In the event, several factors were working against Veblen at the time.

First, Veblen was seen by many classical and neoclassical economists of the day to be promoting socialism and socialist values, and to be working to a political rather than to an academic agenda. His analysis of pecuniary emulation, of conspicuous consumption and of ostentatious waste appeared to many to be a political polemic, a view which was reinforced by the warm reception given to his book by many radicals of the day, who preferred to interpret his work not as a considered explanation of consumption and consumer behaviour, but as an attack on the established order. Certainly, Veblen's views of American finance capitalism were far from sympathetic, but his work suffered nevertheless from being labelled by some as political rather than economic.

Even when this political barrier was overcome, Veblen was often treated as a sociologist rather than as an economic theorist. He had without doubt been influenced by the work of sociologists such as Herbert Spencer and Lester Ward, and had always insisted that sociology and economics had to come together before any credible theory of consumer demand could be developed. This approach, however, gave more conventional economists the opportunity to reject his work, arguing that it was describing the sociology of consumption and not making any recognisable contribution to economic theory. In this way, it could be safely marginalised.

Most economists had a vested interest in distancing themselves from Veblen's work, for it could have presented a very real challenge to conventional economic thought. Classical and neoclassical demand theory had not attempted to accommodate the fact that a significant part of consumption was motivated by status-seeking considerations. Had Veblen's views entered the economic mainstream and been given due weight, then economists would again have had to question the validity of the orthodox demand theory on which much microeconomic analysis was resting.

The potential threat posed to neoclassical economics by *The Theory of the Leisure Class* was underlined by the fact that no effective refutation of 'pecuniary emulation' and its associated theories of consumer motivation was put forward. Some (Moran, 1901) argued that conventional demand theory could, in fact, accommodate such external effects on consumer demand within the catch-all 'tastes and preferences' variable used in neoclassical analysis to explain differences between individuals in their purchase and consumption, but such arguments carried little conviction. For the most part, economists felt it was wiser to label Veblen a populist and sociologist, and to ignore his strictures. So successful was this strategy in the UK, for example, that the first review of *The Theory of the Leisure Class* to appear in the *Economic Journal* was in 1925, some twenty six years after the book was first published.

While economists generally were happy to ignore Veblen's radical economic ideas at the turn of the century, Veblen himself must share some of the blame for this neglect, for while he forcefully, and often correctly, challenged more conventional economics in so far as consumer theory was concerned, he failed to offer a practical alternative or reinterpretation of marginal utility theory. If the concept of additivity and cardinal measurement could be shown to be false, for example, then what alternative approach to the actual measurement of utility was Veblen proposing which would then be of practical use in developing a new 'science' of economics? In the event, he proposed none, and this failure to offer a workable alternative inevitably diminished the force of his argument.

Veblen was right to believe that his work had moved beyond observation and had offered an explanation of observed consumer behaviour. At the same time, he remained open to the criticism that his theories could be taken no further in any operational sense. Many thought that the only conclusion to be reached from his work was that consumer demand was a function of the interaction of culture, society, economics and the environment and that little else could be said. His critics argued that he still needed to translate an essentially sociological interpretation of demand into a parallel economic theory which allowed for the measurement of utility and which could then be used to take economics forward as an evolutionary science. Veblen, it was claimed, had offered, prima facie, a reasoned hypothesis, revealing the inadequacies of conventional neoclassical theory to good effect, yet had failed to construct a replacement theory which offered any practical prospects of successfully measuring utility and value.

Although Veblen was not welcomed into the economic mainstream, he was not alone among American economists in the belief that the discipline had lost its way by the end of the nineteenth century and was offering nothing positive with regard to consumer theory. Patten's contribution to the debate has already been referred to. Similarly, Seligman agreed in 1901 that the values with which economics was dealing were essentially social. 'Social economics', he argued, 'deals with the relation of man to man, class to class. The value with which we have to deal, therefore, is not an individual, but a social matter. It is society as a whole which set a value on things. Society is indeed composed of individuals, but it is the aggregate of individual wants that shapes values in actual life' (1901: 323). Value, he concluded, was not merely the expression of marginal utility, it was the expression of *social* marginal utility, and needed to be considered in this light.

While Seligman was unhappy with economics for ignoring the social dimension in consumption, however, he did not examine or discuss the phenomenon of consuming for status, although his concept of social marginal utility could have accommodated such consumer behaviour with far greater ease than conventional neoclassical analyses of value and utility. However, his attack on the implicit assumption of classical doctrines and of current marginal utility theory that the individual was not unduly influenced by social considerations in coming to decisions on purchasing and consumption put him close to Veblen in his interpretation of consumer demand.

While Seligman did not specifically address forms of status-motivated conspicuous consumption, Keasbey (1903) took up the theme directly. Since the time of Adam Smith, he argued, the value of any product had been seen to have two principal components – one, a consumer value or value in use; the other, a value to producers, or a value in exchange. But he agreed with Veblen that there were, in reality, two reasons why consumers wanted goods, for products not only had a value in use but, as Veblen had argued, a social value, a prestige value, which, though generally recognised and widely observed as having a significant influence on market behaviour, had been ignored in the development of consumer theory. Prestige value only disappeared, argued Keasbey, when society as such disappeared. Alone on a desert island, goods would only be wanted for their value in use. In this case, 'prestige values would disappear as prestige depending upon wealth would be ridiculous with no one to be impressed with our grandeur. Use values alone would remain' (1903: 465).

It would not have been difficult to reconcile Seligman's concept of social marginal utility with Keasbey's notions of Veblenian prestige value, although there was no attempt to do so. In fact, the early years of the twentieth century saw no serious attempt within economics to evaluate Veblen's views of consumption and of the formation of tastes. For the most part, neoclassical demand theory remained undisturbed.

A part of the failure to influence the development of consumer theory lay with Veblen's inability to press home the attack on orthodox economic thought. In fact, he showed no serious desire to do so. He had catholic interests, ranging far beyond economics and certainly beyond theories of consumption, and the contributions which he did make to economics between 1900 and 1910 were limited and often repetitive.

Europe, with its longer traditions, vested interests and academic investment in economic theory and thought, would always have been a difficult citadel to attack. In the United States, however, economics was a younger science, and it was here that the potential existed for Veblen's views to enter the mainstream of economic thinking. Economic theory and the neoclassical orthodoxies had taken far weaker hold in America, and minds were more open and receptive to new ideas. Nevertheless, Veblen's views had little impact on developments in demand and utility theory.

The group which was potentially most receptive to the new Veblenian prospectus were those economists, many German-trained, who identified themselves most closely with the Historical School of economic thought. Their preference for historical-inductive (as opposed to theoretical–deductive) reasoning made Veblen's historical perspective and subsequent explanation of Gilded Age US society a particularly fertile field for research. However, Veblen was never at ease with the School, believing that observation was not being effectively translated into theoretical constructs. He was always critical of those who were able to provide strong empirical evidence of consumer behaviour, yet were unable or unwilling to translate these into a body of consumer theory which would make a real contribution to widening the economic debate. He had been particularly critical of the earlier German Historicists – Roscher, Knies and Hildebrand – who had failed, in his view, to make any significant contribution to economic theory:

> Of constructive scientific work – that is to say, of theory – this elder line of German economics is innocent; nor does there seem to be any prospect of an eventual output of theory on the part of that branch of the historical school, unless they should unexpectedly take advice, and make the scope, and therefore the method, of their inquiry something more than historical in the sense in which that term is currently accepted. The historical economics of the conservative kind seems to be a barren field in the theoretical respect (Veblen, 1901: 72).

This hostility towards the Historicists extended equally to the 'newer' School represented by Gustav Schmoller, who were pushing Roscher's historicism to extremes, arguing that all received theory should be completely discarded as it was full of unrealistic assumptions and theoretical abstraction. While Veblen was promoting a new economic agenda, he was not at all minded to join with those whose anti-theoretical bias was total and who were not prepared to move from observation and report towards theoretical reasoning.

A second and potentially more rewarding way forward for the promotion of Veblen's ideas would have been to persuade more orthodox economists in the United States of the necessity to question many of the conventional neoclassical theories of demand which had successfully crossed the Atlantic. In part, this was never a practical proposition, for most economists had embraced the mathematical economics of Cournot, Jevons and Walras, always notoriously unsympathetic to anything approaching a 'sociology' of demand. Foremost among these was Irving Fisher at Yale, whose commitment to the mathematical method was explicit (1898) and who greatly admired Alfred Marshall's mathematical exposition of neoclassical theory in *Principles*. Ironically, Fisher was the first mainstream economist to (casually) recognise the possibility of status-linked interpersonal utility functions within utility analysis (1892), but he did not attempt any mathematical representation of such phenomena. Not surprisingly, perhaps, Fisher and other American mathematical economists were never persuaded of any significance attaching to *The Theory of the Leisure Class* and effectively ignored its publication.

Veblen could have hoped for a better reception among orthodox, literary (as opposed to mathematical) scholars, and it was here that his efforts, such as they were, became focused. The leading non-mathematical neoclassicist of the day was John Bates Clark of Columbia University. Veblen had been particularly influenced by Clark in his younger days, and had attended Clark's lectures on the philosophy of value many years earlier as an undergraduate at Carleton College.

Although largely mainstream and orthodox in his approach, Clark was open-minded and, like Veblen though for different reasons, had some reservations about the progress being made in economics at the turn of the century (1898: 1907). He was potentially an important ally for Veblen if he could have been persuaded to put a Veblenian interpretation upon the inadequacies and deficiencies of neoclassical demand theory. Clark's work on value and utility had been used as a point of reference by both Seligman (1901) and Keasbey (1903), and his support would have given far greater weight to any reinterpretation of ideas based on Veblen's paradigm. However, his reservations concerning neoclassical theory were centred for the most part on issues relating to distribution rather than consumption. He continued to adhere to what Veblen referred to disparagingly as 'the postulates of current hedonistic economics' and was attacked by Veblen (1908) for his 'passive acceptance of rational schemes of (consumer) behaviour under some notion of Natural Law', which, Veblen claimed, effectively undermined much of Clark's economic analysis. Clark, in the event, was not persuaded to change his views on value and utility, and so gave no greater respectability within economics to Veblen's more radical views.

In 1909, Veblen published perhaps his most focused criticism of conventional economic thought with an attack on the limitations of marginal utility published in the *Journal of Political Economy*. Here again, Clark's work was challenged. 'For all their use of the term "dynamic", claimed Veblen, 'neither Mr. Clark nor any of his associates in this line of research have yet contributed anything at all appreciable to a theory of genesis, growth, sequence, change, process, or the like, in economic life' (1909: 152). Once again, Veblen attacked both classical and marginal utility schools – neither could accommodate arguments working from cause to effect; and neither could deal theoretically with change, only with 'rational adjustments to change which may be supposed to have supervened'. To Veblen, preoccupation with, and unquestioning acceptance of, Bentham's hedonistic calculus was sterile. Only when the pecuniary interest was allowed to intervene in consumption decisions would any real progress be made towards a new, more realistic theory of value and utility, for commercial (or pecuniary) tests and standards were now being widely applied, outside commerce, to matters relating to social standing and prestige.

This commercialisation of taste and appreciation, argued Veblen, may possibly have been overstated 'by superficial and hasty criticism of modern life' – an admission of sorts that reaction to Gilded Age excesses, and to his own work on conspicuous consumption, had perhaps been over-sensational and sometimes ill-considered. At the same time, he challenged critics to say that wealth and its privileges did not secure social status and reputation. He ended again with an appeal for reconsideration:

> It is not simply that the hedonistic interpretation of modern economic phenomena is inadequate or misleading; if the phenomena are subjected to the hedonistic interpretation in the hedonistic analysis, they disappear from the theory; and if they would bear the interpretation in fact, they would disappear in fact (1909: 174).

For the most part, Veblen's appeals fell on deaf ears. There was no academic debate within economics which sought to examine the treatment of status-directed consumption either in classical and neoclassical theories of consumer demand, or which questioned the premises on which theories of value and utility were based. His immediate impact on mainstream economic thought in the early years of the twentieth century was minimal, and although his work was later to form a cornerstone of the dissenting Institutional School of American economists, it posed no immediate threat to the economic certainties of the day. Only later were Veblen's views to receive wider attention and to have some greater impact on economic theory and thought. This 'delayed action' of events is well illustrated by Harvard's John Cummings, among the first to criticise *The Theory of the Leisure Class* in 1899. In a letter written in 1931, some two years after Veblen's death, he wrote:

> It was hard for me to accept him or his philosophy. It went against my grain. I was eager to find it lop-sided and unreal ... My review gives good evidence that I did not at the time fairly appreciate the contribution Veblen was making to our economic and social philosophy. I have often wondered how I could have been so blind. In the years since, we have all seen the accumulating evidence of the widespread influence of Veblen's analysis of social and economic behaviour, as set forth in his *Theory of the Leisure Class* ... I know I should write a very different review today (Dorfman, 1934: 507–8).

Others were to follow Cummings in subsequently revising their opinions of Veblen's work and in crediting him with being among the first to identify many fundamental inadequacies relating to neoclassical theories of consumption and consumer behaviour. Like many before him, Veblen received little academic recognition during his lifetime; with hindsight, however, it is clear that he had opened a debate on the economics of status-linked consumption which was not to go away.

References

Clark, John Bates (1898), 'The Future of Economic Theory', *Quarterly Journal of Economics*, **13** (October), 1–14.

Clark, John Bates (1907), *The Essentials of Economic Theory, As Applied to Modern Problems of Industry and Public Policy*, New York: The Macmillan Co:

Cummings, John (1899), Review of *The Theory of the Leisure Class, Journal of Political Economy*, **8** (September).

Dorfman, Joseph (1934), *Thorstein Veblen and His America*, New York: The Viking Press.

Fisher, Irving (1892), *Mathematical Investigations in the Theory of Value and Prices*, New Haven: Yale University Press.

Fisher, Irving (1898), 'Cournot and Mathematical Economics', *Quarterly Journal of Economics*, **12** (January), 119–38.

Keasbey, Lindley M. (1903), 'Prestige Value', *Quarterly Journal of Economics*, **17** (May), 456–75.

Marshall, Alfred (1897), 'The Old Generation of Economists and the New', *Quarterly Journal of Economics*, **11** (January), 115–35.

Mason, Roger (1981), Conspicuous Consumption: a Study of Exceptional Consumer Behaviour, New York: St Martin's Press.

Moran, Thomas F. (1901), 'The Ethics of Wealth', *American Journal of Sociology*, **6** (May), 823–38.

Patten, Simon N. (1889), *The Consumption of Wealth*, University of Pennsylvania Press.

Patten, Simon N. (1892), *Theory of Dynamic Economics*, University of Pennsylvania Press.

Seligman, Edwin R.A. (1901), 'Social Elements in the Theory of Value', *Quarterly Journal of Economics*, **15** (May), 321–47.

Veblen, Thorstein (1892), 'Some Neglected Points in the Theory of Socialism', *Annals of the American Academy of Political and Social Science*, **2** (November), reprinted in Veblen, T. (1919, edited edition 1961), *The Place of Science in Modern Civilisation*, New York: Russell and Russell, 387–408.

Veblen, Thorstein (1894), 'The Economic Theory of Woman's Dress', *Popular Science Monthly*, (November), 198–205.

Veblen, Thorstein (1898a), 'Why is Economics Not an Evolutionary Science?', *Quarterly Journal of Economics*, **12** (July), 373–97.

Veblen, Thorstein (1898b), 'The Beginnings of Ownership', *American Journal of Sociology*, **4** (November), 352–65.

Veblen, Thorstein (1899a), 'The Preconceptions of Economic Science I', *Quarterly Journal of Economics* **13** (January), 121–50.

Veblen, Thorstein (1899b), 'The Preconceptions of Economic Science II', *Quarterly Journal of Economics*, **13** (July), 396–426.

Veblen, Thorstein (1899c), 'The Barbarian Status of Women', *American Journal of Sociology*, **4** (January), 503–14.

Veblen, Thorstein (1899d), *The Theory of the Leisure Class*, reprinted (1957), London: George Allen and Unwin.

Veblen, Thorstein (1899e), 'Mr.Cummings's Strictures on 'The Theory of the Leisure Class', *Journal of Political Economy*, **8** (December), reprinted in L. Ardzrooni (ed.) (1934), *Essays in Our Changing Order*, New York: Augustus M. Kelley.

Veblen, Thorstein (1900), 'The Preconceptions of Economic Science III', *Quarterly Journal of Economics*, **14** (February), 240–69.

Veblen, Thorstein (1901), 'Gustav Schmoller's Economics', *Quarterly Journal of Economics*, **16** (November), 69–93.

Veblen, Thorstein (1908), 'Professor Clark's Economics', *Quarterly Journal of Economics*, **22** (February), 147–95.

Veblen, Thorstein (1909), 'The Limitations of Marginal Utility', *Journal of Political Economy*, **17** (November), reprinted in W.C. Mitchell (ed.) (1964), *What Veblen Taught*, New York: Augustus M. Kelley, pp.151–75.

Ward, Lester (1900), Book review of *The Theory of the Leisure Class*, *American Journal of Sociology*, **5** (May), 829–37.

Wells, D. Collin (1899), Book review of *The Theory of the Leisure Class*, *Yale Review*, (August).

6   The Resistance to Change

The theories of conspicuous consumption developed by Thorstein Veblen at the end of the nineteenth century failed to generate any significant interest within economics in the years after 1900. At the same time, Veblen was more successful in opening up discussion on the broader issue of economics' relationship with other social sciences. Interest in so-called 'behavioural economics' certainly increased, and less conventional economists, sociologists and psychologists began a search for common ground in attempts to produce a more integrated theory of consumption and consumer demand.

Veblen had used his position as editor of the University of Chicago's *Journal of Political Economy* in the 1890s to actively promote such discussions, both through his own articles and book reviews, and through publication of invited papers from those who were working with him in Chicago and who were sympathetic to the cause. Albion Small, a Chicago sociologist, reviewing the relationship between sociology and economics in 1894, ended with an appeal 'to work in intelligent cooperation in order to approach the common end'. In 1895, Veblen asked Henry Waldgrave Stuart to write an article on hedonism in economics. Stuart also concluded:

> The unsound hedonistic theory ... has been banished already from psychology, and there is no occasion to give it shelter within the neighbouring domain of political economy. Ordinarily, its presence may be a matter of indifference, but at critical moments it will be sure to prove a treacherous guest (1895: 84).

Such contributions, together with Veblen's own papers in the *Quarterly Journal of Economics* (1898–1900) and the *American Journal of Sociology* (1898–1899), pressed the case for greater interdisciplinary research in the social sciences. At the same time, it was a narrowly-based interest, centred on the University of Chicago, and did not, at first, succeed in moving discussion into a wider arena. The subsequent popularity of *The Theory of the Leisure Class,* however, served to focus greater attention on the new behavioural economics after 1900, and highlighted the growing divisions between the social sciences to far greater effect.

The economist and sociologist E.A. Ross had suggested in 1899 that the 'tame' treatment of consumption within economics had been due to a dim perception of many factors which were not primarily economic but social in origin. Reality, he claimed, was increasingly being sacrificed to appearance by consumers, and economics would have to look elsewhere for explanations of economic actions relating to forms of social consumption. These sentiments were carried through into the first decade of the twentieth century, attracting the interest not only of a small but more significant number of academics but also of the popular press, whose fascination with Gilded Age consumption continued unabated. However, although the need for more sophisticated, interdisciplinary explanations of consumer behaviour was being more widely discussed, it still struggled to become an issue within economics.

The proposition that economic behaviour which was social, psychological and economic in its origins would be better explained by research extending across the social sciences, rather than piecemeal within each separate discipline, had found few supporters within conventional economics. Some suspected, even believed, that economic theory relating to consumption was deficient in certain respects, and might need some qualification or a change in approach, given the doubts which were being expressed over its hedonistic assumptions. Their conclusions, however, still favoured relatively minor revisions of orthodox theory in order to accommodate these 'difficulties'.

In reality, economics had been moving in an opposite direction to sociology and psychology for many years. Building on the neoclassical groundwork of Jevons, Fisher, Marshall, Pareto and others, it was becoming increasingly mathematical in approach and content. In the decade after 1900, when Veblen and other radicals were arguing for a more social perspective to be brought to bear on the economics of the marketplace, mainstream economics was not neutral but was actively opposed to such a realignment. Veblen's 1909 attack on marginal utility reflected, in large measure, his frustration with these emerging trends.

Veblen was not alone in feeling such frustrations. Joseph Schumpeter insisted in 1909 that the concept of utility which had been constructed by economic theorists was still proving to be far too narrow to be of any real use. In particular, it ignored the strong social influence on perceived value. Others took up the same theme. Mitchell (1910), a convert to Veblenian economics and an early member of the Institutional School, joined in the attack on the traditional hedonistic concepts of utility. Quoting McDougall (1909), an eminent Oxford philosopher who had argued that, contrary to the assumptions of classical political economy, 'man is only a little bit reasonable and to a great extent very unintelligently moved in quite unreasonable ways', Mitchell supported Veblen's 1909 attack on the limitations of marginal utility, arguing that the traditional assumption of rationality was totally inadequate to explain the behaviour of individuals and markets. The same year, Downey joined the attack, claiming that the hedonism underpinning marginal utility theory had been hopelessly discredited by modern psychology, and that a century and a quarter of diligent research into marginal utility had contributed substantially nothing to the increase and diffusion of knowledge among men:

Marginal-utility economics is an admirable body of dialectics – scarcely surpassed for subtlety, reach, and want of content by the finest products of medieval scolasticism. It affords unrivalled opportunity for the pursuit of refined distinctions between elusive ideas and for the multiplication of strange-sounding terms. 'Economics' of this type strongly attracts men of a metaphysical turn of mind, and will doubtless continue to be cultivated. But it has not contributed, and it cannot contribute, to the elucidation of any practical problem (1910: 268).

Paradoxically, even among the most eminent 'metaphysical' economists, there had been little real dissent from the view that interpersonal effects could have a major influence on utility. Alfred Marshall had conceded as much to Pigou, and others were willing to acknowledge such market realities. Pareto had pointed out (1906) that 'all experience contradicted the notion that people's utility functions were independent of the actions and consumption of others'. Having acknowledged this interpersonal element in consumption, however, he continued to use additive utility functions throughout his work, and never attempted to rework or reformulate utility theory in order to accommodate such phenomena.

This resistance to change continued after 1910, as mathematical economics became more firmly established. Even those who looked specifically at luxury consumption during the period and who did not belong to the mathematical school of economists gave little support to a more behavioural approach. In Germany, for example, Sombart (*Luxus und Kapitalismus*, 1913), whose view of economics was both historical and theoretical, argued nevertheless that while psychology might be useful in supplementing the economist's knowledge, it was no part of the proper study of economics.

Some claimed to detect a slight but positive change in the attitude of economic theorists towards contributions from the other social sciences in theory construction and in a greater questioning of traditional, hedonistic preconceptions. Mitchell (1914) thought that elements of the sociology of consumption were being increasingly recognised as factors in market behaviour. Others, however, were more openly scornful of economic's failure to come to terms with consumption and the consumer. Wieser (1914) held that 'of consumption, (economics) says nothing, or just enough to veil its silence'. Economic theory, he argued, had never been interested in the physical process of consuming commodities and had failed to recognise that 'consumption as such, the satisfaction of needs as such, is not an economic act at all' (1914: 43). This resistance to the concept and consequences of socially-inspired consumption meant that economics was not able to accommodate that part of economic behaviour in the marketplace which was driven by social ambitions.

Those few economists who were prepared to question the economic orthodoxies and, in particular, the validity of the hedonistic calculus which underpinned the treatment of consumer behaviour in neoclassical economics, represented only a small minority of academics and were often branded as eccentrics. In 1918, Carver dismissed their intervention, arguing that, while they were right in pointing to some behavioural inadequacies of conventional economic theory, they had, in fact, taken their argument too far. The new economic man they wished to create was the result of an over-emphasis on the non-pecuniary and the neglect or under-emphasis of conventional pecuniary motives, just as the old economic man was the result of the opposite tendencies. To Carver, the so-called behavioural economists had, in fact, failed to recognise that orthodox economics had made ample allowance, within theories of demand, for instincts, impulses and emotions; the proper criticism was that economists had failed to give sufficient weight to such factors in their analyses, descriptions and cataloguing of individual motives and economic behaviour. No 'new economics' was needed, therefore, only a better application of existing theory:

> What are all these non-pecuniary motives? There is a large question here; and if the behaviourists can answer it in detail, they will have made a significant contribution to economics. But if they think they have built up a complete system and can dispense with all that has gone before, they must be placed in the class of men in other fields, such as chemistry, physics, medicine and zoology, who, because of some new observations, hasten to announce that all previous work is of no account (1918: 200).

Carver's dismissive criticism of behavioural economists was, in a sense, unfair, for none among them had claimed that they had built up a 'complete new system' which made all earlier work redundant. When their more moderate claims were examined, they were increasingly persuasive, and were beginning to influence a very small number of more eminent economists. J.M. Clark was, by 1918, convinced that an accommodation of sorts had to be made between economics and psychology. Economists, he argued, might try to ignore psychology, but it was entirely impossible to ignore human nature, as economics itself was a science of human behaviour (remarkably, this claim itself was controversial: a common defence of the status quo had been to deny that economics necessarily had any foundations in human nature at all (Tugwell, 1922).

Clark believed that closer links to psychology were now essential, and saw dangers in failing to develop such ties. 'If the economist borrows his conception of man from psychology, his constructive work may have some chance of remaining purely economic in character. But if he does not he will not thereby avoid psychology. Rather he will force himself to make his own, and it will be bad psychology' (1918: 4).

Despite the growing reservations of a small number of theorists, Carver's view that the discipline could and would accommodate issues relating to economic sociology and economic psychology was widely held within mainstream economics. Given this continuing indifference to calls for a greater integration of economics with the other behavioural sciences, marginal utility theory and Marshallian interpretations of consumption and consumer demand were not put under any real threat. At the same time, while no significant threat came from within the discipline, neoclassicists still had to explain how and why the well-documented excesses of the Gilded Age – driven, by common consent, by status considerations alone – could fall outside conventional theory.

The explanation was not difficult to construct, for it had always been conceded that significant levels of status-directed expenditure and consumption could be found among the very rich: indeed, Jevons, Marshall and other neoclassicists had made pointed reference to the phenomenon. In the aggregate, however, such consumer behaviour had always been considered to be insignificant and irrelevant to general theory construction, associated as it was only with a small, privileged group within society who were totally unrepresentative of the vast majority of consumers, and whose preferences as consumers were esoteric, trivial in overall terms, and could therefore be safely ignored.

For so long as status consumption could be associated only with this small group of unrepresentative consumers, so it could be marginalised and discounted by economic theorists. However, this policy of containment and neglect was becoming increasingly untenable, for Veblen had demonstrated that the Gilded Age conspicuous consumption of the very rich had been widely emulated and copied, within available resources, at every level of society. At the same time, this 'natural' tendency of people to emulate the behaviour of their perceived social superiors was being actively encouraged by a business community anxious to increase sales of goods and services. So successful were they that, by the turn of the century, status-driven expenditure and consumption could be routinely observed in the stores and high streets not only of the United States but throughout Western Europe. It was no longer possible for economics to argue with any conviction that the 'phenomenon' of conspicuous consumption had no place of any significance in theories of consumer demand.

The years after 1850 had, in fact, seen a remarkable growth in the market for status goods on both sides of the Atlantic – a growth largely attributable to changes in the social, economic and commercial environment (Fraser, 1981; Williams, 1982; Strasser, 1989). As discretionary incomes had risen, so more people were able to move away from patterns of consumption generated exclusively by needs and to acquire and consume luxuries which also served to enhance social status within the community. And this greater interest in status goods was actively encouraged by manufacturers who made every effort to facilitate such purchases.

Demand for goods and services with a high social utility was stimulated firstly by the significant growth and increasing sophistication of advertising. Wall posters had been widely used after 1850 to extol the social virtues of products and to promote many goods for their value as status symbols. Enough psychology was known even then to appreciate the effectiveness of linking socially visible consumption with associated status gains, and these poster campaigns were supporting increasingly effective newspaper advertisements. To coordinate and develop these campaigns, the role and size of advertising agencies (which had, in fact, existed since the late eighteenth century) was substantially increased. Agencies further extended their functions after 1880, as markets grew significantly in size and spending power. By the end of the nineteenth century, a majority of larger companies had contracted out the promotion of their products to agencies which were able to offer comprehensive market analysis and campaign planning services to their clients.

By 1900, many believed that advertising had now become a 'science' and that this new science was rooted primarily in the study of psychology. As interest in the psychology of advertising grew, so also did manufacturers' awareness that sales of many goods and services could be significantly increased if products could be sold not only for their tangible utility but also for their perceived ability to confer social status on the purchaser and consumer. By the turn of the century, a product's social value, whether real or created, was being used as an integral part of the advertising message.

Status-linked consumption was further stimulated in the later nineteenth century by a significant expansion of the credit system, particularly after 1860. Extended credit facilities were initially introduced, and intended, to allow the poor access to goods and services, particularly at times of unemployment or sickness. Over time, however, credit was used to buy luxury items which enhanced social status rather than physical well-being. And as the tally system expanded after 1860, accompanied by what were the beginnings of high-pressure salesmanship, so purchase of seemingly superfluous luxuries grew as households vied with one another to acquire the latest status symbol.

Finally, conspicuous consumption was encouraged by developments in retailing. Traditionally, the ostentation of the rich had been serviced by exclusive retail shops, located in equally fashionable towns, streets and avenues, which offered high fashion goods and services at considerable cost in an appropriate retail environment. Prices were, in fact, kept high enough to act as a deterrent to the 'lower orders', but as a more affluent middle class and working class began to emerge – equally anxious to assert their relative status and status aspirations through pecuniary emulation and conspicuous consumption – so new opportunities in retailing developed. This retail gap was, in fact, filled by the emergence and development of the department store.

Early initiatives in the development of such stores can be traced back to the opening in Paris of Aristide Boucicant's Bon Marché in 1852 and to Macy's in New York in 1860. These French and American initiatives were quickly followed by similar developments in Britain, where department stores of two main types were to emerge. As Fraser (1981) has pointed out, the London department stores which appeared in the decades after 1860 were aimed at middle class customers as they 'struggled to rig themselves out with the "paraphernalia of gentility"'. Outside London, however, where concentrations of middle class buyers were less marked, the department stores targeted the working class as their main customers.

Both middle class and working class stores in Europe and America shared similar business philosophies. Potential customers were encouraged to come in the stores to browse and 'to be seen'. The stores had large staffs, and offered a personal attention to buyers which added to the perceived prestige of the store and, at the same time, enhanced the personal status and self-esteem of potential customers. They were, in essence, offering a high status shopping experience and the opportunity to conspicuously consume within a budget. Together with developments in advertising and the relaxation of credit restrictions, they succeeded in significantly extending opportunities for status-directed consumption (Miller, 1981; Laermans, 1993).

By 1920, improved levels of disposable income, changes in the market and retail environment, and the extensive use of social psychology in stimulating and shaping demand for a wide range of consumer goods, were transforming patterns of consumption. At the same time, economics had nothing to say regarding the growing importance of product symbolism in determining a significant part of consumer demand. Those agreeing with Carver argued still that neoclassical marginal utility theory and the conventional hedonistic calculus were more than able to address such issues, and that the only charge which could be levelled against economics was one of neglect rather than false theory construction. Others claimed that, in any event, the psychology of demand was no part of economics. Certainly, psychological factors were at work in shaping demand but, as Dickinson (1919) complained, economists were entirely sanguine about these trends:

> What of it? is the reply. Granting that people's wants are determined frequently by instincts, and often by imprudent ones at that – what change does it

necessitate in economic principles? We do not need to account for the origin of wants; our business is to study the means of satisfying them, and the conditions under which they may be satisfied ... On the whole, in the hearts of most economic students, no conviction of sin has been awakened, altho the 'psycho-economists' have been pressing their attacks in different quarters for over twenty-five years (1919: 378).

Dickinson noted that recent psychological theories relating to consumer demand offered, in particular, an explanation of 'the wants connected with ostentation, which Veblen has so well characterized' and that 'the critics themselves seem to consider these desires among the strongest motives in the pursuit of wealth' (1919: 400). At the same time, he was forced to conclude that the prevailing attitude within economics seemed to be that no results of social or psychological research had been brought into economic discussion which called for any radical revision of theory.

Some concerns were expressed, in particular that treatment of the effects of advertising and salesmanship as significant determinants of demand was, for the most part, absent from the neoclassical paradigm (Clark, 1918). In truth, a substantial American business literature now existed which allowed psychologists to interpret the results of laboratory research in terms of their advertising applications (Cherington, 1913; Hollingworth, 1913; Tipper et al., 1915). Today, the new use made of psychology in advertising between 1910 and 1920 is widely recognised as a key development in the marketing and promotion of consumer goods and services (Bartels, 1965). Not until the 1930s, however, did economists look at these developments in any detail; in 1920, it was not seen to merit any serious attention by theorists, who chose to stay with Alfred Marshall's assumption that purchasers came to market with predetermined demand schedules which could only be affected by changes in price.

Through the 1920s, a minority continued to protest against a utility theory which, for them, rested on an unsound psychology, and was, consequently, both false and misleading. Most persistent of these critics was Frank H. Knight, an economist based at the University of Iowa, who was far from happy with the mathematical bias which had come into economics, and with what he saw as a growing obsession to turn the discipline into something akin to a pure science:

> The striving after natural science ideals in the social sciences is a false steer. For practical purposes of the prediction and control of human behavior, and finally for the theoretical purpose of understanding it, we can learn more by studying the ways in which *minds* know and influence each other than we ever can by attempting to analyze mechanically the process of interaction between bodies (1925a: 265).

Knight was particularly concerned with economics' treatment of consumer motives and wants, and with the interpretations of classical deductive economics. Like many others, he believed that man's reasons for wanting things came down, in large measure, to the desire to be like other people or the desire to be different. This preoccupation with self, and the 'Machiavellian–Mandevillian standards' it represented, was damaging, he argued, when taken to the excesses which had been observed in the mass markets of the early twentieth century. Economics' failure was that the treatment of consumer demand in neoclassical theory gave little if any recognition to status-driven consumption, and was therefore not able to offer any serious explanation and critique of a phenomenon which was now so important a factor in consumer preference formation (1925b).

Knight's pessimistic view was shared by others. Some (Frank, 1924) took the view that a totally new approach to utility theory and demand creation would need to be taken if any real progress were to be made, while others (Snow, 1924) thought that any attempt to fit psychological concepts into the confines of accepted economic theory (that is orthodox marginal economics) would simply be a waste of time – economics would then 'continue to be entirely superficial, a creation of formal logic rather than of an empirically determined science'.

By the middle of the 1920s, the gulf between economists and other social scientists with regard to consumption and consumer theory was growing wider, and pressures on economics to reconsider first principles increased significantly. The pressure was such that eminent mainstream economists were now forced to respond, but little ground was given.

In his 1925 review of the utility concept in value theory, Jacob Viner described the attacks on economics as 'an unintermittent series of slashing criticisms of the utility economics. Its psychology, it is alleged, is obsolete; its logic faulty; its analysis and conclusions tainted with class bias; its service to economic enlightenment nil'(1925: 371). He then set out to counter many of the attacks which were being made by these critics.

A part of his argument was concerned with the charge that positively-inclined demand schedules were, contrary to received wisdom, readily observable in the real world, particularly in relation to 'fashion and style' commodities which had a social as well as a utilitarian value. Viner argued, as Marshall had done thirty years earlier, that any apparently positive price/demand relationships could only be seen over time, as goods became increasingly fashionable and so offered more value to conspicuous consumers. At any one point in time, however, no positively-sloped demand schedule existed. 'The demand of each individual may rise as the use of a good spreads', said Viner, 'but at any given moment, given the extent of its use, he will take fewer units at a high than at a low price' (1925: 379).

This, in fact, represented the conventional, Marshallian defence of marginal utility theory. But Viner had conceded that, even at any given point in time, demand for a fashion commodity was, in part at least, determined by the consumer's calculation of 'the extent of its use' up to that time – that is, by the extent to which the consumer thought other people had been buying and consuming the good in question. In essence, Viner was acknowledging that interpersonal effects played a role in determining any one individual's demand for a product which had recognisable social value, for in refuting claims that fashion goods could be associated with positively-sloped demand schedules, he had conceded that demand, under static conditions, was a function not only of price but of other people's past consumption, whether real or imagined. Marshall's assumption that demand schedules could be affected only by changes in price was therefore called into question, for, as Viner himself conceded, 'if extent of use and price are closely related, it will be difficult to separate the influence of price from the influence of extent of use on the amount which buyers will take' (1925: 379n).

Viner was prepared to admit that, under special circumstances, certain demand schedules could be legitimately regarded as 'perverse'. The well-known Giffen Paradox (which said that, under given market conditions, the poor could be seen to increase their consumption of bread as its price rose) provided one example. Other special cases, however, were also identified:

> Instances are conceivable of the existence of true, positively inclined demand curves. Commodities which have prestige value derived mainly from their expensiveness may have demands which for part of their range are positive in inclination, as may also commodities whose quality is judged by purchasers mainly from their price (1925: 379).

Viner recognised therefore that, for purposes of social status and ostentatious display, a high price could be seen by buyers as an attractive product attribute which added to its social value and consequently made it more desirable. While he felt able to explain such consumer behaviour within marginal utility theory, arguing that it represented only a divergence between 'demand' and 'desire' schedules, the special case once again raised issues relating to the influence of interpersonal effects on consumer preference formation. Like other contemporary mainstream economists, however, Viner took discussion no further, implicitly dismissing status-directed consumption as eccentric behaviour which did not merit any special consideration.

Viner was not alone in continuing to marginalise interpersonal effects on consumer demand. Through the 1920s and early 1930s, economists generally gave little credence to the proposition that the neoclassical derivation of demand curves relating to goods which offered significant social utility to the consumer could not be convincingly defended. Pigou, once a major critic of Marshall's analysis of utility and value in this respect (1903, 1910, 1913), published a paper in 1930 on the statistical derivation of demand curves which implicitly accepted the concept of additive demand schedules. In 1932, Talcott Parsons produced a robust defence of Marshallian economics, arguing that the degree to which the sociology of demand had been taken into account by Marshall had been greatly underestimated.

Admittedly, there were a few who had become increasingly unhappy with aspects of Marshall's neoclassical approach, but these reservations related in the main to theories of monopoly and competition. Robinson (1933) and Chamberlin (1933) both recognised the influence of advertising and salesmanship on consumer preferences (it was, by now, hardly possible to deny them), and attempted to incorporate these factors into the demand equation. Neither, however, gave any real attention to the psychology or sociology of demand, or to the ways in which advertising was increasingly using imagery and product symbolism to promote sales of socially visible goods. Robinson, while recognising some psychological influences on demand formation, saw these as questions for psychologists and not for economists, implying that the two social sciences were fulfilling separate roles. At the same time, she acknowledged that the psychological naïvety of economists led them to make indefensible assumptions – most notably, 'by assuming that other people have the same psychology as himself, [the economist] can, by an act of blind faith, admit the existence of a definite marginal utility' curve for individuals other than himself' (1933: 213).

This, she argued, was a 'treacherous account' of marginal utility based on a wholly discredited technique of *Gedanken Experimente* which had no rigour or validity. In the final analysis, she acknowledged, marginal utility remained 'a purely formal conception which may be, in some circumstances, devoid of any real or interesting meaning' and this was seen to be particularly true when social and psychological characteristics influenced demand (1933: 217).

Within economics generally, there was, by this time, a growing unease with marginal utility theory, for it was becoming increasingly evident that utility-based theories of demand formation could be taken no further, relying as they did on individual preferences which were rooted in an indeterminate psychology. This unease, however, was entirely unrelated to any Veblenian concerns about the nature of consumer preference formation, and those who now led the attacks on marginal utility moved not towards, but away from, any greater consideration of interpersonal effects and status-seeking as significant influences on demand.

In 1934, Hicks and Allen published their paper challenging the basic assumptions of utility and marginal utility theory, arguing, in effect, that they were of little practical value, and provided no mechanism whereby demand could be effectively measured. They therefore proposed moving away from cardinal to ordinal measures of utility, and from demand for a single commodity to demand for related (complementary and competitive) goods. Their indifference curve analysis, derived from earlier work done by Edgeworth, Slutsky and Pareto, replaced marginal and diminishing marginal utility with marginal rates and diminishing marginal rates of substitution.

Nowhere in this analysis was it thought necessary to address issues relating to interpersonal preferences or to behaviour motivated more by social than by economic, utilitarian considerations. Traditionally, in order to determine the quantities of goods which any individual would buy at given prices under utility-driven neoclassical theory, the individual's 'utility surface' needed to be known. However, under the new approach, only information concerning the individual's indifference map was necessary – something which was capable of being more readily measured and which required no calculations of pleasure, pain, or motivation. In effect, Hicks and Allen had set out to remove what little 'psychology' there was in marginal utility theory, and their work promoted a mathematical analysis of consumer demand which intended to remove any notions of social psychology or of status-motivated consumption from demand measurement.

A further attack on classical and neoclassical demand theory came in 1936, but this time was more sensitive to arguments that demand could often seem to be irrational in purely economic terms. In his *General Theory*, Keynes, like Hicks and Allen, rejected the conventional utility-maximising model. Keynes, however, more concerned to develop a theory of full employment than with the detail of consumer preference formation, recognised the 'very subsidiary aspect' of mercantilist thought which, in the seventeenth century, had argued that thrift, far from stimulating demand and assisting in economic development, actually depressed demand and created unemployment. Luxury consumption, irrespective of any moral objections, added to demand, kept money in circulation, and created jobs for many who would otherwise be unemployed.

Keynes was understandably sympathetic to these views, not because of any belief in, or attachment to, luxury consumption per se, but because he recognised the importance of avoiding under-consumption and the need to sustain demand in order to ensure the highest levels of employment. He explicitly rejected Say's Law (that supply created its own demand), and Ricardo's belief that economists could safely neglect the aggregate demand function. The propensity to consume, he argued, was a major determinant of employment and growth, and anything which contributed to aggregate demand was clearly productive in purely economic terms. In this sense, luxury consumption added to economic growth and prosperity.

Keynes recognised that both objective and subjective factors contributed to the overall propensity to consume. Subjective motives to consumption he defined as enjoyment, shortsightedness, generosity, miscalculation and, significantly, ostentation and extravagance:

> Now the strength of these motives will vary enormously according to the institutions and organisation of the economic society which we presume, according to habits formed by race, education, convention, religion and current morals, according to present hopes and past experience, according to the scale and technique of capital equipment, and according to the prevailing distribution of wealth and the established standards of life (1936: 109).

While Keynes conceded that the reasons for 'subjective' consumption were often rooted more in social and cultural factors than in individual economic circumstances, he was reluctant to digress from what he saw to be the central focus of his work on employment, interest and money:

> We shall not concern ourselves, except in occasional digressions, with the results of far-reaching social changes or with the slow effects of secular progress. We shall, that is to say, take as given the main background of subjective motives to saving and to consumption respectively. In so far as the distribution of wealth is determined by the more or less permanent social structure of the community, this also can be reckoned a factor, subject only to slow change and over a long period, which we can take as given in our present context (1936: 109–10).

It therefore followed that short-period changes in consumption, and the effect such changes had on savings and employment, could be taken to depend, for the most part, only on the rate at which income was being earned and not on changes in the propensity to consume out of a given income (1936: 110). By removing both objective and subjective influences on demand in this way, Keynes was then able to develop an income-driven theory of the marginal propensity to consume.

Unlike most of his contemporaries, Keynes was prepared to allow that ostentation and extravagance could and did have an effect on the overall propensity to consume. At the same time, he argued that such motives changed only slowly over time, and saw no reason to explore the motives underpinning such behaviour – more particularly, how an individual's decision to conspicuously consume may well be directed towards others in order to secure status gains. By focusing on the shorter term, Keynes was, in fact, put under no obligation to concern himself with explanations of subjective, socially-determined incentives to consume. It was sufficient, he argued, 'if we give a catalogue of the more important, without enlarging on them at any length' (1936: 107). Although some reservations were later expressed as to whether the subjective factors could safely be assumed to be stable in the short period (Gilboy, 1938), the Keynesian view prevailed within mainstream economic thought.

In effect, the revised theoretical treatment of consumer demand proposed by Hicks and Allen, coupled with Keynes' recognition but removal of subjective influences on demand from short-term considerations of the consumption function, conspired to ensure that the neglect of whatever psychology and sociology did, in fact, underpin consumer preference formations was legitimised at both the micro and macro levels. Through the remaining years of the 1930s, economic analysis, therefore, moved away from any serious concern with interpersonal effects on consumer demand. Only in the field of social welfare economics were economists addressing some issues of interdependence, but this necessary concern with interpersonal comparisons was never extended into the realm of status-driven consumption.

After 1936, the economics of consumption and consumer demand developed along two principle and predictable lines. First, considerable effort was focused on the relevance and legitimacy of the Keynesian consumption function in the context of macroeconomic demand management. Second, the successful move away from traditional utility-based demand analysis orchestrated by Hicks and Allen fostered an increasing interest in the new theory of consumer demand based on indifference curve analysis.

The attack launched by Hicks and Allen on the utility concept of demand formation was welcomed in particular by Samuelson who, between 1937 and 1945, developed a comprehensive, mathematical theory of consumer's behaviour which built on the Hicks and Allen paper. Samuelson was singularly unimpressed with utility theory, and saw it as a sterile concept:

> The consumer's market behavior is explained in terms of preferences which are in turn defined only by behavior. The result can very easily be circular, and in many formulations undoubtedly is. Often nothing more is stated than the conclusion that people behave as they behave, a theorem which has no empirical implications, since it contains no hypothesis and is consistent with all conceivable behavior, while refutable by none (1947: 91–2).

In so far as interdependence of demand was concerned, only in the field of welfare economics did Samuelson explore individual preferences which were influenced by the preferences and consumption of others. 'As Veblen characteristically pointed out', he noted, 'much of the motivation for consumption is related to the fact that others do or do not have the same thing. Conspicuous expenditure, "keeping up with the Joneses", snob appeal, maintenance of face, are important in any realistic appraisal of consumption habits' (1947: 224). Having acknowledged these influences, however, he then ignored them. If such assumptions relating to demand formation were not made, he argued, the conclusions of welfare economics still remained valid, 'although they required modifications to allow for certain "external" consumption economies'. Not surprisingly, perhaps, such modifications were never seriously explored and the 'nuisance' of interdependent preferences was taken no further.

In 1938, Samuelson had attacked the Hicks and Allen concept of marginal rates of substitution for having 'vestigial traces' of the utility concept within it. Approaches based on such marginal rates, he argued, had not removed all of the psychology of utility or at least were ambiguous. He set out to remove any last traces of utility, and began to develop a theory of revealed preference which lacked any psychological overtones.

While Samuelson was working on this further refinement, Hicks published his results and proposed a new 'Theory of Subjective Value' (1939) which, notwithstanding Samuelson's reservations that it was not radical enough, moved substantially away from the hedonistic calculus of traditional utility theory. By now, the gap between economic demand theory and the status-driven consumption, often actively promoted by advertising campaigns, which had become commonplace in many consumer goods markets, was seemingly unbridgeable and becoming a cause of major concern among more heterodox economists. This concern was particularly evident in the United States where, unlike Europe, faculties of academics specialising in business and management studies were, by then, well established, and were becoming increasingly frustrated with the treatment of consumption within theoretical economics.

At Harvard, faculty members of the Graduate School of Business Administration were highly critical of the irrelevance of much economic doctrine to the realities of the marketplace. Tosdal (1939) contrasted the progress made by psychology in establishing appropriate bases for the study of consumer demand with that of economics, where consumption remained a largely peripheral issue and was typically discussed only in connection with the treatment of production. General economic treatises, protested Tosdal, rarely go beyond the point of discussing certain general characteristics of human wants, and 'nothing in the businessman's general training in economics fits him for any sort of detailed understanding of consumer demand which will so vitally affect him' (1939: 8). Economics, he argued, was producing laws and generalisations which were so broad as to be worthless for the solution of most specific problems.

Criticism was not confined to Harvard. In December 1938, a group of academics with primary interests in consumption economics had come together for a meeting in Detroit to voice their concern with current economic theory in its treatment of consumption and consumer demand. Chaired by

Benjamin Andrews, an economics professor at Columbia University, the meeting reviewed all books on consumption economics which had appeared since 1920, although this literature itself was remarkably 'thin'. Bowman (1939) later attempted a synthesis of the group's discussions, a process which only served to emphasise the confusion within economics itself concerning the proper treatment of consumption and consumer theory. Overall, the Detroit initiative raised more questions than answers, and proposed no vision or strategy for the future. 'The problem', Kyrk (1939) noted, 'is still, how to explain consumers' choices, the "why" of consumers' desires and their relative intensity'.

Given the continuing, privileged position of the very rich, and the significant developments in advertising, access to credit, and retailing which had taken place in the early years of the twentieth century in order to encourage status-directed consumption at all social and economic levels, it is, at first sight, difficult to understand the particular neglect of status consumption within economics through the 1920s and 1930s. This neglect was, however, due in no small measure to the fact that economic conditions and consumer priorities over the two decades had done little to heighten interest in the subject. Although it was not difficult to identify examples of status-driven consumption at all social levels, aggregate expenditures on conspicuous consumer goods intended solely for ostentatious display fell significantly over the period. This decline had, in fact, come about for two particular reasons.

First, the nature and direction of status consumption among the very rich had undoubtedly changed since the Gilded Age years which had effectively ended in the first decade of the new century. The exponential growth of nouveau riche conspicuous consumption in America between 1890 and 1910 had become so great that there was a strong public reaction to such excessive display. The new rich were increasingly seen as the idle rich, and public rejection of their consumer behaviour began to deepen. The press, always sensitive to swings in the public mood, now changed their coverage, abandoning their former deference and admiration of the social behaviour of the rich, and introducing a sharp note of disapproval into their reporting. Editorials began to demand changes in social and economic structures, and a political philosophy of 'progressivism' began to establish itself, a philosophy which actively promoted community welfare programmes and radical social change.

The rich, sensitive to this changing political and social climate, responded in kind. Overt, personal displays of wealth had become a social liability, and other, more acceptable yet still effective means of status-linked consumption needed to be found. Also, having secured considerable status gains in the period to 1910, they were now increasingly preoccupied with status consolidation rather than status achievement. The means to this consolidation was to move away from personal indulgence and towards the funding of philanthropic projects.

Conspicuous philanthropy was not new. Andrew Carnegie, who had never condoned the excessive conspicuous consumption of many of his contemporaries, had set up the Carnegie Institute, the Carnegie Corporation, and many other charitable trusts between 1902 and 1911 (Schlesinger, 1951). The Rockefeller family had, similarly, invested heavily in projects directed at social improvement. But after the First World War, the rich turned to conspicuous philanthropy with a new-found enthusiasm.

By 1920, 100 personally financed foundations, agencies and charitable trusts had been established in the United States, but by 1931, the number had risen to over 350. The rich had, in fact, found an ideal vehicle to consolidate their status, while at the same time being seen to contribute significantly to social and community welfare programmes which fitted well with the political sentiment of the day.

While the rich had discovered new, politically acceptable directions for their status-motivated expenditures, the incidence of conspicuous consumption among those less fortunate members of society had dropped also. To some limited extent, this could be explained in Veblenian terms as a diminished desire to emulate a higher social class who were consuming fewer status goods and services. More likely, however, it owed more to the worsening economic conditions of the 1920s, culminating in the Wall Street Crash, which set in train a recession which drove millions of people into desperate poverty. And as America's economy collapsed, so Europe was plunged into an equally severe recession which persisted for the greater part of the inter-war years. While the business community continued to promote the status attributes of their products – indeed, status emphasis in American advertising was particularly strong during the 1920s and 1930s (Belk and Polloy, 1985) – reductions in levels of discretionary income among the general buying public meant that only a fortunate few, mostly middle class, people had the means to indulge in status consumption. And these few, again aware of the social and economic conditions of those around them, often adopted a policy of 'conspicuous reserve' rather than risk the opprobrium of those less fortunate than themselves.

As the 1930s drew to a close, therefore, excessive levels of status-driven consumption had not appeared as a significant element in consumer spending for some two decades. This, in part, explained the lack of urgency with which economic theorists were treating the subject, preferring instead to believe that conspicuous consumption, whilst briefly important as an influence on the consumption behaviour of the very rich in the Gilded Age period, was now a diminishing force on consumer preference formation.

In the early 1940s, this lack of real interest continued. This was not at all surprising, for the Second World War focused attention well away from the niceties of personal consumption and consumer preference formation. For the most part, and particularly in Europe, there was a greater concern to see consumption restricted to necessaries, and rationing was introduced to control overall demand. These restrictions on consumption, however, caused some economists to revisit consumer theory. Robinson, who, in 1933, had given some limited recognition to the influence of social and psychological factors on demand, now explicitly identified the refusal to recognise the importance of interdependent preferences as the one great weakness of orthodox consumer demand theory – a weakness which, ironically, had been revealed by wartime privation:

> Latter-day experience of the restrictions of consumption has brought into a clear light one great weakness of the traditional theory of demand, that is, the erroneous assumption of individualism. When a given cut in consumption has to be made, traditional theory teaches that the minimal sacrifice is imposed on consumers if the requisite amount of general purchasing power is taken away, and each consumer is left free to economise on what he feels he can best spare. In reality, it is obvious that less sacrifice is caused by a total disappearance from the market of certain commodities, such as silk stockings, which are bought by each consumer mainly because other people have them ... Perhaps the spread of Austerity to the United States will soon be suggesting a still more radical reconsideration of traditional theory (1943: 116).

A few others recognised similar deficiencies in the theoretical treatment of demand. In 1945, James Meade, a conservative economist from well within the economic mainstream, admitted that it now had to be conceded that 'the consumer's present enjoyment depends on what others are at present consuming'. The same year, Scitovsky, in one of the first papers to look specifically at price-dependent preferences, examined the relationship between price and perceptions of product quality, and asked economists to show a greater awareness of the demonstrable correlation between price and social status. Consumers were often prepared to put a premium on certain goods and services merely for the sake of their expensiveness, as the ability to pay high prices was an effective way of raising and maintaining social status. Manufacturers, moreover, were well aware of such attitudes, and had quickly realised that high prices were often no barrier to sales. Such contributions were welcome, but were, in essence, only repeating what had already been said by earlier critics of demand theory. Nonetheless, they pointed again to omissions which had received little or no attention in the economic literature over many years.

In truth, consumer demand theory received little attention in the early 1940s; not surprisingly, supply-side issues had come to the fore as the need to sustain wartime production became paramount. At the end of hostilities. however, Paul Samuelson published his *Foundations of Economic Analysis* (1947), a book which was to have a profound influence on conventional mainstream economics for many years to come. Included in his work was a proposed new theory of consumer behaviour which, as promised, moved beyond Hicks and Allen and abandoned all links to traditional utility theory. In 1946, Hicks published a revised second edition of *Value and Capital*, in which he acknowledged the 'new construction' which Samuelson had been reporting in the literature since 1937 – a construction which, as Samuelson himself acknowledged, owed much to Hicks' own work. In recognising Samuelson's contribution, however, Hicks took issue with him for taking the attack on utility too far:

> It may well be that for econometric work a theory of Professor Samuelson's type is all we need; it gives a superb model for statistical fitting. But for the understanding of the economic system we need something more, something which does refer back, in the last resort, to the behaviour of people and the motives of their conduct. It may well be that ways will be found by which we can retain these advantages as well as the advantages of a mechanical theory; but I do not think that they have been found just yet (1946: 337).

Both Samuelson and Hicks had been developing and reworking their new consumer theories throughout the war years, at a time when market behaviour and patterns of consumer demand were, of necessity, managed and heavily controlled. This consumer environment, recognised as artificial, posed no real challenge to economic theorising, for it was seen to be contrived and unrepresentative. As war ended, however, and the economies of the United States and Europe began, slowly at first, to allow greater degrees of freedom in consumer choice, so the limitations of Hicksian indifference analysis and Samuelson's revealed preference theory, particularly with regard to socially-motivated consumption, soon became evident.

References

Bartels, Robert (1965), 'Development of Marketing Thought: A Brief History', in G. Schwarz (ed.), *Science in Marketing*, New York: John Wiley & Sons, pp. 47–69.
Belk, Russell W. and R.W. Polloy (1985), 'Images of Ourselves: The Good Life in Twentieth Century Advertising', *Journal of Consumer Research*, **11** (March), 887–97.

Bowman, M.J. (1939), 'Considerations in Developing a General Course in Consumption', *Journal of Marketing*, **4** (July), 20–22.

Carver, T.N. (1918), 'The Behavioristic Man', *Quarterly Journal of Economics*, **33** (November), 195–201.

Chamberlin, E.H. (1933), *The Theory of Monopolistic Competition*, reprinted (1969), Cambridge Mass.: Harvard University Press.

Cherington, Paul T. (1913), *Advertising as a Business Force*, New York: Doubleday, Page.

Clark, J.M. (1918), 'Economics and Modern Psychology', *Journal of Political Economy*, **26** (January), 136–66.

Dickinson, Z. Clark (1919), 'The Relation of Recent Psychological Developments to Economic Theory', *Quarterly Journal of Economics*, **33** (May), 377–421.

Downey, E.H. (1910), 'The Futility of Marginal Utility', *Journal of Political Economy*, **18** (April), 253–68.

Frank, L.K. (1924), 'The Emancipation of Economics', American Economic Review, **1** (March), 17–38.

Fraser, W. (1981), *The Coming of the Mass Market, 1850–1914*, London: Hamish Hamilton.

Gilboy, E. (1938), 'The Propensity to Consume', *Quarterly Journal of Economics*, **53** (November), 120–40.

Hicks, J.R. (1939), *Value and Capital*, 2nd Edition (1946), Oxford: Clarendon Press.

Hicks, J.R. and R.G.D. Allen (1934), 'A Reconsideration of the Theory of Value', *Economica*, **1** (New Series) (February), 52–76.

Hollingworth, H.L. (1913), *Advertising and Selling*, New York: Appleton–Century.

Keynes, John Maynard (1936), *The General Theory of Employment, Interest and Money*, London: Macmillan.

Knight, Frank H. (1925a), 'Fact and Metaphysics in Economic Psychology', *American Economic Review*, **15** (June), 247–66.

Knight, Frank H. (1925b), 'Economic Psychology and the Value Problem', *Quarterly Journal of Economics*, **39** (May), 372–409.

Kyrk, Hazel (1939), 'The Development of the Field of Consumption', *Journal of Marketing*, **4** (July), 16–19.

Laermans, R. (1993), 'Learning to Consume: Early Department Stores and the Shaping of Modern Consumer Culture, 1860–1914', *Theory, Culture and Society*, **10**, 79–102.

McDougall, William (1909), *An Introduction to Social Psychology*, Oxford: Clarendon Press.

Meade, J.E. (1945), 'Mr. Lerner on the Economics of Control', *Economic Journal*, **55** (April), 51–6.

Miller, M.B. (1981), *The Bon Marché: Bourgeois Culture and the Department Store, 1860–1914*, Princeton, NJ: Allen and Unwin.

Mitchell, Wesley C. (1910), 'The Rationality of Economic Activity II', *Journal of Political Economy*, **18**, 197–216.

Mitchell, Wesley C. (1914), 'Human Behavior and Economics: A Survey of Recent Literature', *Quarterly Journal of Economics*, **29** (November), 1–47.

Pareto, Vilfredo (1906), *Manuale d'Economia Politica*, Milan: Societa Editrice Libraria.

Parsons, Talcott (1932), 'Economics and Sociology: Marshall in Relation to the Thought of His Time', *Quarterly Journal of Economics*, **46** (February), 316–47.

Pigou, A.C. (1903), 'Some Remarks on Utility', *Economic Journal*, **13** (March), 58–68.

Pigou, A.C. (1910), 'Producers' and Consumers' Surplus', *Economic Journal*, **20** (September), 358–70.

Pigou, A.C. (1913), 'The Interdependence of Different Sources of Demand and Supply in a Market', *Economic Journal*, **23** (March), 19–24.

Pigou, A.C. (1930), 'The Statistical Derivation of Demand Curves', *Economic Journal*, **40** (September), 384–400.

Robinson, Joan (1933), *The Economics of Imperfect Competition.*, Second Edition (1976), London: Macmillan.

Robinson, Joan (1943), Review of Norris, R.T. 'The Theory of Consumer's Demand', *Economic Journal*, **53** (April), 115–17.

Ross, E.A. (1899), 'The Sociological Frontier of Economics', *Quarterly Journal of Economics*, **13** (July), 386–95.

Samuelson, Paul (1938), 'A Note on the Pure Theory of Consumer's Behavior', *Economica*, **5** (New Series) (February), 61–71.

Samuelson, Paul (1947), *Foundations of Economic Analysis*, Cambridge, Mass: Harvard University Press.

Schlesinger, A.M. (1951), *The Rise of Modern America 1865–1951*, New York: Macmillan.

Schumpeter, Joseph (1909), 'On the Concept of Social Value', *Quarterly Journal of Economics*, **23** (February), 213–32.

Scitovsky, Tibor (1945), 'Some Consequences of the Habit of Judging Quality by Price', *Review of Economic Studies*, **11/12**, 100–105.

Small, A.W. (1894), 'Relations of Sociology to Political Economy', *Journal of Political Economy*, **3**, 169–84.

Snow, A.J. (1924), 'Psychology in Economic Theory', *Journal of Political Economy*, **32** (August), 487–96.

Sombart, Werner (1913), *Luxus und Kapitalismus*, Munich & Leipzig: Duncker & Humblot.

Strasser, S. (1989), *Satisfaction Guaranteed: The Making of the American Mass Market*, New York: Pantheon Books.

Stuart, H.W. (1895), 'The Hedonistic Interpretation of Subjective Value', *Journal of Political Economy*, **4**, 64–84.

Tipper, H., H.L. Hollingworth, G.B. Hotchkiss and F.A. Parsons (1915), *Advertising: Its Principles and Practices*, New York: Ronald Press.

Tosdal, Harry R. (1939), 'Bases for the Study of Consumer Demand', *Journal of Marketing*, **4** (July), 3–15.

Tugwell, R.G. (1922), 'Human Nature in Economic Theory', *Journal of Political Economy*, **30** (June), 317–45.

Viner, Jacob (1925), 'The Utility Concept in Value Theory and Its Critics', *Journal of Political Economy*, **33** (August), 369–87.

Wieser, Freidrich von (1914), *Social Economics*, reprinted (1927, A. Ford Hinrichs (trans.)), London: George Allen and Unwin.

Williams, R. (1982), *Dream Worlds: Mass Consumption in Late Nineteenth Century France*, London: University of California Press.

7   Demand Reconsidered: External Effects and the Relative Income Hypothesis

In the years following the Second World War, a major shift in US living standards and in levels of consumption occurred. Between 1941 and 1950, the average increase in family income after taxes (in dollars of 1950 purchasing power) was 20.8 per cent, but this figure concealed some more remarkable upward shifts in purchasing power. Increases in income were particularly marked at the lower end of the social scale. The lowest fifth of all families saw their real purchasing power increase by some 42 per cent, while the second lowest increased by 37 per cent. Only among the highest 5 per cent of families did real after-tax income fall and then only by 2 per cent (Goldsmith et al., 1954).

As incomes rose, so the immediate post-war years began to see a significant increase in consumption. The war years had offered few real opportunities to spend, but the deferred demand was translated into significant increases in consumption after 1945. Katona (1949) measured levels of dissaving (that is spending in excess of income) in 1946 and 1947, finding them to be significantly raised, for not only had real disposable income increased, but the ability to spend more than one's income had been provided by large liquid asset holdings and the small size of consumer debt outstanding at the end of the war. 1946–47 saw full employment coupled with high production as resources were switched out of war production and into the manufacture of consumer goods. Over the period, incomes increased and savings fell as consumption rose. High levels of dissaving were also in evidence across all social and economic groups.

As spending increased, so an across the board desire to emulate others in their consumption behaviour became increasingly evident. This emulation had become possible and significant because higher levels of real disposable income had greatly improved the ability of relatively less affluent families to indulge in levels of conspicuous consumption which had hitherto been denied to them. For the first time, opportunities for significant status-directed consumption were available to all social and economic groups, and these new opportunities began to change the nature and pattern of consumer demand. And as discretionary incomes rose and dissaving generated demand for consumer goods, so interest grew in the alleged and true motives which underpinned the conspicuous consumption it generated.

Katona (1951) observed that, if analysts were always to believe in the superficial reasons which were given in the years after 1946 to explain socially-visible purchases, then the immediate gratification of desires, based on measures of personal utility, seemed to be strong. However:

> From what he [the analyst] knows about the situation prevailing during those years, he may speculate further about the psychological impact of shiny new automobile models seen on the street, in advertisements, and in the possessions of neighbours, about the role of suggestion, salesmanship, and, above all, prestige (1951: 75).

In short, Katona suspected that the immediate post-war years were becoming remarkable for the degree to which status and prestige were being actively used in the promotion of consumer goods and services, and, although difficult to measure, were beginning to have a profound effect on a population whose ability to indulge such motives had never been greater.

In this new world, the economic models of consumer behaviour developed in the 1930s by Hicks and Allen and by Samuelson began to look increasingly impotent in the face of socially-motivated consumer demand. This in due course prompted some revaluation. In 1948, Morgenstern looked again at demand theory and pointed to the inadequacies of current economic thinking on the subject. In particular, he revisited a subject which had first been raised in the 1890s, but which had been effectively sidelined for some fifty years – namely, the assumption that measures of aggregate demand could be obtained by the simple summation of individual demand curves:

> Additivity is only valid if the demand functions of the various individuals are independent of each other. This is clearly not true universally. Current theory possesses no methods that allow the construction of aggregate demand curves when the various constituent individual demand curves are not independent of each other. The problem does not even seem to have been put. If there is interdependence among individual demand functions, it is doubtful that aggregate or collective demand functions of the conventional type exist ... The inability to deal with non-additivity satisfactorily – still worse, the neglect of this empirically important case – constitutes a most serious limitation of demand theory. It has far-reaching ramifications (1948: 175; 191).

Morgenstern was clearly mistaken in claiming that 'the problem does not even seem to have been put' as Cunynghame, Pigou, Veblen and others could have testified. But he was aware of the dangers associated with additivity, and of the risk that entirely erroneous assumptions and predictions concerning consumer demand and the aggregate demand function could easily be made. Most importantly, he recognised that non-additivity, in the context of the US post-war experience, could no longer be seen as a trivial, esoteric matter, as Marshall and the great majority of early twentieth century economists had supposed. In truth, he argued, the larger part of consumer demand was non-additive:

> It is a serious shortcoming of the current treatment of aggregate demand curves that their study has not been extended to the most important case where additivity is absent. Even if everything were completely known for additive aggregate demand curves and found to be in order, that knowledge would only apply to a small part of aggregate demand; in the majority of empirical cases, non-additivity seems to prevail (1948: 175).

Even in those few cases where the summation of demand curves was defensible in principle, argued Morgenstern, no legitimate conclusions as to the nature of demand could be drawn, as aggregate demand assumed that all individual demand curves were the same in terms of desires. It was never seen to be necessary to go behind an aggregate curve, which itself could be obtained in a number of different ways.

The inability of theory to deal satisfactorily with non-additivity, and the persistent neglect of a case which was, by then, generally conceded to be empirically important had, in Morgenstern's view, compromised consumer demand theory. And by arguing, as he did, that 'virtually all' aggregate demand was non-additive, yet almost without exception calculated on the additive principle, so virtually all aggregate demand curves were wrong.

Others were more constrained in their view of the degree to which additivity was invalid, but nevertheless shared Morgenstern's reservations. Stigler wrote in 1950:

> Economists long delayed in accepting the generalised utility function because of the complications in its mathematical analysis, although no one (except Marshall) questioned its realism. They refused to include in the individual's utility function the consumption of other individuals, although this extension was clearly unimportant only in the social life of Oxford (1950: 150–1).

These omissions, argued Stigler, were attributable to the fact that choices between economic theories had, until then, been driven above all by the criterion of 'manageability'. Economists had, in fact, tacitly agreed that it was better to have a poor, useful theory than a rich useless one. Nevertheless 'the faithful adherence for so long to the additive utility function strikes one as showing at least a lack of enterprise. I think it showed also a lack of imagination: no economic problem has only one (mathematical) avenue of approach' (1950: 151).

Disquiet with the state of consumer theory, and with the concept of additivity in particular, was heightened by the changing economic and social environment of the post-war world, which was placing increasing strains on existing theories of consumption. In the event, the late 1940s produced two of the most significant contributions to the debate over interpersonal effects on demand and the concept of additivity – contributions which are today still widely recognised in the literature.

The first to examine the importance of so-called external effects on consumer demand was Harvey Leibenstein (1950) who observed that 'the desire of some consumers to be 'in style' the attempts by others to attain exclusiveness, and the phenomena of 'conspicuous consumption' had as yet not been incorporated into current theories of consumers' demand. Prompted by Morgenstern's paper, he set out to explore matters in greater detail.

The past literature, argued Leibenstein, seemed to divide into three categories. First, sociologists had, since the late nineteenth century, been concerned with the social causes of such behaviour, and with the consequences for society at large. (He was careful to categorise Veblen as a sociologist rather than as an economist, so distancing himself from the need to explore Veblen's theoretical explanations of such behaviour, while at the same time recognising that 'Veblen effects' were, by then, a part of the economic literature). Second, interpersonal effects on consumption had been explored within the field of welfare economics, but not in the context of conspicuous, status-driven display. Finally, such effects had, from time to time, been examined by consumer theorists, but with little real impact or consequence. Leibenstein acknowledged that Pigou had questioned Marshall over the issue; Marshall had, in fact, chosen to ignore any theoretical consequences, in Leibenstein's view, simply because any serious consideration of such effects on utility would have made the diagrammatical treatment of consumers' surplus too complex. Geometrical convenience, in short, had taken precedence over inclusive representation.

Leibenstein began his own analysis of interpersonal effects by drawing a distinction between functional and nonfunctional demand. The latter he further classified into three types. First, as demand driven by external effects on utility; second, as speculative demand, when consumers respond to their expectations of future market conditions; and finally as irrational demand, defined as a catchall category, and referring to unplanned purchases made on a whim which served no real rational purpose. He did not argue that consumption in pursuit of external effects was in any sense irrational, and this in itself ran counter to many of the prejudices and beliefs of more conservative, mainstream economists who had often claimed, for whatever reason, that such behaviour was both eccentric and trivial.

Leibenstein's subsequent thesis centred on the bandwagon, snob and Veblen effects which he identified as significant social influences on demand. Bandwagon effects he defined as representing the desire of people to purchase a commodity in order to get into 'the swim of things'; in order to conform with the people they wished to be associated with; in order to be fashionable or stylish; or in order to appear to be 'one of the boys'. Given such motives, demand for a commodity was increased because others were also consuming it. (Social taboos, argued Leibenstein, were, in a sense, bandwagon effects in reverse – some people would not buy and consume particular products simply because others were not buying and consuming them.)

Snob effects, in contrast, were seen to represent the desire of people to be different and exclusive, and to wish to distance themselves from the 'common herd'. Here, demand for any good decreased if the intending snob recognised that others were consuming the same commodity, or that they were increasing their consumption. Finally, Veblen effects were defined, narrowly, as that form of conspicuous consumption where demand was a function not of the consumption of others but only of product price. Here, consumption was intended only as a means of displaying wealth to others in order to gain in status and prestige.

Leibenstein attempted to incorporate these three effects into consumer demand theory, but quickly recognised the limitations of any efforts to do so by conceding that it was only possible to offer a static explanation of such consumer behaviour. The static situation he used was one in which the order of events was of no significance, and he borrowed Hicks's notion that the analysis should deal with 'those parts of economic theory where we do not have to trouble about dating'. In addition to these limiting assumptions, Leibenstein went further:

> In order to preserve internal consistency, it is necessary to assume that the period of reference is one in which the consumer's income and expenditure pattern is synchronized. And, we have to assume also that this holds true for all consumers. In other words, we assume that both the income patterns and the expenditure patterns repeat themselves every period. There is thus no overlapping of expenditures from one period to the next. This implies, of course, that the demand curve reconstitutes itself every period. The above implies also that only one price can exist during any unit period and that price can change only from period to period. A disequilibrium can, therefore, be corrected only over two or more periods (1950: 188).

These further restrictions were considered necessary 'in order to take care of some of the difficulties raised by Professor Morgenstern'. In essence, Leibenstein assumed away many of the problems which Morgenstern had identified as major stumbling blocks to further progress in the development of demand theory. As a result, his subsequent analysis was of limited value.

In fairness to Leibenstein, he himself conceded that his work lacked any demonstrable rigour. 'As is customary in economic theory ... the analysis is carried out on the basis of a number of simplifying assumptions ... and the analysis of more complex situations must await some other occasion'. He acknowledged that the formulations of his static analysis were necessarily very tentative and that, hopefully, they might pave the way for future work that was more directly applicable to behaviour in the real world. At best, his diagrammatical representations provided a starting point for more sophisticated work: at the same time, he certainly recognised the inadequacy of existing theory and attempted, however tentatively, to incorporate status-driven consumption into conventional demand theory.

Leibenstein offered new ideas relating to so-called external effects on consumer behaviour. He suggested that there was a diminishing marginal external consumption effect on demand, analogous to the principle of diminishing marginal utility but which implied that, beyond a certain point, incremental increases in the demand for a commodity by others had a decreasing influence on a consumer's own demand; and that a point was reached at which these increases in demand by others had no influence on his own demand. The equilibrium demand curve was then the curve that existed when the marginal external consumption effect for every consumer but one, at all alternate prices, was equal to zero. This equilibrium position, he argued, could (theoretically) be identified through successive market surveys.

Leibenstein claimed that, when bandwagon effects were significant, it would be possible to distinguish a bandwagon demand curve from the more conventional functional demand curve. For given changes in price, the bandwagon demand curve would, other things being equal, be more elastic than the functional curve, because any reaction to price changes would be followed by additional reactions in the same direction. Moreover, once bandwagon and functional demand curves had been derived through market surveys, so bandwagon and price effects on demand could be separately identified and assessed. In a similar fashion, when the market was driven by snob effects rather than by bandwagon effects, a snob demand curve could be identified which, working in the opposite direction, would be more inelastic than the conventional utility demand curve. Leibenstein held, in fact, that the snob effect was an opposite but completely symmetrical relationship to the bandwagon effect.

With regard to Veblen effects on demand, Leibenstein introduced the price-sensitive marginal Veblen effect, similar to the demand-sensitive marginal external consumption effect of bandwagon and snob markets. He also argued that the price of a Veblenian commodity could be separated into two component parts, namely a 'real price', paid by the consumer in money terms; and a 'conspicuous price', being the price that other people think the consumer paid for the good in question. This conspicuous price, according to Leibenstein, gave a product its conspicuous consumption utility:

These two prices would probably be identical in highly organized markets where price information is common knowledge. In other markets, where some can get 'bargains' or special discounts, the real price and conspicuous price need not be identical. In any case, the quantity demanded by a consumer will be a function of both the real price and the conspicuous price (1950: 203).

Again, Leibenstein argued that it was possible to separate the effects of any given price change into two component parts – the price effect and the Veblen effect. Like snobs, conspicuous consumers were attracted by higher prices but, unlike the snob demand curve, the Veblen demand curve could be positively inclined, negatively inclined or a mixture of both, depending on whether, at alternate price changes, the Veblen effect was greater or less than the price effect.

The possibility of mixed effects was also recognised. Four significant influences had been identified – price, bandwagon, snob and Veblen effects; and every price change created two positive and two negative effects, two which increased quantities demanded and two which decreased demand. Which effects dominated, argued Leibenstein, depended on the relative strengths of the Veblen effect and the price effect:

The Veblen and the price effects will depend directly on the direction of the price change. An increase in price will therefore result in price and bandwagon effects that are negative, and in Veblen and snob effects that are positive, provided that the price effect is greater than the Veblen effect; that is, if the net result is a decrease in the quantity demanded at the higher price. If, on the other hand, the Veblen effect is more powerful than the price effect, given a price increase, then the bandwagon effect would be positive and the snob effect negative. The reverse would of course be true for price declines (1950: 205).

Leibenstein's 'brief essay' on external effects on consumer demand was significant if only because it was a first attempt to incorporate such effects into consumer theory. He himself recognised the limitations of his work, but the limitations were, in a sense, made more severe because he tried to accommodate external effects entirely within a conventional economic framework. His analysis was derived from the neoclassical view of consumer demand and his orthodox interpretation of external effects was in no sense threatening to established theory. Leibenstein, indeed, claimed to have shown that such consumer behaviour could in fact be accommodated within the neoclassical tradition, and that non-additivity was no insurmountable obstacle in effecting a transition from individual to collective demand curves.

He also agreed with mainstream opinion that it was no part of an economist's responsibilities to be concerned with the motives underpinning such consumer behaviour, observing only that the factors involved in encouraging and creating external effects 'may be the history of the community, the people's conservatism or lack of conservatism, or the type and quantity of advertising about the commodity under consideration'. Such considerations, he stressed, were matters for social psychologists rather than for economists.

In essence, Leibenstein's approach and analysis was entirely orthodox, and represented an attempt to introduce only an additional external dimension to marginal utility analysis. The constraints of neoclassical theory, however, were such that this added dimension could only be accommodated within a static analysis heavily overlaid with other limiting assumptions. So limiting was this approach that Leibenstein's work could not be effectively carried forward by others, although he himself had anticipated that his paper would stimulate discussion and that his treatise 'may in some small way pave the road for future formulations that are more directly attributable to problems in the real world'(1950: 206).

In a footnote to his paper, Leibenstein referred to other work which was then being carried out into external effects, but which had come to his attention 'too late to be given the detailed consideration it deserves'. This was a reference to James Duesenberry's *Income, Saving and the Theory of Consumer Behavior* (1949), a book which took a radically different approach to the phenomenon of interpersonal effects on demand, but which was helping, in Leibenstein's view, to fill an important gap in current theory.

Duesenberry's work was, in fact, a critique of consumption theory in general but, more particularly, of the Keynesian consumption function. It argued that two fundamental assumptions of aggregate demand theory were invalid – first, the assumption that every individual's consumption behaviour could be taken as independent of that of every other individual; second, that consumption relations were reversible over time.

Keynes had avoided discussion of the interdependence issue in formulating his *General Theory*, realising that demand theory was not able to derive aggregate demand functions when the opinion or consumption of others entered into an individual's decision to buy. Duesenberry, however, believed that it was possible to obtain a theorem which allowed for interdependent consumer preferences, namely:

> that for any given relative income distribution, the percentage of income saved by a family will tend to be a unique, invariant and increasing function of its percentile position in the income distribution. The percentage saved will be independent of the absolute level of income. It follows that the aggregate savings ratio will be independent of the absolute level of income (1949: 3).

This alternative to the Keynesian analysis was necessary, in Duesenberry's view, because theories based on any assumed independence of different individuals' preferences could not be sustained. Such independence was, he conceded, implicit in most economic theory, but it had 'slipped in during the course of the historical development of consumer behavior theory'. Casual observation would quickly establish that it could not be seriously defended.

While both Jevons and Marshall, the 'classical' neoclassicists, had acknowledged interpersonal effects in their non-analytic discourses, but had taken no account of such behaviour in their more mathematical interpretations, writers such as Veblen and Knight had attacked orthodox neoclassical economists for their neglect of the subject. However, these attacks failed, according to Duesenberry, because they did not offer an alternative, positive and analytical theory of consumption which could take account of interdependent preferences and yet still be useful in practical terms. Their comments were always seen to be negative and carping and, Duesenberry suggested, most people would rather have a bad theory than no theory at all (1949: 15). Moreover, the issue of interdependent preferences was then considered to be such a special case that it did not, in any event, seem central to an overall theory of utility, value and consumption. Duesenberry set out to put matters in better perspective.

For any individual or family, he argued, social status was a key factor influencing the process of choice and the purchase of goods, and this status was measured by comparing the amount and pattern of consumption with that of others with whom they compared themselves. As some changed and improved their overall consumption rating, so others broke habit patterns in order to emulate them, and these breaks could be independent of changes in income and prices. For any particular family, therefore, the frequency of contact with superior goods increased primarily as the consumption expenditures of others with whom they came into contact increased. Duesenberry called this the 'demonstration effect', an effect which was put to the test by consulting one's own experiences:

> What kind of reaction is produced by looking at a friend's new car or looking at houses or apartments better than one's own? The result is likely to be a feeling of dissatisfaction with one's own house or car. If this feeling is produced often enough it will lead to action which eliminates it, that is, to an increase in expenditure (1949: 27).

Duesenberry argued that this increased expenditure to secure social status came about because the maintenance of self-esteem was a basic drive in every individual. And in a society in which improvements in the standard of living were a social goal, so this drive to maintain self-esteem expressed itself in a drive to acquire higher quality goods. Moreover, the 'quality' of such goods need not relate to any measure of practical value in use; indeed, the goods in question could be expensive yet largely useless items, reflecting a high degree of conspicuous waste.

This need for acquisition and the display of wealth came about, as Veblen had argued, because income had become one of the principal status criteria. Yet income alone was not enough – it had to be visibly displayed through consumption. High standards of consumption, therefore, came to be established as criteria for high status, and the mechanism whereby needs to increase or improve consumption were recognised by the individual came through association. Each person or family had strong social relationships with those of equal status, but would have some contact also with those of higher or lower status. As a result, they were able to 'place' themselves in the social order, and unfavourable comparisons with others led to a greater impulse to buy goods and services.

This impulse to buy or to conspicuously consume could come from three principal sources. First, it was possible that others within the individual's own social group who were perceived as social equals could significantly improve their consumption standard. This, in turn, would encourage a 'catching up' process, the phenomenon of 'keeping up with the Joneses' which had long been observed. Second, increases in the consumption standard of those perceived to be in a lower social group could lead individuals to increase consumption in order to preserve the social distance between groups. Finally, people could well aspire to join higher social groups themselves and so raise their consumption levels in order to gain membership of such groups. Overall, changes in social consumption by any individual were determined by the frequency with which he or she made unfavourable comparisons with groups of equal, lower or higher status with whom they came into contact. After some minimum level of income (above subsistence) was reached, therefore, the frequency and strength of impulses to increase expenditures for one individual depended entirely on the ratio of his expenditures to the expenditures of those with whom he associated. By the same token, dissatisfaction arose from the rejection (for whatever reason) of impulses to spend and the level of this dissatisfaction was again a function of comparative expenditure ratios.

While Duesenberry recognised that incentives to increase consumption could arise from contacts with equal, lower or higher status groups, he believed that it was the frequency of association which gave greater or less impetus to the impulse to consume for status. The greatest social contacts for any individual would be those of similar (equal) social and economic status, and it was this group which would have the greatest influence on consumption standards. However, the ambitions of this membership group would themselves determine the degree and direction of conspicuous spending:

> Consider two groups with the same incomes. One group associates with people who have the same income as they have. The other group associates with people who have higher incomes than the members of the group ... The two groups have the same income but the first will be better satisfied with its position than the second. Its members will make fewer unfavourable comparisons between their consumption standard and that of their associates (1949: 48).

People, in short, could aspire to join higher status groups either as individuals with ambitions to leave their existing membership group, or as a member of a group which itself aspired to 'move up' in terms of perceived status.

Duesenberry claimed that the consumption patterns of individuals or families were a function of their position in the income distribution, and that this result was produced by social factors which were local in character. Savings ratios were also, by definition, independent of the absolute level of income – a claim which ran counter to the Keynesian thesis of savings and consumption. He also argued that there was a ratchet effect on consumption which ensured that, when income levels fell, individual consumers' expenditures did not fall pro rata as they struggled to maintain past (better) standards of living. Consumption, in short, was a function of both present and past income.

Consumers' preferences were, therefore, both interdependent and irreversible: in particular, consumption was largely conditioned by the process of emulation which Veblen had described many years earlier. In support of his argument, Duesenberry tested his assumptions regarding income, aspirations and social status by examining published data on the consumption expenditures of blacks and whites in New York who were at the same income level, yet whose savings levels turned out to be significantly different (blacks saving more than whites). He also examined patterns of savings, consumption and income in other cities and again found nothing to disprove his theories. He concluded:

> The view that preferences are a matter of individual personality alone is certainly untenable. The differences in consumption patterns between societies and the similarities within them require us to regard consumption behavior as a social phenomenon (1949: 112).

In particular, he again stressed that a significant proportion of a family's consumption expenditures was always strongly influenced by comparisons with other people's consumption behaviour, and that, as a consequence, notions of deriving any measure of utility by assuming independent consumer preference formation were necessarily invalid.

Duesenberry's work on the 'demonstration effect' and on the interpersonal effects which affected consumer demand was, by any measure, an original contribution to consumer theory. Taken together, *Income, Saving and the Theory of Consumer Behavior* and Leibenstein's 1950 paper on external effects had opened up new avenues for exploration and research at both empirical and theoretical levels. The general response, however, was decidedly muted.

In the event, it was Duesenberry's macroeconomic rather than Leibenstein's more limiting microeconomic analysis which received the greater attention. Prompted by Duesenberry's relative income hypothesis, Johnson (1952) explored the probable effects of income distribution on aggregate consumption in societies where consumer preferences were significantly interdependent. Redistribution of income, he argued, would produce not only an income effect but also an interdependence effect related to the observed consumption patterns of all members of the community. In a 'competitive society' in which an individual's influence on everyone else's consumption varied inversely with his position on the income scale, the interdependence effect of any redistribution of income would always have the same sign as the income effect, so that the total change in consumption would be in the same direction as, and larger than, the change that would have occurred in the absence of any interdependence of consumption. In contrast, in an 'emulative society', where an individual's influence on everyone else's consumption varied directly with his position on the income scale, the income effect and interdependence effect would be of opposite sign, so that the total effect of any income redistribution might be in the same direction as, and larger than; in the same direction as, but smaller than; or in the opposite direction to the change that would have occurred in the absence of interdependence. These cases were, to Johnson, largely theoretical, however, and he agreed with Duesenberry that in reality income effects could be overstated:

> Both of the cases are extremely unrealistic, however, because in any actual society the influence of an individual's consumption on the consumption of others is not likely to be correlated exactly with income. Interdependence of consumption is likely to be either a matter of contact with the consumption habits of others, or of comparison of one's own consumption habits with an ideal standard identified in practice with the consumption habits of a social class about whom there is a relatively great amount of social information (through magazines, films, advertisements, novels etc.) (1952: 141).

Because of these realities, Johnson argued that those individuals who were close to the middle of any income scale would have the most influence on social consumption, and that this influence might be positively correlated with income in the lower half of the income range, but negatively correlated with income in the upper half. (This in turn raised 'the interesting possibility' that redistribution from rich to middle class would raise consumption more than any redistribution from rich to poor.)

To Johnson, Duesenberry had been right to argue that social contacts could have an important influence on consumer behaviour and that this needed to be taken into account in adopting any income-redistribution policies in order to influence and change the aggregate propensity to consume in any society. However, these conclusions were subsequently questioned (James and Beckerman, 1953). First, Johnson's use of what was referred to as 'the sociological method' came under attack for being too loose to be of any real value; second, when the analysis was reworked using more conventional 'psychological methods', results were claimed to be far less persuasive. James and Beckerman concluded that:

> In the absence of strong evidence to the contrary, it does not appear that theoretical analysis of interdependence effects can modify to any significant degree the usual conclusions regarding policy for redistribution of income (1953: 83).

Johnson replied that, even on their own assumptions, he could find no argument to support his critics' conclusions that the interdependence effects on income redistribution could in practice be ignored, but this particular aspect of policy-making subsequently received little real attention. Duesenberry's demonstration effect had, however, brought the complexities of consumer choice, in particular as they related to status-seeking consumption, to a wider audience.

In addition to the implications for income redistribution, Duesenberry's book had another, quite different, impact on economic thought, for the 'demonstration effect' was seen by some to have significant consequences for the consumption behaviour of developing countries. Hoyt (1951) argued that want development in underdeveloped areas was heavily influenced by exposure to the status goods of the developed economies – goods which, over time, tended to be absorbed into the consumer culture of the developing nation or region. The demonstration effect was therefore observable not only within but across nations.

Nurkse (1953) took this further, arguing that the effect played the role of villain in developing societies, syphoning savings away from much-needed investment and into the purchase of imported consumer goods of little real value. Capital formation suffered accordingly and this acted as a damper on real economic growth and development. 'The presence or the mere knowledge of new goods and new methods of consumption', argued Nurkse, 'tends to raise the general propensity to consume' and this could only be at the expense of saving and investment.

The claim that the demonstration effect raised the general propensity to consume was too ambitious for some. Chiang (1959) later pointed out that developing countries usually consisted of two distinct cultural sectors which were also distinguishable from each other geographically and economically, and that it was the commercial centres rather than the hinterlands which were most exposed to external cultural influences. These few centres, with their highly-developed commercial and industrial establishments, were culturally receptive to outside influences and provided the contact point with outside values, goods and services which Duesenberry had stressed was essential to the well-being of status-driven consumption. In contrast, the rural hinterlands offered no such basis for the development of status consumption. The proper interpretation of the impact of the demonstration effect was therefore:

> that it is the foreign-induced luxury and semi-luxury imports of one sector of the economy, which may be very small in land area and in population size, when superimposed upon the basic essential imports of the whole nation, that must be held chiefly responsible for the balance of payments difficulties of many poorer nations (1959: 254).

Chiang also claimed that the demonstration effect could serve as a force for good in the longer term if it encouraged greater investment in import substitution industries and if, at the same time, it widened the consumption horizons of the hinterland populations. Properly managed, he, along with others, saw it as a potential catalytic function in the process of economic development.

Notwithstanding the (limited) interest shown in Duesenberry's work with regard to the implications for income distribution and for economic development, there was no evidence of a more general concern for the importance of interpersonal effects on consumer demand by the end of the 1940s. Some writers (Katona, 1951, 1953) attempted to promote a more heterodox approach but, for the most part, orthodoxy prevailed. Stigler (1950) certainly recognised the past neglect of external effects on demand in his review of utility theory – a neglect which 'seemed to have stemmed partly from a belief in the unimportance of the effect and partly from the obstacles it would put in the way of drawing specific inferences from utility analysis'.

At the same time, he made no explicit appeal for its inclusion in future economic analyses of consumer demand, and implied that it continued to be of marginal interest. Mack (1952), reviewing work carried out into the economics of consumption over the past half century, acknowledged Duesenberry's contribution but, looking to the future, worried that any assumption of non-additivity of consumer demand 'would involve, in a sense, redrawing schedules' and that interdependence was best included 'loosely' as a possible additional dimension. The issue was clearly still being avoided and a continuing neglect was being tacitly encouraged; Duesenberry's and Leibenstein's foresight in anticipating the changing market conditions of post-war America had, for the moment, made little impact on economic theory and thought.

In truth, Duesenberry's work had attracted considerable criticism among economists because it appeared to relegate savings to a residual activity which only occurred after all culturally required consumption had been met. This, to most economists, seriously overstated the importance of the consumption function. Second, he was accused of placing far too much emphasis on emulation as the primary underlying motive of consumption by assuming that social competitiveness and social pressures were unrelenting. Again, most economists thought such an interpretation to be extreme and unsustainable, and were this time joined by some anthropologists who pointed out that many primitive cultures actively discouraged and often condemned excessive competition between individuals.

While non-economic behavioural scientists wanted to promote a better understanding of the complexity of cultural values and norms in seeking to explain consumption, economists generally were determined to refute Duesenberry by finding a more plausible, yet entirely 'economic' explanation for patterns of consumption and saving. This new interpretation arrived in 1957 with the publication of Milton Friedman's *A Theory of the Consumption Function*. Friedman introduced his 'permanent income' hypothesis, claiming that savings were not residual but a provision for the future and that, contrary to the assumptions of Duesenberry's relative income hypothesis, the real constraint for consumption decisions was the long-run expected yield from wealth (or permanent income).

Friedman believed that an individual's decisions regarding saving and consumption were informed by estimates of permanent income over their whole life span. While these income estimates might exist only as a vague guideline in the minds of consumers, they tended, nevertheless, to even out expenditures over the life cycle, with consumers using savings as a part of this process. This life span approach to consumption was attractive to economists, not only because it gave to savings a more important role than Duesenberry had acknowledged, but, at the same time, successfully removed any need to become concerned with the sociology of consumption. Friedman rejected the argument that variations in consumption were, in any sense, dictated by emulation or by a 'demonstration effect', and he at no point recognised interpersonal effects as a potentially significant determinant of consumer demand. Nowhere also was there any mention or discussion of the possible effects of status-directed product advertising and promotion, nor of the changes in consumer preferences which these might generate. Like Samuelson before him, he proposed a new theory of consumption couched in exclusively economic terms, at a time when market activity and manufacturing production were being increasingly sustained by non-economic consumer demand.

In his 1961 review of consumption theory, Houthakker gave some greater consideration to interpersonal effects on demand and to the status-seeking consumption which often resulted. A part of his review was given over to problems of aggregation, including the possible interactions between consumers' preferences, and he conceded that these social interactions could and did have a marked effect on consumer choice:

> Powerful though the assumption of random variation of preferences is, it also contradicts many intuitive notions on the social nature of human behavior. The formation of preferences is to some extent a social process, in which imitation and differentiation are important elements (1961: 733).

The process of preference formation was therefore significant, argued Houthakker, but had traditionally been dismissed as lying outside the remit of the economist. 'There is much to be said for this', he thought, but the danger was then that psychologists would not find the subject of sufficient interest, with the result that it would either be neglected or not studied at all (in reality, psychologists had been researching consumer preference formation for some fifty years, and their work had been largely ignored by economists).

With regard to the evidence of interpersonal effects offered by existing empirical research, Houthakker was less impressed. Duesenberry's work on the demonstration effect was consistent with casual observation but had not been rigorously tested; and a preliminary examination he himself had conducted with Prais (1955) into family expenditures had suggested that social interactions were more complex than Duesenberry had suspected. Houthakker also believed that the historical persistence and universality of consumption preference patterns indicated that they were not easily changed, and that this was as true in the 1950s as it had been in the past:

> This may seem surprising to those who, taking the claims of the more irresponsible advertisers or the best-sellers of popular sociologists at face value, believe that the preferences of modern man are largely shaped by Madison

Avenue and its equivalents in other countries. In fact, a large part of advertising does no more than inform the public of changes in prices and products. Most of the remainder is merely an attempt to sway consumers from one brand to another ... Examples of advertising that changed the demand for a substantial commodity are hard to find. The prudent marketer tries to exploit consumer's preferences, not to change them (1961: 734).

To Houthakker, advertising generated brand-switching or brand loyalty, but had no significant effect on the consumer's 'indifference' between one product class and another. It followed that advertising effects were 'of little relevance to those interested in basic patterns of consumption, which is the proper concern of the economics of consumption'. Overall, Houthakker felt that, on current evidence, it was questionable whether social interactions and interdependent effects on consumer demand were of sufficient importance for the economist to be unduly concerned with their influence. Considerations of product price and of income and budget constraints were still, he argued, the overwhelmingly important factors determining levels of demand at both micro and macro levels, and it was not at all clear that the neglect of any social influences on consumer preferences was a cause for concern.

Houthakker's effective dismissal of these social effects on demand was the more remarkable in that it came at the end of a decade which had seen the emergence in the United States of socially-motivated, mass conspicuous consumption on the grand scale. By now, the realities of the marketplace sat more easily with the theories of Duesenberry and Leibenstein than with traditional interpretations of utility and of individual consumer preference formation, yet orthodoxy prevailed. Economics was, in fact, offering no explanation for a phenomenon which could no longer be considered as trivial and peripheral. In reality, the promotion of status-seeking consumption was now a major preoccupation of business and commerce, and economists were well aware of the changes which had taken place in the post-war years. At the same time, for whatever reason, they failed to come to terms with the new consumer demand and held to assumptions and attitudes which had persisted since neoclassical theory was first developed.

References

Chiang, A.C. (1959), 'The "Demonstration Effect" in a Dual Economy', *American Journal of Economics and Sociology,* **18** (April), 249–58.

Duesenberry, James (1949), *Income, Saving and the Theory of Consumer Behavior*, reprinted (1967), Cambridge, Mass.: Harvard University Press.

Friedman, Milton (1957), *A Theory of the Consumption Function,* Princeton: Princeton University Press.

Goldsmith, S., G. Jaszi, H. Kaitz and M. Liebenberg (1954), 'Size Distribution of Incomes since the Mid–thirties', *Review of Economics and Statistics*, **36** (February).

Houthakker, H.S. (1961), 'The Present State of Consumption Theory', *Econometrica*, **29** (October), 704–39.

Hoyt, Elizabeth E. (1951), 'Want Development in Underdeveloped Areas', *Journal of Political Economy*, **59** (June), 194–202.

James, S.F. and W. Beckerman (1953), 'Interdependence of Consumer Preferences in the Theory of Income Redistribution', *Economic Journal*, **63** (March), 70–83. (Comment: H.G. Johnson, p.83).

Johnson, H.G. (1952), 'The Effects of Income Redistribution on Aggregate Consumption with Interdependence of Consumers' Preferences', *Economica*, **19** (May), 131–47.

Katona, George (1949), 'Analysis of Dissaving', *American Economic Review*, **39** (June), 673–88.

Katona, George (1951), *Psychological Analysis of Economic Behavior*, reprinted (1963), New York: McGraw Hill.

Katona, George (1953), 'Rational Behavior and Economic Behavior', *Psychological Review*, (September), 307–18.

Leibenstein, Harvey (1950), 'Bandwagon, Snob and Veblen Effects in the Theory of Consumers' Demand', *Quarterly Journal of Economics*, **64** (May), 183–207.

Mack, Ruth P. (1952), 'Economics of Consumption', in B.F. Haley (ed.), *A Survey of Contemporary Economics*, vol. II, Homewood, Illinois: Richard D Irwin Inc.

Morgenstern, Oskar (1948),'Demand Theory Reconsidered', *Quarterly Journal of Economics*, **62** (February), 165–201.

Nurkse, R. (1953), *Problems of Capital Formation in Underdeveloped Countries*, Oxford: Basil Blackwell.

Prais, S.J. and H.S. Houthakker (1955), *The Analysis of Family Budgets*, Cambridge University Press.

Stigler, George (1950), 'The Development of Utility Theory', *Journal of Political Economy*, **58** (August and October). Reprinted (1965) in *Essays in the History of Economics*, Chicago: University of Chicago Press, pp. 66–155.

8 Consumer Theory and the Economics of Affluence

The first era of generalised conspicuous consumption which had begun in the United States in the later 1940s was soon well established, and a part of the unprecedented growth in consumer demand could be directly attributed to the fact that business organisations were now explicitly selling the widest possible range of products as symbols of social status. This appeal to status aspirations found a ready audience with American consumers who were benefiting from a remarkable increase in individual wealth. Average after-tax incomes had more than doubled in real terms between 1950 and 1956. In one year in the same period, the number of Americans with annual incomes of more than $100,000 increased by 20 per cent over the twelve months. By 1959, the number of American families with a net worth of $500,000 had doubled since 1945; and it had been the 1950s rather than the 1940s which had shown the most remarkable improvements in earnings and living standards.

A further stimulus to the conspicuous consumption of goods and services came from the marked improvements in manufacturing productivity which, in turn, had led to significant increases in leisure time – increases which effectively devalued the 'consumption' of leisure as a symbol of rank and social position. The rise in disposable incomes, however, coupled with an ever-increasing emphasis on the status symbolism of products, meant that a significant proportion of customer purchases were made for social rather than for purely utilitarian reasons. This heightened interest in status-directed consumption had also made shopping itself a social event and, in much the same way as department stores had attempted many years earlier, a wide range of retail organisations now went to considerable efforts to project store images appropriate to the goods they stocked and promoted.

The increased incomes which were enjoyed at all levels of society again created shifts in the relative propensities to conspicuously consume at different social levels. The long-established, very rich, whose money was now 'old' rather than 'new' and who had been more circumspect in the ways in which they had chosen to spend their money through the Depression and the New Deal, continued to adopt a more reserved lifestyle as the 1950s arrived. However, the reasons for this reserve had now changed. In the 1920s and 1930s, they had been responding to a much-changed social and political climate which condemned rather than applauded ostentatious consumption; by the 1950s, as far greater numbers of people began to enjoy newly acquired wealth, they refrained from excessive conspicuous consumption because it was becoming increasingly ineffective as a means of securing status and social position. Indeed, the ostentatious display of wealth now came to be seen as vulgar by the old money élites. As Galbraith observed:

> Vulgar means: 'Of or pertaining to the common people, or to the common herd or crowd'. And this explains what happened. Lush expenditure could be afforded by so many that it ceased to be useful as a mark of distinction ... In sum, although ostentatious and elaborate expenditure in conjunction with the wealth that sustained it, was once an assured source of distinction, it is so no longer (1958: 72–3).

While the old-established 'American of wealth' now saw little to gain and much to lose from overt displays of affluence, those made newly-rich in the 1940s and 1950s had no such inhibitions, and responded happily to commercial signals which were encouraging them to consume for status. As wealth increased and incomes rose across the economy, so conspicuous consumption itself grew. To many economists, this appeared to be of little real consequence; to others outside the mainstream, including Galbraith, it had major implications not only for the management of production and consumption within affluent societies, but also for existing conventional theories of consumer demand.

Galbraith argued that many consumer wants no longer originated with the individual, as economic theory had always implied, but were increasingly being contrived by manufacturers, advertisers and retailers in order to sustain production. The nature of this new status-linked demand, however, still appeared to be of no concern to those who remained loyal to the traditional view that it was not the business of the economist to explore how consumer wants were formed. Marshall himself had famously laid down the rule that 'the economist studies mental states rather through their manifestations than in themselves; and if he finds they afford evenly balanced incentives to action, he treats them prima facie as for his purposes equal'. This evasion, argued Galbraith, could no longer be defended.

In an affluent society, when basic physical needs had been satisfied for the great majority of the population, psychologically-grounded desires took over and these desires were, in fact, never satisfied if manufacturers contrived continually to create new ones and to plan for the social obsolescence of products. America was now in the grip of a consumer culture which promoted the sale of goods and services which were far from necessaries in the traditional sense, but which nevertheless helped to ensure increasing levels of production.

The arrival of this new society had, in fact, been foreseen many years earlier, for in 1930 Keynes had written:

> The needs of human beings may seem to be insatiable. But they fall into two
> classes – those needs which are absolute in the sense that we feel them whatever
> the situation of our fellow human beings may be, and those which are relative in
> the sense that we feel them only if their satisfaction lifts us above, makes us feel
> superior to, our fellows. Needs of the second class, those which satisfy the desire
> for superiority, may indeed be insatiable; for the higher the general level, the
> higher still they are. But this is not so true of the absolute needs – a point may
> soon be reached, much sooner perhaps than we all of us are aware of, when these
> needs are satisfied in the sense that we prefer to devote our further energies to
> non-economic purposes (1930: 326).

It was no longer good enough, in Galbraith's view, for economists to ignore
the nature of wants and want formation, for this seemingly insatiable desire
for Keynes's 'needs of the second class', prompted and promoted by
manufacturers, advertisers and distributors, had significantly changed the
nature and direction of demand. Furthermore, this status-inspired
consumption cut across all social and economic groups, for those who could
not afford to finance such expenditures out of savings or income were now
more than willing to incur substantial levels of debt in order to sustain their
consumption lifestyles. Banks and other financial institutions were no less
willing to extend the necessary loans and credit facilities to these consumers.

Galbraith saw advertising and emulation as the two dependent sources of
desire which were working across society, operating both on those who could
afford and those who could not. The resultant status-seeking consumption
was, to his mind, clearly sustainable over the long term, as new wants and
desires were created, promoted and financed. As far as economic theory was
concerned, this development had far-reaching consequences, for it suggested
that, contrary to received wisdom, the effect of increasing affluence had been
to substantially reduce the importance of purely economic wants. This, in
turn, suggested that production and productivity would become less and less
important, unless they could be sustained by other (non-economic) means.

Economists had traditionally avoided this problem by refusing to admit to
any diminishing urgency of economic wants, arguing that there was an
infinite variety of goods on the market and that the arrival of new products
would always widen opportunities for introducing variety into purchasing
decisions. Moreover, there was seen to be unlimited opportunity for adding
to the range of new products and brands. However, the consumer preferences
of 1950s America, and the parallel 'repositioning' of goods and services by
US manufacturers and retailers, all indicated a major shift away from
economic goals and towards a consumer culture based on product symbolism,
store image and status-directed conspicuous consumption with its roots in the

sociology and psychology of demand. Economics was offering no explanation or analysis of these new market realities.

While economics largely chose to ignore the socially-directed consumption of the later 1940s and the 1950s, the new patterns of production, advertising and consumption were attracting considerable interest elsewhere. By the middle of the 1950s, motivation researchers were exploring the social psychology of consumer preference formation in affluent societies; marketing specialists began to focus on the process of conspicuous consumption and on other forms of status-seeking consumer behaviour (Leavitt, 1954; Katz and Lazarsfeld, 1955; Levy, 1959); and, at the theoretical level, major texts were published which began to explore models of social psychology which could explain and accommodate the new consumerism.

Four interpersonal models of consumer behaviour had their origins in the theoretical writings of the 1950s and early 1960s, all of which could be counted as social psychological in the Veblenian sense and were clearly influenced by the new market realities of the time. Riesman (1950) developed a model which centred on the concept of social character, itself shaped by the type of society (tradition-directed, inner-directed or other-directed) in which the individual operated. The model implied that society was capable of directing consumer behaviour in a predictable way. A second model (Festinger, 1957) was derived from the family of concepts called cognition consistency theories (balance, congruity and cognitive dissonance) in which people were assumed to be trying to maintain a state of balance in their relationships with other people and hoping to remove stress from their lives by purchasing products which established such balances.

Goffman (1959) developed a third model from role theory, arguing that individuals were actors who were playing a role in society. Here the focus was on overt social conduct where products became vehicles for image projection as well as symbolic representations of status. According to this theory, buyers purchased goods in accordance with their expectations of their 'audience' and not because the goods in question had any intrinsic attributes. Finally, McClelland (1961) attempted to explain socially-directed consumption in terms of achievement-oriented activity. Such activity was seen to be affected by the conflict between the tendency to achieve success and the tendency to avoid failure, and the implications for consumer behaviour centred on the resolution of these two opposing tendencies.

The theoretical writings of the 1950s gave further impetus to other social psychologists who were more directly concerned with product symbolism and consumption for status. Woods (1960) insisted that, in the light of American experience over the previous decade, it had to be recognised that many purchases were now being made not for cognitive (rational) motives, but in response to other, non-cognitive forces. He identified two types – behaviour in response to affective appeal and to symbolic appeal, both often grouped together as irrational.

The response to affective appeals was categorised as impulsive behaviour in which consumers reacted to physical product qualities such as colour and design. Response to symbolic appeals, in contrast, was seen as emotional behaviour generated by:

> thinking about the meaning of a product purchase rather than the function of the purchase. Thus the perceived prestige of ownership comes to be more important in bringing about a purchase than the function which the product would serve (1960: 17).

The market for consumer products could therefore be broken down into two basic buyer groups, one rational, the other seemingly irrational. Irrational buyers comprised an impulse group, insensitive to brand name, and a group of 'emotional reactors', responsive to what products symbolised and heavily swayed by images.

Complementing these rational and irrational categories of buyers, several product groups were then identified which catered to their specific needs – in particular, 'prestige' products which were essentially symbols and whose function was to extend or identify the ego of the consumer consistent with his or her own self-image; and 'status' products which served the function of imputing class leadership to their users.

Whilst prestige products connoted leadership, Woods argued, status products connoted membership, and both types of social need led the individual to prefer and consume products with status connotations. It followed, therefore, that the emotional reactors identified as a major buying group would tend to identify, purchase and consume both prestige and status products for their symbolic and social value, a process much in evidence in 1950s America. Moreover, not only could irrational motives dictate consumer attitudes, but certain products were put on the market to cater specifically for these seemingly irrational needs. In this context, products became symbols rather than bundles of utilities, and could bear little if any resemblance to those supplied for conventional (rational and economic) purposes.

Study of the role of products as symbols was taken further by others who explored in greater detail why such symbols had come to play such a significant part in consumer demand (Bourne, 1963; Lazer, 1964; Sommers, 1964). In his work on the diffusion of innovations, Rogers (1962) calculated that the adoption of highly visible new product innovations was especially likely to be status motivated, and questioned why these motives had been consistently understudied in past diffusion research. He attributed this to the fact that respondents were always reluctant to admit that they had adopted a new product in order to secure status, and so such aspirations and intentions were significantly underreported in consumer research findings. Nonetheless, he placed ambitions to reinforce or to achieve a higher socioeconomic status at the heart of many decisions to adopt new products, arguing that early adopters either enjoyed a higher social status or had a greater degree of upward social mobility than later adopters. To Rogers, 'socioeconomic status and innovativeness appear to go hand in hand' (1962: 252).

By the mid-1960s, the importance of status-motivated consumer behaviour was well established. Further, it could now no longer be seen as a purely American phenomenon for, as the European economies completed their recovery from post-war austerity, the same patterns of conspicuous consumption were now in evidence elsewhere.

Status-motivated consumption had historically always been recognised within sociology and psychology, and the writers of the early 1960s were continuing a well-established interest. When the first behavioural models of consumer demand began to appear in the later 1960s, therefore, it was realistic to expect that this interest and belief in status-linked consumer preference formation would be fully accommodated. In the event, and somewhat surprisingly, status-driven consumption was once again marginalised.

The first general model of consumer decision processes to attract wide attention in the 1960s was that of Nicosia (1966). The Nicosia model explored the process of product or brand choice, and identified four fields of activity – consumer attitude formation, information search and evaluation, the act of purchase and, finally, post-consumption feedback.

Within the model, there was some recognition that certain purchases could be generated by a desire to secure social status rather than by any consideration of direct utility. The role of reference groups and the importance of socially visible products were acknowledged, as was the need for store image and reputation to complement product status and visibility. For the most part, however, status consumption was seen as a special case which arose when a (status-inspired) 'future state of affairs' was the goal orientation of the act of purchase.

In looking (too briefly) at conspicuous consumption, Nicosia claimed, controversially, that the social attributes of products appealed more to relatively poorer social and economic groups within the community:

> Social attributes have also become relevant variables in establishing the rapport between consumer and product ... Ultimately, what counts is the presence or absence of these perceptions in the decision process ... Only in this sense can we understand, for example, the finding that people of lower socioeconomic status have a higher tendency to buy more 'conspicuous' items. This suggests that the

attribute 'conspicuousness' is a relevant variable in the decision process of consumers of a lower socioeconomic class (1966: 138–9).

The claim that conspicuous consumption was more marked among poorer rather than richer sections of society was clearly at odds with much earlier research by observation. In defence of his claim, Nicosia cited work by Martineau (1958) which had explored the differences in spending behaviour between various social classes and which Nicosia claimed to have substantiated the point (in reality, Martineau's work only demonstrated that conspicuous consumption was evident at *all* social and economic levels, although consumption patterns differed between social classes and income groups). Nicosia then went on to suggest that it was always important to distinguish between 'technical' and 'social psychological' product attributes, because when considerations of status were important, these lower class consumers would inevitably trade off objective and subjective product properties in reaching any purchase decision.

In 1968, a second general model of consumer behaviour was proposed by Engel, Kollatt and Blackwell, but again the attention given in the model to status-seeking consumption was minimal. What limited reference there was to the subject, however, stood in marked contrast to Nicosia's interpretation.

Social risk was recognised as a potentially important factor in encouraging an 'external' search for information concerning a product or product group, and advertising which stressed social approval rather than specific product characteristics was seen to play a role in directing consumers towards certain goods and services which were considered to be socially acceptable. Conspicuous consumption itself was regarded as a phenomenon which was stimulated entirely by social class differences, and, in contrast to Nicosia's claims, described as a predominantly lower-upper class (nouveaux riches) activity. This class, it was argued:

> use products as symbols or badges of their wealth. They bought the largest homes in the best suburbs, the most expensive automobiles, swimming pools, yachts and other symbols that were perceived as obvious indicators of wealth (1968: 290).

Later, in a revised edition of their work (1973), this narrow view of conspicuous consumption for wealth display was moderated by the authors in the light of new research. Laumann and House (1970), for example, had found significant consumption differences between nouveaux riches groups and 'old money' social élites whose wealth had been inherited rather than earned. The former group:

> have a strong need to validate their newly found status yet have not been accepted socially by the traditional upper classes. They turn to conspicuous consumption

but with 'taste' if it is to validate their claim to high status in respects other than mere money (1970: 336).

This need for taste, it was argued, was provided by a class of professional taste makers (architects, fashion designers and others) and by a taste-setting media which was able to promote socially acceptable products and innovations to potential buyers. In essence, the 1973 definition of status-inspired consumption moved away from 'pure' conspicuous consumption, in which the display of wealth was the sole criterion for purchase and consumption, and towards a first-order modification of such behaviour, in which the display of wealth alone was not enough and had to be complemented by an acceptable display of taste. In 1968, however, only wealth display had been seen as important.

While Engel et al. acknowledged that status considerations could, exceptionally, influence consumer purchase decisions, there was no specific attempt to accommodate such behaviour. In truth, the 'phenomenon' was briefly described and implicitly discounted as a perverse form of consumption observed, for the most part, within one small socio-economic grouping.

A third major model developed in the later 1960s was that of Howard and Sheth (1969). Again, references to status-motivated consumption were minimal. There was no attempt to integrate such consumption within a general theory, although, once again, the increasing promotion of products as status goods was acknowledged:

> Conspicuous consumption (expressive behavior) seems to have enabled companies to differentiate brands and inject them with actual or perceived quality differences so that there are a number of brands that have become status symbols with which to identify and which service the expressive function (1969: 343).

Howard and Sheth (unlike Galbraith) saw the impetus for the promotion and sale of status symbols as consumer-led, rather than as a 'manufactured' demand driven by the imperatives of production and productivity. In this they were closer to the Veblenian view that such demand was socially and culturally inspired. However, they took discussion of such consumer behaviour no further, implying, like Nicosia and Engel et al., that it had no place of central importance in the development of a general theory of consumer decision processes concerned, for the most part, with classical utility rather than with the social consumption of goods.

Overall, therefore, the treatment of status consumption by behavioural scientists through the 1960s was mixed, for while some had attempted partial theoretical explanations of what was, by then, a widespread interest on the part of the buying public in the role of goods as status symbols, the general models of consumer behaviour which emerged in the latter part of the decade gave little weight to the phenomenon as a significant influence on consumer decision making. In this respect, at least, they were closer to neoclassical economists than to the many sociologists and psychologists who believed that status-seeking consumption was now significant enough to merit more serious consideration within demand theory.

In economics, also, the general neglect of status-linked consumption continued. There was some mild interest in the degree to which consumers and markets could become occupied with matters of status and social prestige, and the occasional paper looked at issues of luxury consumption directly (Robinson, 1961). Katona (1960, 1964) looked at the changing values of a mass consumption society, and at the need to revisit many of the assumptions implicit in neoclassical consumer economics. For most economists, however, there was no 'problem' to be addressed.

Whilst mainstream economics remained, for the most part, disengaged, there were two significant contributions to demand theory in the 1960s which, while very different in content and approach, both explored the possibility of refining and further developing theories of consumer behaviour. First, Becker (1962, 1965) looked at the nature and behaviour of the household as an economic unit, seeing the individual neoclassical consumer not as an isolated buyer but as part of household production and consumption activity. Becker saw the household, in fact, as a miniature factory, which combined market goods and time to produce ultimate consumption goods. As household wages and earnings increased over time, so more goods and less time came to be used in household production, a phenomenon which, according to Becker, helped to explain the increasing emphasis and success of time-saving appliances and services which had become increasingly evident in later 1950s and early 1960s America. While Becker did not directly address status-driven consumption choices at the time, the issue of household taste stability was to be revisited at a later date.

A second major and original contribution to the exploration of consumer preference formation came in 1966 when Kelvin Lancaster published a paper in the *Journal of Political Economy* which departed radically from orthodox economics and proposed a new approach to consumer theory. While this new approach addressed general problems associated with demand and consumption, it offered the potential for a far better accommodation of status-motivated consumption within economics.

Lancaster's disillusionment with demand theory was first evident in the 1950s. Reviewing Hicks' book *A Revision of Demand Theory* published in 1956, he pointed to the sterility of current economic thought:

Professor Hicks seems to have been seduced by the ghosts of Marshall and his followers. They attempted to squeeze the last drop out of demand theory, but they did not realise that they were squeezing a stone, nor that the drops were water and not blood; by now we should all know better (1957: 354).

Lancaster believed that the current state of demand theory omitted any consideration of the intrinsic properties of particular goods, notwithstanding the fact that market researchers, advertisers and manufacturers commonly acted on the well-founded belief that such intrinsic properties were relevant to the way consumers reacted to products. Traditional theory still had nothing to say either on new commodities or on quality variations between goods, and it manifestly could not deal with many important aspects of actual relationships between goods and consumers.

Lancaster suggested that these deficiencies came about because the traditional view of goods was that they were the direct objects of utility. If utility could instead be taken to derive from the properties or characteristics of goods, then far more progress could be made in understanding the nature and preferences of consumer demand. Any particular good in fact possessed more than one characteristic, so consumption was therefore characterised by joint outputs. Further, a characteristic present in one good could be present in many others; consumers chose their purchases on the basis of the 'bundle' of characteristics offered by any one particular product in comparison to others.

In 1966, Lancaster proposed three new assumptions (1966a), each of which represented a break with tradition. First, a good per se did not give utility to consumers, rather it possessed characteristics, and it was these several characteristics which gave rise to utility. Second, a good would, in general, possess more than one characteristic, and many characteristics were typically shared by more than one good. Finally, combinations of goods could possess characteristics different to those offered by the same goods separately (Lancaster illustrated this last claim by arguing that a meal and a social setting, brought together through the medium of a dinner party, offered a bundle of characteristics – nutritional, aesthetic, intellectual – which was entirely different from a meal and a social gathering consumed separately).

Lancaster's new definition of goods and commodities was intended to have wide application, and it was potentially able to accommodate status-seeking consumer behaviour with far greater ease than more traditional interpretations of consumer demand. To some limited extent, Lancaster himself recognised certain aspects of the sociology and psychology of consumer preference formation. In another 1966 paper on change and innovation in the technology of consumption (1966b), he had acknowledged that the typical consumer inherited many consumption traditions from his social background and that it was often difficult to adopt appropriate and expected patterns of consumption when moving to a higher social and economic level. 'We are all aware that the *nouveau riche* may consume differently from persons already established in the higher income group', he argued, and suggested that they were undergoing a process of socialisation which, over time, would equip them to spend and consume in a more appropriate manner (1966b: 19). Beyond such general observations of social and hierarchical effects, however, his analysis of consumer demand stayed well within the confines of traditional economic discussion, and he showed no interest in applying his consumer theory to explanations of status-motivated consumption.

This relative lack of interest in the more sociological aspects of consumer demand was made clear when, in 1971, he drew his work together in the book *Consumer Demand*. Nowhere in the text was any reference made to the role of interpersonal effects on consumer preference formation. In explanation, Lancaster argued that, generally speaking, it was better to avoid explicit 'psychologizing' about goods, and to concentrate only on their utilitarian rather than on any social characteristics. Many cases of apparent non-additivity came about as the result of such unnecessary psychologizing, he said, and when such speculation was removed so 'non-additivity presents no particular problem' (1971: 107).

The determination to avoid interpersonal effects on demand was evident in Lancaster's application of his theory of 'revealed relevance' to the United States' automobile market, where the relevant product characteristics determining consumer choice were taken as accommodation (size and comfort), ride quality, handling and steering, engine quality, brakes, frequency of repair record, and manufacturer's suggested retail price. Neither social status and prestige, nor the opinion of 'relevant others' were seen to be of any significance. Summarising results, Lancaster argued that his analysis 'suggests that the automobile market is readily amenable to rational analysis in terms of straightforward physical characteristics of cars, without using such imponderables as "style" or any sex at all'(1971: 174). In short, his perspective on consumer preference formation, even in a market which was by then being seen as particularly susceptible to social engineering and to product symbolism, was that demand was both rational and economic and that any sociology of consumption could be safely ignored.

While Lancaster himself showed no enthusiasm for adopting a more heterodox view of consumer demand, his 'revealed relevance' model did offer a potentially more constructive framework for analysing the nature and consequences of interpersonal effects on preference formation. In particular, the concept of products as bundles of characteristics could have been extended to include such elements as prestige, high price, snob value, social visibility or the consumption of others as relevant factors which, in many markets, had certainly become major influences on purchase decisions after 1950. In the event, the model was not used, either by Lancaster or by other economists, as a vehicle to explore these more psychological influences on consumer demand.

This relative lack of interest in testing and applying Lancaster's new consumer theory extended into the 1970s. Lipsey and Rosenbluth (1971) used the model to attempt a rehabilitation of Giffen goods, arguing that when products were seen as bundles of characteristics, existing presumptions in the demand literature that the Giffen Effect was an extremely unlikely one rested on shaky foundations. For the most part, however, the new approach to consumer demand received little attention. And, by the mid-1970s, what little attention was given to the subject was, on balance, critical rather than supportive.

By 1975, several writers were commenting on what they saw as the limits of Lancaster's new theory. Hendler (1975), Ratchford (1975), Lucas (1975) and Pekelman and Sen (1975) all argued that, once Lancaster's special assumptions were removed, his conclusions were hard to sustain and the model could not be considered to be operational in any real sense. Others, more positively, were attempting to adapt Lancaster and to revise his model accordingly.

A major difficulty in applying the original model to any examination of status-inspired consumption was that Lancaster saw the characteristics associated with products as 'objective properties' which were both observable and measurable. To the conspicuous consumer, however, it was the opinion of third parties (in particular, significant others and reference groups) which determined whether a good held any real, if abstract, utility value. Lancaster had explicitly removed any social or psychological considerations from his own analysis, and so these external effects were not a part of the equation.

Ladd and Zober did, in fact, recognise such social effects on demand in proposing a revised model (1977). Lancaster's objective characteristics of products were acknowledged but were complemented by what they defined as consumer 'services' obtained from the consumption of these products. Status gains were given as an example of such product services but no attempt was then made to accommodate these status-linked benefits in their revised model. While the influence and effect of advertising on consumer demand was also acknowledged, its role in promoting social symbolism and prestige value was not developed, nor was any attempt made to explore the price paid for status as a product service or to describe and measure the quantities of 'status' being bought as a product characteristic. Indeed, having included status as a potential product benefit, the revised model moved back towards a Lancaster-type analysis based on objective properties – properties which they had earlier seen as only a partial explanation of consumer demand.

While Ladd and Zober had hinted at the possibility of using Lancaster's new consumer theory to develop a better theory of status-motivated consumption, Hayakawa and Venieris (1977) attempted a more ambitious reworking which adapted the Lancaster model specifically in order to accommodate consumer interdependence. They argued that 'the insights of Veblen and Pigou can be most effectively abstracted for economic analysis in terms of a theory of interdependent choice via reference groups'. These significant others were, they suggested, ordered by individual consumers in terms of social status and relative importance, factors which then determined patterns of consumption.

Two fundamental axioms were proposed. First, that social groups existed with distinct life styles and associated clusters of wants. Second, that a consumer, as a function of his social status, identified himself with, and emulated, a social group as his reference group. Life style was then seen in terms of Lancaster-type consumption of characteristics associated with particular products, with individuals consuming to patterns dictated by the group.

In the short run, Hayakawa and Venieris argued, an individual's desired bundle of characteristics was predetermined by the preferences and approval of the relevant reference group and was relatively stable. This bundle would, however, vary over the longer term as the reference group itself changed its consumption tastes and preferences. And if the social status of the individual consumer itself changed over time, so targeted reference groups changed and the desired bundle of life style characteristics would in turn be modified.

It was argued that, at the core of individual consumption, there was, for status-sensitive products, an optimal bundle of characteristics 'ray' (in Lancaster's terms) which represented the life style of an emulated social group. Accepting this notion, then certain assumptions followed. First, that in the consumption set (the space of characteristics) of a consumer, there was an optimal ray that he wished to maintain. Second, that for two intensities of a given life style, the more intensive was always preferred to the less intensive, and that any bundle of characteristics closer to a more intensive representation of a given life style was preferred to a less intensive alternative. Third, that given any optimal life style, the further the consumer deviated from it the worse off he became, and that there existed a completely unacceptable life style over which any sub-optimal level of intensity was preferred. Finally, that for any intensity of an arbitrarily given life style, there was an intensity of the optimal life style which was indifferent to it.

Hayakawa and Venieris presented four theorems which, under static conditions, characterised these suggested preference structures. They were at pains, however, to point out that their presentation and results were less radical in terms of economic theory than might at first sight be supposed. The substitution of characteristics space for commodity space still produced convex indifference curves of a type associated with neoclassical theory. Furthermore, the preference map contained a relevant range over which marginal rates of substitution were positive and diminishing and, as prices changed, both income and substitution effects came into play to affect the consumer's equilibrium response.

It has already been noted that Lancaster removed 'psychologizing' from his analysis and that his study of US demand for automobiles had focused exclusively on objective product characteristics. Hayakawa and Venieris now took issue with this interpretation:

> Complementarity in the theory of consumer behavior is seldom mentioned except in the case of clear-cut technical complementarity (such as between bodies of cars and tires) ... Once the notion of a reference group is introduced into consumer choice calculus, we need another type of complementarity, psychological complementarity (1977:612).

Reference groups, they argued, could no longer be ignored as 'even a casual glimpse of advertising strategy seems to reveal an effort to appeal to the attractiveness of a reference group rather than to the inherent qualities of the product in question'. And if these advertising campaigns were having any measurable effect on an individual's life style 'rays', so reference groups needed to be put at the centre of consumer demand theory.

While the Hayakawa and Venieris paper had outlined an application of Lancaster's new consumer theory which explored the nature and direction of status-directed consumption, it made no attempt to propose how the preferences and influence of reference groups could be measured in order to derive the life style ray which lay at the core of their analysis. However, other researchers had, independently, begun to explore how such measurements could be made. Wind (1976) had widened Becker's concept of the household as a buying centre to include not only family members but also other individuals and relevant others whose views shaped the buying decisions of individuals and groups within the family. He then outlined a procedure, based on conjoint measurement analysis, which would allow researchers to quantify the specific role of these relevant others and so bring greater precision to reference group analysis. More work needed to be done, however, for Wind's experimental approach did not offer the necessary statistical inferential apparatus which could then extend such measurement into empirical analysis. Nonetheless, it demonstrated that adaptations of Lancaster's consumer theory offered some hope of defining and interpreting status-driven consumption at both theoretical and practical levels.

The Hayakawa and Venieris paper represented the only work of any significance in the 1970s which attempted to explore status consumption directly through Lancaster's new consumer theory. In reality, there was little interest in further developing such work, not least because Lancaster's new approach had made little impact on mainstream economic treatments of consumer demand. Most other significant contributions to the study of status consumption over the decade came not from any extension of Lancaster's thesis but from economists working to improve and extend the more conventional theories of consumer preference formation. Some now recognised that social influences on consumer demand needed to be better described and explained within the corpus of economic theory, and began the search for a better treatment of status-seeking behaviour within economics.

In Europe, Krelle (1972) looked at the utility function as it had evolved from the work of Menger, Jevons and Walras, an exercise which could only confirm that, in the light of observed consumer behaviour in the marketplace, it offered, at best, a partial and severely limited explanation of consumer preference formation in the real world. In essence, it was static, extremely individualistic, and entirely neglected any mutual interdependence of preferences in society. Crucially, it did not provide a connection between the satisfaction level of a person as measured by psychologists, and the utility index used by economists.

Krelle proposed a theory of social interdependence of consumer evaluations, arguing that mutual utility interdependence had to be recognised and accommodated in any economic analysis of consumer demand. This interdependence inevitably resulted from the networks of personal contacts developed by people and from the persuasive and informative power of media messages and product advertising. All information received was processed by the individual and subsequently had a significant influence on personal preferences by bringing interpersonal effects to bear on consumption choices.

The parameters of utility functions were therefore decided by the nature and effectiveness of a society's information system. Krelle then outlined a new treatment of consumer preference formation which attempted to link conventional utility theory to the social psychology which had been largely removed from economic analysis since the 1930s. The proposed model, however, needed to be both dynamic and also able to map changes in preferences which were themselves continually changing. Krelle concluded that it would never be possible to consider the utility function of any individual as determinate or given, as demand was always a function of complex networks of perceived values. This raised questions as to whether consumer demand could ever be realistically measured.

Krelle's attempts to develop dynamic representations of a utility function which incorporated both psychological and economic influences on consumer choice were taken further by Gaertner (1973), who constructed a more detailed model of consumer and consumption interdependence. Elsewhere in Europe there was little interest in such reformulations, but in the United States, a greater level of interest in the subject was being shown among some more eminent economists.

In 1974, Becker acknowledged that, while nineteenth-century economists had given far greater recognition to social influences on preference formation, and while sociologists (among whom he included Veblen 'for these purposes') had long emphasised the central role of interactions on individual wants, twentieth-century theorists had, for the most part, avoided such market realities. Certainly, Duesenberry and Leibenstein had attempted to discuss and analyse interpersonal effects, but their efforts had been effectively marginalised. Becker now attempted to develop a theoretical framework for the analysis of consumer demand, a theory of social interactions which explored demand for a single commodity described as 'distinction'.

Becker maintained that a key factor in determining demand for distinction was the individual's social environment, an environment which, while largely beyond the individual's control, could nevertheless be managed to some degree by decisions to buy or not to buy certain distinction-giving goods. An individual's social distinction, he argued, was determined firstly by the contribution to his distinction of his social environment, and secondly by his own contribution. Each person then maximised a utility function comprising the product 'social distinction' and other utilitarian commodities subject to a budget constraint that depended on income and the exogenously given social environment.

An attempt was then made to incorporate these social effects into conventional economic theory. The subsequent analysis, however, was open to the criticism that the chosen definition of utility assumed a strong stability of 'tastes' which was hard to defend. In particular, with regard to social distinction, it understated the influence of fashions and fads in making the demand for goods of social distinction unstable rather than stable over time. Becker was prepared to argue that patterns of demand for products of social distinction were, in reality, far more stable than was commonly recognised. In 1977, together with George Stigler, he looked in greater detail at the stability of tastes and at consumer preference formation over time. With regard to social distinction they focused, in particular, on the claim that changes in 'fashions and fads' did, in fact, make the market for status goods markedly unstable.

The commodity produced by fashion goods, they argued, was certainly social distinction, achieved by 'demonstration of alert leadership, or at least not lethargy, in recognizing and adopting that which will in due time be widely approved'. This commodity could also be termed *style* and was not secured simply by change – it depended, in fact, on a correct prediction of what would subsequently be approved. Style was 'social rivalry, and it is, like all rivalry, both an incentive to individuality and a source of conformity'. However, while changes in fashions and styles might seem to occur with great frequency, Stigler and Becker (1977) argued for a stability of tastes by claiming that while current fashions could and did change patterns of demand between competing products, demand for the generic commodity remained essentially unchanged and the stability of the commodity's utility function remained stable. Tastes, in short, might vary between brands, but fashion changes did nothing to weaken the essential stability of tastes for the commodity itself. Further, even when individuals were fashion conscious, markets for brands themselves still tended to be relatively stable, because the flow of information regarding new tastes and trends was neither full nor free (Stigler, 1961): in effect, seeking, collecting and processing information about rapidly changing markets was difficult and costly and worked to slow down any tendency towards instability of tastes.

By removing any unstable tastes from the equation, the demand for social distinction in goods could then be analysed purely in terms of price and income effects, and all changes in behaviour explained by changes in prices and incomes, 'precisely the variables that organise and give power to economic analysis'. Market dynamics could then be introduced and explained in more conventional form, even in relation to the market for distinction-giving luxury goods, and the demand for fashion systematically analysed without assuming a shift in tastes:

An increase in I's own income, prices held constant, would increase his demand for social distinction and other commodities. If his social environment were unchanged, the whole increase in his distinction would be produced by an increase in his own contributions to fashion and other distinction-producing goods. Therefore, even an average income elasticity of demand for distinction would imply a high income elasticity of demand for fashion (and these other distinction-producing) goods, which is consistent with the common judgment that fashion is a luxury good.

If other persons increase their contributions to their own distinction, this may lower I's distinction by reducing his social environment. For distinction is scarce and is to a large extent simply redistributed among persons: an increase in one person's distinction generally requires a reduction in that of other persons. This is why people are often 'forced' to conform to new fashions. When some gain distinction by paying attention to (say) new fashions, they lower the social environment of others. The latter are induced to increase their own efforts to achieve distinction, including a demand for these new fashions, because an exogenous decline in their social environment induces them to increase their own contributions to their distinction.

Therefore, an increase in all incomes induces an even greater increase in I's contribution to his distinction than does an increase in his own income alone. For an increase in the income of others lowers I's social environment because they spend more on their own distinction: the reduction in his environment induces a further increase in I's contribution to his distinction. Consequently, we expect wealthy countries to pay more attention to fashion than poor countries like India, even if tastes were the same in wealthy and poor countries. (1977: 88–9).

Stigler and Becker attempted a purely economic interpretation of status-motivated consumption and did not succumb to the 'psychologizing' which had so concerned Lancaster. They explicitly discounted John Stuart Mill's claim, developed by Veblen and others, that custom and tradition were significant factors in demand formation. Similarly, they gave little weight to claims that advertising could have a profound effect on generalised patterns of demand and on the stability of tastes, arguing that brand-switching was relatively trivial and ought not to be confused with changes in demand for a generic commodity, where markets displayed a far greater stability over time. This emphasis on the stability of demand for the commodity rather than for the brand implicitly rejected Lancaster's approach based on consumer searches within any given commodity group for competing bundles of characteristics.

While they themselves had refrained from speculating about the social psychology of status-driven consumption, they were, at the same time, not complacent about the extent to which their analysis could be considered comprehensive and took issue with those economists who, over many decades, had argued that matters associated with the psychology or the sociology of tastes and of consumer demand were best left to others. 'Our hypothesis is trivial', they conceded, 'for it merely asserts that we should apply economic logic as extensively as possible. But the self-same hypothesis is also a demanding challenge, for it urges us not to abandon opaque and complicated problems with the easy suggestion that the further explanation will perhaps someday be produced by one of our sister behavioral sciences' (1977: 89–90). To this extent, they located a part of the future study of the motives which underpinned status consumption within economics itself.

Work on developing applications of Lancaster's new theory and, less controversially, on the construction of new economic theories of social interactions and consumer demand within more conventional economic paradigms, were complemented in the 1970s by some limited additional work on status consumption which focused more narrowly on the role and influence of product price and of price-dependent preferences on consumer demand for socially-visible goods and services. Interest in the relationship between high prices and associated snob or status value was not new (Scitovsky, 1945), and Leibenstein's 1950 analysis of external effects on consumer demand had placed price at the centre of status-linked external effects on demand. Much earlier, Veblen had emphasised that prices which made products and services unaffordable to others lay at the heart of conspicuous consumption and conspicuous waste.

The consequences for consumer demand which could arise when prices entered the utility function were now being more actively explored (Kalman, 1968; Allingham and Morishima, 1973). A special case theorem was developed which attempted to accommodate the fact that a high price could be seen as a positive product attribute. However, this was of limited value in so far as status-driven consumption was concerned because it drew no clear distinction between two very different forms of price–quality association – those of the Veblenian conspicuous consumer who saw price per se as an element of product quality, and those of the more 'rational' buyer who took price to be an indicator of tangible product worth unconnected with any notions of social value.

Alcaly and Klevorick (1970) did, in fact, distinguish between this physical and social utility of products in examining the proposition that price could well be seen by the conspicuous consumer as a positive characteristic of goods within a Lancaster-type model. Later, Pollak (1977), regretting the paucity of theoretical literature, explored, inter alia, the importance of price-dependent preferences 'when a higher price enhances the "snob appeal" of a good'.

Leibenstein had argued that, to understand the effects that conspicuous consumption has on the demand function, it was necessary to divide price into two categories – 'real' price, being the price paid by consumers in money terms; and 'conspicuous' price, referring to the price that other people would think had been paid for the commodity. Pollak, similarly, separated out two elements of price, distinguishing between 'market prices', which entered the budget constraint, and 'normal prices', which influenced preferences. Unlike Leibenstein, however, his subsequent discussion was more limiting in that it did not introduce the opinions of 'significant others' into the analysis of individual or market demand functions for status goods.

This neglect of interpersonal influences was surprising in that, one year earlier, Pollak had developed a model of interdependent preferences, defined as preferences which depend on other people's consumption, and had examined its implications for demand theory. 'It is a commonplace that preferences are influenced by other people's consumption, but this insight has never been incorporated into demand analysis in a satisfactory way ... The lead provided by James Duesenberry was never systematically explored' (1976: 309; 310).

Pollak's 1976 paper, (which built on earlier research into habit formation and its influence on dynamic demand formation (1970), as well as on Gaertner's earlier (1973) thesis), had looked in some detail at Duesenberry's work, using it to develop a model of interdependent preferences. In two important respects, however, he qualified Duesenberry's analysis. First, instead of specifying that an individual's preferences depended on other people's past and present consumption, it was assumed that interdependent preferences operated only through past consumption, whether influenced by, or independent of, habit formation. This more limiting assumption offered the advantage of analytical tractability – 'a virtue not to be despised' – and was also seen to be consistent with the belief that the acquisition of preferences formed part of the process of socialisation. Pollak was suspicious of so-called simultaneous interdependence, arguing that it was difficult to accept that a complete adjustment of tastes could realistically take place in a single period. Second, he assumed that a simple model of interdependent preferences needed to be built on the assumption that an individual was concerned only with the consumption of the man one rung above him in the hierarchy (this ruled out any consideration of bandwagon effects, where individuals were influenced in their consumption behaviour not by their superiors in the hierarchy but by their peers and social equals).

The remarkable feature of Pollak's 1976 and 1977 papers was that there was no linkage between the two, for the analysis of price-dependent preferences associated with conspicuous consumption in fact made no reference to interdependent preferences nor to the importance of reference groups and significant others on patterns of consumption. Duesenberry's relative income hypothesis and the 'demonstration effect', the focus of the 1976 paper, were not seen to be relevant to issues relating to the potential snob appeal of goods and services. In truth, Pollak was demonstrating a commonplace ability among economists to discuss social influences on preference formation, yet to remove all discussion of such influences from economic and econometric models of price and income effects on consumer demand. For their part, a clear majority of economists found such separation easy to justify: most continued to believe, as they had two decades earlier (Chipman, 1960), that, as economics entered the 1980s, concern with interdependent and price-dependent utilities was 'hairsplitting' and 'of little practical difference'.

References

Alcaly, R.E. and A.K. Klevorick (1970), 'Judging Quality by Price, Snob Appeal and the New Consumer Theory', *Zeitschrift fur Nationalekonomie*, **30** (July), 53–64.

Allingham, M.G. and M. Morishima (1973), 'Veblen Effects and Portfolio Selection', in M. Morishima (ed.), *Theory of Demand: Real and Monetary*, Oxford: Oxford University Press, pp. 242–70.

Becker, Gary S. (1962), 'Irrational Behavior and Economic Theory', *Journal of Political Economy*, **70** (February), 1–13.

Becker, Gary S. (1965) 'A Theory of the Allocation of Time', *Economic Journal*, **75** (September), 493–517.

Becker, Gary S. (1974), 'A Theory of Social Interaction', *Journal of Political Economy*, **82** (November/December), 1063–93.

Bourne, F.S. (1963), 'Different Kinds of Decisions and Reference Group Influence', in P. Bliss (ed.), *Marketing and the Behavioral Sciences*, Allyn & Bacon, pp. 247–55.

Chipman, J. S. (1960), 'The Foundations of Utility', *Econometrica*, **28** (April), 193–24.

Engel, J.F., D.T. Kollat and R.D. Blackwell (1968),*Consumer Behavior*, New York: Holt, Rinehart, Winston.

Festinger, Leon (1957), *A Theory of Cognitive Dissonance*, Evanston, Ill.: Row, Peterson & Co.

Gaertner, Wulf (1973), 'A Dynamic Model of Interdependent Consumer Behaviour', PhD dissertation, University of Bonn.

Galbraith, J.K. (1958), *The Affluent Society, reprinted* (1965),Bombay: Asia Publishing House.

Goffman, E. (1959), *The Presentation of Self in Everyday Life,* Garden City: Doubleday Anchor Books.

Hayakawa, H. and Y. Venieris (1977), 'Consumer Interdependence via Reference Groups', *Journal of Political Economy*, **85** (3), 599–615.

Hendler, R. (1975), 'Lancaster's New Approach to Consumer Demand and Its Limitations', *American Economic Review*, **65** (1),194–9.

Howard, J.A. and J.N. Sheth (1969), *A Theory of Buyer Behavior*, New York: John Wiley & Sons.

Kalman, P.J. (1968), 'Theory of Consumer Behavior When Prices Enter the Utility Function', *Econometrica*, **36** (July/October), 497–510.

Katona, George (1960), *The Powerful Consumer,* New York: McGraw-Hill.

Katona, George (1964), *The Mass Consumption Society*, New York: McGraw-Hill.

Katz, E. and P.F. Lazarsfeld (1955), *Personal Influence*, Free Press of Glencoe.

Keynes, John Maynard (1930), 'Economic Possibilities for Our Grandchildren', in The Collected Writings of J.M.Keynes,. Vol IX Essays in Persuasion, Royal Economic Society: Macmillan, pp. 321–32.

Krelle, W. (1972), 'Dynamics of the Utility Function', *Zeitschrift fur Nationalekonomie*, **32**, 59–70.

Ladd, G.W. and M. Zober (1977), 'Model of Consumer Reaction to Product Characteristics', *Journal of Consumer Research*, **4** (September), 89–101.

Lancaster, Kelvin J. (1957), 'Revising Demand Theory', *Economica*, (New Series) **24** (November), 354–60.

Lancaster, Kelvin J. (1966a), 'A New Approach to Consumer Theory', *Journal of Political Economy*, **74** (April), 132–57.

Lancaster, Kelvin J. (1966b), 'Change and Innovation in the Technology of Consumption', *American Economic Review*, **56** (Papers and Proceedings) (May), 14–23.

Lancaster, Kelvin J. (1971), *Consumer Demand*, New York: Columbia University Press.

Laumann, E.O. and J.S. House (1970), 'Living Room Styles and Social Attributes: The Patterning of Material Artefacts in a Modern Urban Community', *Sociology and Social Research*, **54** (April), 321–42.

Lazer, W. (1964), 'Life Cycle Concepts and Marketing', in S.A. Greyser (ed.), *Toward Scientific Marketing*, Chicago: American Marketing Association, pp. 130–9.

Leavitt, H.J. (1954), 'A Note on Some Experimental Findings about the Meaning of Price', *Journal of Business*, **27** (July), 205–10.

Leibenstein, Harvey (1950), 'Bandwagon, Snob and Veblen Effects in the Theory of Consumer's Demand', *Quarterly Journal of Economics*, **64** (May), 183–207.

Levy, S.J. (1959), 'Symbols by Which We Buy', in L.H. Stockman (ed.), *Advanced Marketing Efficiency*, Chicago: American Marketing Association, pp. 409–16.

Lipsey, Richard G. and G. Rosenbluth (1971), 'A Contribution to the New Theory of Demand: A Rehabilitation of the Giffen Good', *Canadian Journal of Economics*, **4**, 131–63.

Lucas, R.E.B. (1975), 'Hedonic Price Functions', *Economic Inquiry*, **13** (June), 157–78.

McClelland, D.C. (1961), *The Achieving Society*, Princeton: Van Nostrand.

Martineau, Pierre (1958), 'Social Classes and Spending Behavior', *Journal of Marketing*, **23** (October), 121–30.

Nicosia, F.M. (1966), *Consumer Decision Processes: Marketing and Advertising Implications*, Englewood Cliffs, NJ: Prentice-Hall.

Pekelman, D. and S. Sen (1975) 'A Lancastrian Approach to Multiattribute Marketing Models', paper presented to the American Marketing Association, Rochester, New York.

Pollak, Robert A. (1970), 'Habit Formation and Dynamic Demand Functions', *Journal of Political Economy*, **78** (July/August), 745–63.

Pollak, Robert A. (1976), 'Interdependent Preferences', *American Economic Review*, **66** (June), 309–20.

Pollak, Robert A. (1977), 'Price Dependent Preferences', *American Economic Review*, **67** (March), 64–75.

Ratchford, B.T. (1975), 'The New Economic Theory of Consumer Behavior: An Interpretative Essay', *Journal of Consumer Research*, **2** (September), 65–75.

Riesman, David (1950), *The Lonely Crowd*, New Haven: Yale University Press.

Robinson, D.E. (1961), 'The Economics of Fashion Demand', *Quarterly Journal of Economics*, **75** (August), 376–98.

Rogers, Everett M. (1962), *Diffusion of Innovations*, reprinted (1983), London: The Free Press.

Scitovsky, Tibor (1945), 'Some Consequences of the Habit of Judging Quality by Price', *Revue of Economic Studies*, **2** (12), 100–105.

Sommers, M.S. (1964), 'Product Symbolism and the Perception of Social Strata', in S.A.Greyser (ed.), *Toward Scientific Marketing*, Chicago: American Marketing Association, 200–216.

Stigler, George J. (1961), 'The Economics of Information', *Journal of Political Economy*, **3** (June), 213–25.

Stigler, George J. and Gary S. Becker (1977) 'De Gustibus Non Est Disputandum', *American Economic Review*, **67** (March), 76–90.

Wind, Yoram (1976), 'Preference of Relevant Others and Individual Choice Models', *Journal of Consumer Research*, **3** (June), 50–57.

Woods, W.A. (1960), 'Psychological Dimensions of Consumer Decisions', *Journal of Marketing*, **24** (January), 15–19.

9 Status, Identity and Style: Towards a New Theory of Consumption

In the later 1970s and throughout the 1980s, the importance of status-motivated consumption increased significantly. A new kind of consumer had emerged for whom consumption itself came to play a central role in constructing new senses of identity based on and around the possession and ownership of status-conferring goods (Giddens, 1991). Traditional concepts of social class based on education and occupation were breaking down; social life was, in effect, becoming increasingly deregulated, with social relationships more variable and less structured by stable norms. 'Lifestyle' grew in importance as an indicator of social group membership, and these group identities, freed from the old restrictions imposed by social class and fixed status groups, were secured by adopting appropriate patterns of consumption.

The extended use of products to mark social differences and to act as status communicators represented a major shift away from cultural and social identity linked to production and towards new interpretations centred on consumption and the 'commodity sign'(Baudrillard, 1970; Bourdieu, 1984). Evident, too, was a far greater preoccupation with 'style' (Featherstone, 1991; Ewen, 1990) as a device of conformity or of opposition, where projection depended crucially, again, on the use and display of products. Considerations of style began to overlay the world of goods, and certainly influenced consumer choice to a far greater extent than previously.

The new fluidity of relationships meant that an individual's identification with one or more social or cultural groupings became an increasingly elective process. Consumers now felt free to declare, at their own discretion, their social position and status, and group membership became far more a matter of personal choice. Individuals were now, in a sense, what they claimed to be, even when these claims might appear unconvincing to others.

The new found freedom to establish identity had the effect of destabilising markets, making them liable to constant and rapid change. This, in turn, allowed business interests a far greater degree of manipulation:

> Social groups can seek to change their place in the categorical scheme, while marketers can seek to establish a new cultural category of person (e.g. the 'yuppie') in order to create a new market segment. Cultural categories ... are subject to rethinking and rearrangement by several parties (McCracken, 1986:72)

These new patterns of consumer behaviour and market management served to confirm heightened concerns with lifestyle, with image and with symbolic consumption, and prompted the less stable and relatively unstructured social groupings which had begun to take shape in the 1970s.

With the arrival of the 1980s, display consumption and product symbolism were well established in the new 'postmodern' societies. At the same time, the significant economic growth and more widespread affluence which had been increasingly evident through the 1960s and 1970s meant that changes were occurring in the ways in which status itself was pursued.

First, by the 1980s, it was clear that status gains could no longer be made through the purchase and consumption of generic commodities alone. By this time, ownership of traditional status symbols – automobiles, fashion clothes, furniture, jewellery and many other items whose ownership had formerly indicated wealth and position – was widespread and commonplace and conferred no particular status. But as ownership of the commodity per se declined as a status signifier, consumers' attention turned to the relative status value of individual brands within commodity groups. The era of brand image and the designer label had arrived.

Within conventional economics, the importance of the brand in demand theory had either been ignored or understated. Houthakker's (1961) review of consumption economics had continued to emphasise the importance of product price and of income and budget constraints as the factors which overwhelmingly determined levels of demand, even for status goods, at both micro and macro levels. Later, Stigler and Becker's (1977) interpretation of status-motivated consumption had largely dismissed brand preference as a relatively trivial element in determining patterns of demand for status goods, preferring instead to stress the importance of demand for a (status-conferring) generic good. By the 1980s, however, the importance of brand rather than commodity status was self-evident, and manufacturers, through their advertising agencies, increasingly competed for market share on the basis of the claimed social status of their branded products.

This competition within commodity groups was paralleled by a significant expansion in the number and variety of product categories within which status-generated sales opportunities were now available to producers. Certainly, goods seen as traditionally status-conferring were now within reach of a far greater number of consumers and had lost much of their prestige value (their importance was sometimes retained on quantity rather than on quality criteria; the three-home, four-car family still remained impressive in status terms). At the same time, a wider range of goods now came into play as potentially status-conferring. Product categories as diverse as footwear, jeans, stereo equipment and fashion accessories – often relatively inexpensive in absolute money terms – now came to have substantial status value when the right socially approved and status-giving brands were acquired. These new status symbols were available to anyone who had the money or credit to buy them, and as affluence spread to those who had formerly had little opportunity to conspicuously consume, so the pressures on social class and on traditional concepts of rank and status within communities were similarly increased:

> The status symbols of earlier generations have become increasingly unable to convey their former meanings, as the names of the high-status fashion houses appear on the clothing and body accessories, which are purchased by anyone who can afford them and who wishes to purchase them. Everyone who has the money may buy top designer labels under these conditions, regardless of their occupation or social status. Alternatively, those without enough money may steal such items from shopping centres (Bocock, 1993).

The new sociology of consumption significantly increased the importance of interpersonal effects on consumer demand, for now 'lifestyle projection' preoccupied many millions of people who felt able to create personal identities through consumption. And as the number of product categories used to secure social status widened, so it became increasingly evident that it was neither sensible nor profitable to attempt to identify the status-conferring value of any one good in isolation, and that patterns of consumption extending across a range of product categories would more accurately identify status-motivated consumption.

The belief that patterns of consumption were more indicative of conspicuous display than single purchases was not new. Veblen had emphasised the importance of looking at the purchase and consumption of bundles of goods in attempting to isolate and confirm status-seeking behaviour, just as Simon Patten had insisted in the 1890s that 'goods ... are consumed in groups, and the utility of individual articles must be measured in the group of which they are a part'. By the 1970s, it was increasingly difficult to ignore such claims, and the theme was once again taken up in 1978, when Douglas and Isherwood (a social anthropologist and an economist) explored ways in which Lancaster's consumer theory could be given greater application and relevance.

It would never be possible, they argued, to determine the meaning or value of goods in postmodern consumer societies by taking them individually, item by item, for goods revealed their purpose and usefulness only when taken together. They therefore proposed a new approach to consumption and consumer spending which supposed that, in order to protect status at each social position over the life cycle, a certain grade of consumption was obligatory. Goods were used for 'marking' (in the sense of classifying categories) as a part of the social process, and both individuals and families needed to conform to expectations if they were not to be excluded from the group. The authors focused, in particular, on consumption periodicities, claiming that it was possible to identify, over the social scale, low-frequency, high (status) value consumption at the top, and high-frequency, low (status) value consumption at lower levels. As individuals and families progressed over the life cycle and, hopefully, up the social scale, so their consumption behaviour moved toward the first pattern and away from the second. Further, variations in income and wealth between included individuals at any point on the scale allowed for differences in the 'quality', though not in the categories, of purchases made.

At any given time, therefore, with social position known, the appropriate consumption pattern, allowing for quality variations, could be identified:

> By finding a status relationship that holds between periodicities in use and a scale of consumption rituals, the technology of consumption can be mapped onto socially significant properties. Thus Kelvin Lancaster's approach can acquire sociological content. He need no longer restrict his analytic technique to cars and washing machines, but can extend it to dinner parties, as originally intended (1978: 123).

Douglas and Isherwood's new formulation represented a marriage of economics with social anthropology, and attempted to move Lancaster's consumer theory over a substantial hurdle. It offered an explanation of the 'keeping up with the Joneses' phenomenon among groups of social equals. At the same time, it was written in terms which suggested that consumers were still motivated by ambitions which were constrained by 'old' class-linked restrictions. It also implied that status consumption, though widespread, was, for the most part, a within-group rather than a between-group activity, and placed little emphasis on the ambitions of individuals to acquire membership of 'higher' social groups through emulation and conspicuous consumption. However, it had reopened a channel of research into status consumption.

The claim that patterns of consumption across product categories revealed attempts to secure and consolidate social position over the life cycle was empirically verifiable and invited further research. Levy (1981), McCall and Simmons (1982), Hirschman and Solomon (1982) and others now began to explore the nature of interrelationships among product symbols, explicitly recognising that too great a focus on one individual product in the past had not been productive. By the later 1980s this work was drawn together, and in 1987 Solomon and Assael, acknowledging the Douglas and Isherwood contribution, introduced the concept of 'consumption constellations', defined as clusters of complementary products, specific brands and/or consumption activities used by consumers to define, communicate and enact social roles.

Preliminary empirical research did establish correlations between product symbolism, constellations and perceived or actual social status, and in 1991 Soloman and Buchanan reported the results of a far larger study involving 20,000 respondents, which examined the consumption constellations of individuals recognising themselves and/or being recognised as, American 'yuppies'. The research findings showed that social role did, in fact, demonstrate a degree of consumption constellation effects, and suggested that a tighter definition of role and consumables could further strengthen the correlation.

The interest in consumption constellations in the late 1970s and through the 1980s was certainly heightened by evidence from the marketplace which showed that an increasing preoccupation with identity and style was encouraging the purchase and consumption of socially acceptable goods and services across a range of product categories. At the same time, while behavioural scientists in general were interested in exploring the identity/style phenomenon, it created little, if any, sustained interest among economists.

This lack of engagement was disappointing, for the relevance of Lancaster's new consumer theory to such studies had been identified. Research into constellation effects also posed fewer potential difficulties than more traditional explorations of demand for a single product: economic theory had always recognised and accounted for 'complementary goods', and this complementarity was not controversial. Many goods were jointly consumed in order to satisfy some particular need, and there was no reason, in principle, why joint consumption should not extend over several products instead of being restricted to the two-good case typically used in economic analysis. Further, by focusing on choices across product categories, consumption constellation theory sat well with the economist's traditional reluctance to explore market behaviour and consumer choice at the level of the brand.

In the final analysis, the opportunity to draw status consumption further into mainstream theory by extending research into complementary goods was not taken primarily because it required recognition of symbolic as well as of functional complementarity – a concession which would have required far greater recognition of the role of interpersonal effects in shaping consumer demand. An opportunity was therefore lost to bring economics more closely in tune with the behaviour of consumer societies preoccupied with image, identity, status and prestige.

The growing importance of consumption in social and economic affairs was, by the 1980s, not seriously questioned, and patterns of consumer choice were now making their impact on the nature and direction of economic development. While economists were still reluctant to invest time and effort in exploring status-linked consumption at the level of the individual, there was more concern with the possible macroeconomic consequences of such behaviour.

A growing unease with traditional interpretations of consumer preference formation and with the neglect of status consumption had found expression in 1976, when Hirsch offered a new perspective on the difficulties faced by advanced nations in securing continuing high levels of economic growth. To Hirsch, consumer demand for goods and services consisted of two components. First, demand for 'nonpositional' goods – goods which carried no social status value and which could be supplied by the material economy, without risk of scarcity, through improvements in mechanisation or technological innovation. Second, and no less important, a growing demand for 'positional' goods, whose value to the individual depended strongly on how they compared with things owned by others, and hence to the degree of scarcity attached to the products in question. This scarcity could result either from absolute scarcity, as with antiques, original paintings, limited editions and so on, or, for those products where supply was not limited, by the extensiveness of product use. In this latter case, however, social congestion or 'crowding' could diminish the perceived scarcity of the product or service:

> Consumer demand is concentrated on particular goods and facilities that are limited in absolute supply not by physical but by social factors, including the satisfaction engendered by scarcity as such. Such social limits exist in the sense that an increase in physical availability of these goods or facilities, either in absolute terms or in relation to dimensions such as population or physical space, changes their characteristics in such a way that a given amount of use yields less satisfaction. This is equivalent to a limitation on absolute supply of a product or facility of given "quality", and it is in this sense that it is ... a social limitation (1976: 20).

The 'positional economy' described by Hirsch was, therefore, concerned for the most part with those goods and services whose physical production was not seriously limited, but whose social value necessarily declined as physical supplies increased. And while Hirsch was then interested in recognising such goods as a potent social limit to growth, and in exploring the policy implications, it was evident that, for many of these goods and services, reductions in social value were linked to attempts to secure social position and prestige in the eyes of others. Many consumers in the positional economy were, in short, consuming for status, and this status depended to a great extent on product exclusivity or scarcity. As affluence increased and as product scarcity was reduced, so competition was being redirected and further intensified: the process, in short, became self-defeating, and imposed a very real social limitation on economic growth.

Hirsch was at pains not to condemn those who competed for positional goods, arguing, as Adam Smith had done, that the need for high relative standing was instrumental to the realisation of numerous legitimate human objectives. This view was later endorsed by Frank (1985a) who pointed out that disdainful attitudes towards people's efforts to keep up with the Joneses could not be allowed to obscure the fact that concerns about relative standing were entirely consistent with the economist's belief in the individual's rational pursuit of self-interest.

Frank looked in more detail at the nature of demand for positional and nonpositional goods, and was particularly interested in the implications of such consumer behaviour for the relationship between consumption, savings and income. Hirsch's recognition of the socially controlled elements of consumer behaviour which now influenced a significant proportion of total demand, coupled with empirical findings that the need to secure social status weighed more heavily on people with lower incomes (Mayer, 1966), convinced Frank that Friedman's permanent income hypothesis could not fully explain the positive relationship between savings and income, and that Duesenberry's largely discounted relative income approach had much to commend it. Duesenberry's work had been abandoned prematurely by the economics profession, argued Frank, primarily because economists had felt uncomfortable with what they regarded as a sociological theory of the consumption function.

Satisfaction derived from positional goods was seen to depend on the social rank they were able to generate, and this theme was subsequently taken up by others who began to explore the nature of status-seeking games. Congleton (1989) identified two types of games – macro-status games, in which all members of society gain or lose socioeconomic status in competition for relative wealth, education and influence; and micro-status games, played at a more local level and concerned with achieving merit within a small segment of society. With both macro and micro games, however, the common element was that relative rather than absolute performance ultimately determined individual utility levels, 'performance' being measured by the status-assigning rules of the game of interest.

Like Frank, Congleton presented a Hicksian two-good model of status-seeking behaviour, based on interpretations of indifference between status and non-status goods. Frank had claimed that any one status-seeking activity which affected only the welfare of others in the status game was essentially only redistributive and generated no real social gain. Congleton, however, argued that, particularly with respect to micro-status games, third parties were, in reality, liable to benefit or to suffer as non-participants through 'spillover' benefits or costs generated by the participants.

This ability of some, though not all, micro status-seeking behaviour to produce wider benefits to society was, in Congleton's view, recognised and promoted by non-players, and encouraged the 'benign evolution' of micro-status games. 'The non-participating majority', he argued, 'can easily promote status games that provide positive externalities and discourage those that generate negative externalities by changing the returns of alternative status games'. Additionally, players tended to prefer status-seeking activities which served altruistic purposes while at the same time generating status, other things being equal. This then encouraged donations to charities and other philanthropic projects, so accelerating the movement towards spillover benefits resulting from status competition and moving expenditure and consumption away from less productive conspicuous display.

While micro-status games could therefore be seen as a potential force for good, the same could not be said for macro games, since essentially all members of society were directly involved. Here, Frank's view that status competition often only redistributed a fixed pool of status was seen to hold. However, while opportunities for shaping the nature and direction of status-seeking were clearly not as great as with micro-status games, it was still possible for society to promote wealth-creating rather than wealth-destroying activities at the macro level. Overall, Congleton thought that an increasing preoccupation with status consumption could be seen as positive rather than negative, and claimed that, at minimum, 'many, if not most, status-seeking games are less wasteful than one would imagine based on an analysis of the quest for personal status alone'.

With regard to policy implications relating to the demand for positional goods, there was little common ground among those who had researched and written on the subject. Hirsch had taken a pessimistic view of the effects of status consumption, and had argued that a policy change to suppress such behaviour was urgently needed:

> Excess competition in the positional sector has been seen to involve important external costs. If these costs are allowed to become large, a point will come where the damage to society appears too great to justify the individual freedom of action that results in such damage. The individual freedom will then be seen to be socially destructive and ultimately self-destructive, and pressure to restrict such freedom will become irresistible (1976: 187).

A major adjustment needed to be made, in Hirsch's view, in the legitimate scope for individual economic striving, and the key to this was to engineer a change in social ethics. Social interest, in short, had to condition self-interest, but social benefits could be secured when individuals acted *as if* they put the social interest first, even if their primary interest was still selfish. What was certain, in Hirsh's view, was that a new social ethic would never evolve through the independent responses of individuals and this problem could not just be ignored. While there were no easy solutions, he emphasised the need to reduce individual competition in the positional sector by working to persuade individuals that 'position' in society was less important than commonly supposed. Second, status-seeking behaviour needed to be directed so that it contributed positively to recognised social needs. How this direction was to be achieved was not made clear, and Hirsch conceded that the solution was not easy, for the evils associated with collective action to prevent self-seeking consumption could be as destructive as unfettered status-seeking itself.

In contrast to Hirsch, Frank believed that any attempts to engineer changes in the pattern of demand for status-linked positional goods would be counterproductive and would not succeed in significantly changing consumer behaviour with respect to the products and services they chose to buy. The preferred policy was to recognise and concede that consumer choice could not be substantially altered through appeals or exhortations to consumers to be more socially aware, but could be more effectively changed by introducing taxes on those activities which were generally considered to be working against the public interest. To this end, a consumption tax could be introduced on those consumption categories which imposed significant external effects on others. The tax would also create incentives for people to spend less of their incomes on status-conferring positional goods and more on nonpositional goods, so improving the allocation of resources within the economy as a whole.

The countries of Western Europe, as Frank acknowledged, had, in fact, embraced consumption taxation for many years: however, there was considerable opposition to such tax regimes in the United States, where they were seen by many as introducing unnecessary distortions into economic life. Frank argued, nonetheless, that a host of interventionary regulations had been used in their place to 'manage' patterns of US consumption, and that:

> If consumption externalities do indeed motivate many of the command-and-control regulatory interventions we currently observe, then a simple tax on positional consumption expenditures might attenuate the need for many of these interventions. If consumption externalities are as important as they appear to be, then supply-siders have got matters turned completely around when they insist that income and consumption taxes introduce serious distortions into the labour-leisure choice. When relative standing is important, such taxes serve, on the contrary, to mitigate an already present distortion in that choice (1985b: 115)

Both Hirsch and Frank believed that status-seeking consumer behaviour, when expressed through the demand for positional goods, was inherently harmful to the wider interests of the community and to the economy in general. Others, like Congleton, were prepared to argue that, at the micro level at least, such behaviour could often be a force for good if wider, positive externalities resulted, and that there was, in any event, a natural preference among status-seekers to favour status games which generated such positive spillovers. Even at the macro level, opportunities existed to channel status-seeking into wealth-creating activities, but recourse to taxation to achieve these ends was seen as self-defeating:

> It is also difficult to tax or otherwise regulate unproductive macro-status generating activities. Taxation is difficult to motivate for two reasons. Since each person or subgroup benefits if their status-seeking costs are reduced relative to others, coalitions favoring taxation of macro-status generating activities tend to be unstable. Moreover, the required consensus that a particular status generating activity is undesirable, and should be taxed, is difficult to obtain (Congleton, 1989: 187).

More positively, the potential of subsidies in successfully directing status activity was noted: tax preferences and special tax treatment covering many philanthropic investments and expenditures were widespread and charitable contributions were, as of right, recognised as deductible from taxable income. The extension of such schemes offered a significant means of selective subsidy but, as Congleton observed, in practice levels of subsidy tended to be indiscriminate and 'appear to be nearly the same whether the macro-status game is productive or not'.

Recognition of the policy implications of positional goods and associated patterns of consumption extended into the 1990s. Ireland (1992), like Hirsch, took the view that a surfeit of positional spending driven by consumers' concerns with their relative standing within communities generated an unacceptable welfare loss and needed to be controlled. Preoccupation with status had the effect of biasing consumption bundles, leading to inefficient utility levels. More importantly, status-seeking had relatively more damaging consequences for those with low incomes.

Three possible ways of reducing the incidence of positional expenditures were considered. First, an appropriate tax on status-conferring goods and services; second, provision of cash or kind as a flat rate benefit to consumers; finally, the introduction of legislation designed to restrict or remove certain areas of status-seeking consumption, so reducing opportunities to conspicuously consume. Taxes and subsidies were seen to be positive in reducing the incidence of status signalling, although appropriate tax/subsidy policies were recognised as being far more complex to implement practically rather than theoretically. With regard to legislation:

> If consumers seek status their consumption pattern will deviate from that which

a benevolent observer would think appropriate, and create negative externalities for others. Indeed the consumers would wish for a policy which protected them from themselves by reducing the need to signal status. An example would be the family in financial difficulties which is stopped from taking on more debt by protective legislation. Since the legislation operates on all families excessive expenditure is curbed without changes in status (Ireland, 1992: 14).

The various policy recommendations which stemmed from greater recognition of status-seeking behaviour and the demand for positional goods, therefore, reflected significant differences in attitude to socially-inspired consumer behaviour. They succeeded more in emphasising that, while there was now a consensus that social standing and prestige were surely major factors in determining individual and group preferences for goods and services, how and whether such behaviour should be managed and controlled remained a controversial issue.

Work on consumer preoccupations with status and prestige in the 1970s and 1980s led to renewed interest in the implications of such behaviour for international economic development. Duesenberry's earlier (1949) work on the demonstration effect had stimulated limited academic discussion as to the relative importance of status-seeking on the propensity to consume in developing countries (see Chapter 7). While Hirsch and others had confined their attention to developed market economies, it was now possible to consider their work in the context of less developed industrialising economies, and to then identify any policy implications.

The international demonstration effect had been recognised as a significant influence on consumption and saving in developing economies for many years. Nurkse (1953) had argued that the attraction of advanced consumption standards was evident in most developing countries, although their influence was patchy and uneven. At the same time, he was adamant that the demonstration effect was in no way associated with Veblenian notions of conspicuous consumption. Preference formations in rich and poor countries were, to his mind, interdependent rather than independent, with consumers in poorer societies simply imitating the behaviour and expenditures of those in richer countries without giving any thought to the original motives underpinning such consumption. 'We can leave out Veblen's point that the propensity to spend is partly based on the desire for conspicuous consumption', he argued, 'I do not think that on the international plane the effect of unequal living standards depends on the idea of 'keeping up with the Joneses'. All it depends on is demonstration leading to imitation' (1953: 61).

In Nurkse's view, the effect of advertising and of other forms of communication between developed and developing economies was not to change tastes per se but simply to inform consumers in developing countries of those products which exhibited 'modern' characteristics (and which were therefore taken to be intrinsically better). However, Hirsch's work on positional goods and the positional economy sat more easily with Veblen's view of status competition between individuals, where the value of any individual's possessions depended strongly on how these goods compared with things owned by others. In this analysis, the demonstration effect between rich and poor was status-related, and emulation occurred in attempts to gain in social standing and prestige rather than as acts of uncomplicated imitation.

Some felt that this Hirsch–Veblen view of the demonstration effect was the more credible, and that the consequences of such behaviour would be to shift demand over time in favour of visible consumption of potentially high status value (James, 1983, 1987). Changes in taste, it was argued, arose from a process of social learning which did not come from any 'internal' source in developing countries, but through exposure to Western values and lifestyles transmitted through education, industrial occupation and urban residence (Portes, 1973). Further, these values were channelled into self-regarding individual objectives through the pervasive influence of advertising which emphasised self-interest and social status in persuading people to buy.

The end result of such activity was to shift the direction of taste change away from necessary goods towards the more superfluous, highly visible products which characterised Veblenian waste and conspicuous consumption. Given the often severe limitations on income which were typically found in developing countries, the welfare consequences of such taste shifts were immediately apparent for, as Veblen had also pointed out, the desire for status could be so intense that even the poor would tolerate considerable degrees of personal privation in order to secure what they came to see as a 'decent amount of wasteful consumption'.

The need to conspicuously consume even on subsistence incomes also helped to explain the proliferation of 'counterfeit' status goods which were manufactured and sold in both developed and developing countries. Controversially, perhaps, the availability of cheap imitation status goods could be seen as a force for good in one important respect, for by allowing the poor to display what, to others, appeared to be a high-value positional good at very little cost, any taste changes towards positionality led to little real loss in welfare.

Overall, recognition of the existence of a positional economy, characterised by significant levels of demand for status-conferring goods, led to a revaluation of the process and direction of international economic development with respect to consumption and consumer behaviour. It questioned the received wisdom of the previous twenty years centred, for the most part, around Nurkse's hypothesis of a status-free international demonstration effect. Increasingly, evidence suggested that status *was* a significant factor in consumer preference formation in the developing countries of the world, and that status values were shaped by a Western culture which was easily transmitted through global advertising and other forms of international communication.

The market changes of the later 1970s and 1980s prompted widespread reconsideration of the nature of consumption. Sociologists, in particular, had become increasingly concerned with postmodernism and with the new consumer culture which placed consumption at the centre of everyday life. This new emphasis on lifestyle and on relative standing secured through consumption had prompted Hirsch to talk of the 'positional economy' and to explore, with others, the macroeconomic consequences of consumer behaviour directed at securing status and prestige. At the macroeconomic level, however, a narrower, more cautious approach was taken to the new consumer radicalism.

The principal strand of status-related microeconomic theory which was developed through the 1980s and 1990s continued the work on price-dependent preferences which had been carried out earlier by Kalman (1968) and Pollak (1977). A marked difference after 1980, however, was that the process whereby prices could become an integral part of utility functions was recognised and defined as 'Veblen effects' – a term which, for many years, had been treated (and avoided) by more orthodox economists as a sociological concept of dubious merit or interest. The term 'conspicuous consumption', similarly, entered the microeconomic literature to a far greater extent than previously – recognition, again, that the market realities of the 1980s were making it increasingly difficult to persist with the neglect of Institutionalist thought within economics in general, and with Veblenian interpretations of consumer behaviour in particular. At the same time, orthodox suspicion of Institutionalists remained, for the latter had never attempted to analyse consumer behaviour through the use of standard economic theory, and many mainstream economists were convinced that they would not, and could not, do so.

In the early 1980s, following work by Liebhafsky (1980), who demonstrated that Veblen effects were concerned with relative rather than with absolute prices and with the marginal utility of individual goods, attempts were made to measure primary and secondary Veblen effects on preference formation (Basmann et al., 1983, 1985). Looking at expenditures on eleven commodity groups, the marginal rates of substitution of the groups with respect to each other were calculated, using a generalised Fechner–Thurstone direct utility function. Findings indicated that Veblen effects were statistically significant in 82 out of 110 cases. These effects were, moreover, at their strongest when there were clear ceremonial aspects associated with the commodity in question, and where it offered a high level of visible consumption. Similarly, it could be shown (Phillips and Slottje, 1983) that it was possible to obtain elasticities relating to such marginal rates of substitution, further confirming the existence of Veblen effects, and offering additional statistical support for the view that conspicuous consumption was, by then, a ubiquitous element in economic activity.

Basmann et al. returned to the subject again in 1988, this time estimating and testing the effects of secondary (Veblenian) utility on five commodity groups (food, clothing, housing, durables and medical care products) distilled from the bigger group of eleven which had formed the basis of the earlier research. Analysis of data in the study again showed that, as Veblenian theory would have predicted, the greatest secondary effects were associated with the demand for durables, where ownership and consumption was highly visible to the community, and were weakest with regard to medical services, where consumption was usually screened from public view.

Earlier work had been confined to data relating to the United States and, although persuasive, was open to the criticism that it demonstrated the existence of Veblen effects in the American economy, but had no legitimate universal application. In 1991, however, Creedy and Slottje looked at the incidence of conspicuous consumption in Australia, replicating the US methodology and again using a generalised direct utility function, which allowed for the specification of any parameter to be a preference changer.

Australian data for a thirty year period 1959–1989 was used in the study, and five broad commodities groups examined – food, other non-durables, motor vehicles, household durables, and rent. Two periods were considered separately, 1959 to 1974 and 1974 to 1989, and significant Veblen effects were found in both. The study, in effect, established that such effects were not confined to the American market, and that the research findings had a far wider relevance and application.

Research in the 1980s had demonstrated, therefore, that conventional microeconomic analysis was capable of identifying and measuring Veblen effects, provided the necessary data was available and accessible. In parallel, others (Bagwell and Bernheim, 1991,1992) were now seeking to incorporate Veblen effects into a new theory of conspicuous consumption. This work was subsequently drawn together and published in 1996 in the *American Economic Review*.

By the 1990s, the statistical and continuing anecdotal evidence that Veblen effects were significant, particularly in the market for luxury goods, was now widely accepted, and a growing body of literature and research in the social sciences attested to the importance of such consumer behaviour. Nevertheless, it remained difficult to transpose these new market realities into the body of economic theory, and the 1996 theoretical interpretation of conspicuous consumption reflected these difficulties.

Veblen effects were defined as 'a willingness to pay a higher price for a functionally equivalent good, arising from a desire to signal wealth'. In attempting to isolate these effects, luxury brands were not seen as intrinsically superior to budget brands, but taken only to be goods of identical quality, sold at a higher price. By making such assumptions, the economic profits of luxury goods manufacturers, selling at prices above, rather than at, marginal cost could then be calculated. The model assumed also that all potential sellers of a given conspicuous good had access to the necessary production technologies, and that an acceptably conspicuous product could therefore be offered by a large number of firms, each able to produce the same range of qualities. Brand names were not seen to directly affect utility, rather consumers and social contacts observed the prices announced by all firms and made their conspicuous purchase decisions on the basis of these prices, using their ability to pay as a signal of wealth and status. Finally, it was assumed that each household acquired any given conspicuous good from a single vendor, and would choose, ceteris paribus, to purchase at the lowest quality-weighted price.

This theoretical treatment of Veblen effects and conspicuous consumption, while allowing, perhaps, for a greater subsequent level of mathematical elegance, was not convincing in its description of the market for status goods. First, it is not realistic to discount the value of a brand name or a designer label as major influences on a consumer's decision to buy. All evidence suggests that, in the market for status goods, company, designer and/or brand reputation affects utility to a significant degree, and their value needs to be incorporated into any realistic treatment of status-motivated consumption and display. This is true even when the preferred brand is in no way intrinsically superior to competing goods which may be made to identical quality standards, yet which lack the 'cachet' associated with the status-conferring product.

Second, the assumption that sellers and potential sellers are perfectly competitive in terms of technology and of their ability to provide goods which are status-assigning in the eyes of conspicuous consumers, can not be sustained. In reality, corporate reputation, when linked to a recognised high-status brand name, often confers near-monopolistic market advantages with respect to the supply of status goods, and this advantage cannot be removed over the short to medium term.

Third, the model did not recognise the importance of distribution and retail reputation on consumers' purchase decisions. The assumption that households choose to purchase through a single vendor was seen as natural 'as long as there is some cost associated with consummating each transaction', but this 'cost' was clearly taken to be economic rather than psychic or social. In reality, a part of the value of modern conspicuous display is derived from being seen to purchase status goods through exclusive retail outlets which themselves confer prestige on the buyer. The cost of shopping, measured in purely economic terms, seldom enters the consumer's calculations: image is all, and extends to the retail transaction.

Within its restricting limitations, the model was able to isolate a set of theoretical conditions which succeeded in producing Veblen effects. It was conceded that real market conditions could and often did contrast sharply with the assumptions made in the model. However, it was also implied that, unrealistic though they may be, it was only under such assumptions that there was any chance of observing Veblen effects in the marketplace, and that they might well not exist at all in the 'real world':

> the fact that it is possible to produce Veblen effects under some appropriate set of assumptions does not necessarily imply that one is likely to observe these effects in practice. Indeed, the conditions required to generate Veblen effects may strike the reader as implausible (Bagwell and Bernheim, 1996: 364).

In reality, a more market-oriented set of assumptions could have been expected to increase rather than decrease the theoretical incidence of conspicuous consumption and, in this sense, the model understates rather than overstates household propensities to conspicuously consume for status.

There was certainly no lack of awareness of the market realities surrounding, and impinging upon, status consumption. The authors explicitly acknowledged the role of the 'prestige' retailer; the importance of brand reputation and associated snob values; the significance of consumption constellations and consumer tendencies to select from an array of conspicuous goods. Like others before them, however, they did not find it easy to explain an exceptional form of consumer behaviour, rooted strongly in the sociology and psychology of human behaviour, in terms of conventional econometric analysis.

Turning to policy implications, the model promoted a new perspective. Above all, it recognised that market behaviour relating to conspicuous consumption was driven by demand rather than by supply. This, in turn, had important consequences with respect to perceptions that excess (and excessive) profits accrued to companies which collaborated to exploit such markets. Since supranormal profits resulted from the characteristics of demand rather than from any strategic interaction among firms, evidence of high profitability did not therefore support inferences of collusion or of oligopoly. Further, the demand-driven characteristics of the market had equally important implications for tax policy:

> the equilibrium prices of luxury brands are demand driven rather than supply
> driven – that is, luxury brands are sold at the consumer's preferred price, which
> is tax inclusive, and does not vary with the tax rate. Thus, as long as the tax per
> unit does not exceed the difference between the consumer's preferred price and
> the marginal cost, and as long as the tax does not fall on budget brands, an excise
> tax on conspicuous goods amounts to a nondistortionary tax on pure profits (ibid.,
> 1996: 368).

While the tax effect on one specific product taken in isolation could be seen as nondistortionary, however, it was recognised that an increase in the tax rate applied to any single luxury good could be indeterminant because of conspicuous consumers' propensities to spread demand across many goods which together formed a coherent consumption constellation. Consequently, there were significant advantages in adopting a broad-based luxury tax, embracing most products within such constellations, in order to stop demand-switching intended to avoid paying a specific tax increase levied on only one particular item within the constellation.

Analysis of status consumption within economics in the early 1990s focused almost exclusively on Veblen effects and on those aspects of conspicuous consumption which were directly related to those circumstances where price entered the consumer's utility function. It was assumed that, in consuming for status, individuals wished to make or to consolidate status gains, that is, their purchases and consumption were intended either to confirm an existing social superiority or to secure an improvement in social standing through upward mobility. In essence, Veblen's two motives for consuming conspicuous goods – 'invidious comparison', where individuals in a higher group sought to distance themselves from others, and 'pecuniary emulation', where consumers aspired to membership of higher groups – were accepted as providing the stimuli for conspicuous economic behaviour.

The emphasis on vertical mobility, achieved by signalling wealth through the payment of excessive prices for conspicuous goods, inevitably focused economists' attention on product prices and on income and wealth differentials in attempting to explain and analyse such behaviour. However, while ambitions for vertical status gains were certainly still in evidence after 1980, display consumption was, in reality, becoming more broadly based and extended beyond the relatively narrow Veblenian interpretations which had been adopted by economists.

In 1950, Leibenstein had identified three 'nonfunctional' external effects on utility – Veblen effects, certainly, but also snob effects, generated by an individual's desire to be exclusive, and bandwagon effects, produced by consumer needs to conform with people or groups with whom they particularly identified and wished to be associated.

This last external effect, the need to conform, was, as we have seen, not new to economic thought. In the eighteenth century, Adam Smith had conceded that 'established rules of decency' and concern for the opinion of others was something more than vanity, and justified the possession, ownership and display of certain status-linked commodities. Others after Smith were similarly aware of this need to conform to group norms. Being an essentially social and psychological need, it was never happily accommodated within economic theory, but by 1980, increased affluence, coupled with a relaxation of traditional class barriers and a greater freedom of association and identity, gave Leibenstein's bandwagon effects an added significance in determining patterns of consumption.

The influence of conformism on economic and social behaviour was explored by several writers in the early 1980s (Akerlof, 1980; Jones, 1984), but emphasis was placed on the nature of workplace relationships and on the occupational effects of conformist behaviour. By the end of the decade, however, academic attention had also turned to the individual as consumer, and to the consumption effects of this perceived need to conform.

Hirschman (1985) acknowledged the importance of bandwagon effects, arguing that an individual's sense of belonging was often an end in itself and took a high priority in economic and social life. Goods bought and consumed out of a need to conform were described as 'association goods' (Basu, 1989), and attempts were made to incorporate the concept of social norms into economic models, and to look at ways in which status-linked nonmarket decisions could sensibly be interpreted within such models (Cole, Mailath and Postlewaite, 1992). The consequences of what was termed the 'localized conformity of behavior' in which individuals, without regard to their own information, simply follow the behaviour of relevant others within a given community or membership group were also examined (Bikhchandani, Hirshleifer and Welsh, 1992). These relevant others were often seen as fashion leaders and, in situations where such leadership was concentrated on one individual or small group, large shifts in consumer behaviour could occur in response to changes in behaviour signalled by a numerically insignificant number of fashion or fad leaders. These 'informational cascades' were then often responsible for major shifts in aggregate patterns of consumption. Further, because of the largely blind reaction to changes in fads and fashions which could occur without apparent reason, the response was, in classical economic terms at least, irrational rather than rational.

This need to conform, heightened by 1980s conditions and attitudes, and coupled with changes in fads and fashions, could clearly generate large and rapid changes in patterns of demand, and trigger significant movements in market prices as demand/supply equilibria changed over a range of products and services. That part of the market for status goods generated by bandwagon effects, therefore, was seen to be relatively unstable and prone to significant short-term fluctuations. However, there was disagreement over the degree to which this market was unstable.

Sociological research in the 1980s had suggested that society itself was becoming less stable in conventional terms, and was increasingly subject to rapid changes in values, beliefs and norms. In analysing the importance of such changes in economic terms, it was argued that, as the pace of social and cultural change increased, so consumer choice was itself liable to sudden and frequent change. Others disagreed with this interpretation, arguing that the degree of underlying stability in social and economic affairs was being seriously understated:

> In practice, the degree of conformity and persistence of norms vary greatly over activities. Indeed, the difference between a social custom and a fad is primarily one of degree. Customs have two distinguishing features: they are respected by a large fraction of the population, and they are very persistent. In contrast, a much smaller segment of the population follows fads and fashions, and these norms are much more transient (Bernheim, 1994: 862).

Controversy over the degree to which conformist behaviour was relatively stable or unstable, however, did not disguise the fact that the need to identify with social groups and with fashion trends within the wider community was, by the 1990s, a powerful influence on consumer behaviour and consumer choice. As a result, what Leibenstein had described as bandwagon effects were now commonly observed and had become highly significant in terms of shaping and directing consumer demand.

These changes in market behaviour were, at a general level, well understood and increasingly commented upon in the economics literature, but theories of conformity were, nevertheless, not incorporated into parallel theoretical treatments of status-motivated consumption and display. By far the larger part of the literature on conspicuous consumption continued to define such behaviour in traditional terms, as consumption which produces price-dominated Veblen effects and which generates expenditures which are intended to emphasise difference rather than conformity or membership. What was still needed was a more comprehensive economic analysis of socially-inspired purchase and consumption which was able to draw together Veblen, snob and bandwagon effects within a unified model of consumer decision making. In particular, the interaction and interdependence of 'vertical' (between group) and 'horizontal'(within group) status-seeking needed to be described and explained in the context of a new consumer theory.

References

Akerlof, G. (1980), 'A Theory of Social Customs, of which Unemployment May be One Consequence', *Quarterly Journal of Economics*, **94** (June), 749–75.

Bagwell, L.S. and B.D. Bernheim (1991), 'Conspicuous Consumption, Pure Profits and the Luxury Tax: Some Surprising Consequences of Perfect Competition', Working Paper in Economics, The Hoover Institution, Stanford University.

Bagwell, L.S. and B.D. Bernheim (1992), 'Conspicuous Consumption, Pure Profits and the Luxury Tax', Working Paper 4163, National Bureau Of Economic Research.

Bagwell, L.S. and B.D. Bernheim (1996), 'Veblen Effects in a Theory of Conspicuous Consumption', *American Economic Review*, **86** (June), 349–73.

Basmann, R.L., D.J. Molina and D.J. Slottje (1983), 'Budget Constraint Prices as Preference Changing Parameters of Generalized Fechner-Thurstone Direct Utility Functions', *American Economic Review*, **73** (June), 411–13.

Basmann, R L., D.J. Molina and D.J.Slottje (1985), 'Measuring Veblen Primary and Secondary Effects Utilizing the Fechner-Thurstone Direct Utility Function, mimeo, Texas A & M University.

Basmann, R.L., D.J. Molina and D.J. Slottje (1988), 'A Note on Measuring Veblen's Theory of Conspicuous Consumption', *Review of Economics and Statistics*, **70** (August), 531–35.

Basu, K. (1989), 'A Theory of Association: Social Status, Prices and Markets', *Oxford Economic Papers*, **41** (October), 653–71.

Baudrillard, Jean (1970), *La Société de Consommation*, Paris: Gallimard.

Bernheim, B.D. (1994), 'A Theory of Conformity', *Journal of Political Economy*, **102** (5), 841–77.

Bikhchandani, S., D. Hirshleifer and I. Welsh (1992)'A Theory of Fads, Fashion, Custom, and Cultural Change as Informational Cascades', *Journal of Political Economy*, **100** (5), 992–1026.

Bocock, R. (1993), *Consumption*, London: Routledge.

Bourdieu, P. (1984), *Distinction: A Social Critique of the Judgement of Taste*, (R.Nice (trans.)), Cambridge: Harvard University Press.

Cole, H.L., G.J. Mailath and R. Postlewaite (1992), 'Social Norms, Savings Behavior and Growth', *Journal of Political Economy*, **100** (6), 1092–1125.

Congleton, Roger D. (1989), 'Efficient Status Seeking: Externalities and the Evolution of Status Games', *Journal of Economic Behavior and Organization* **11**, 175–90.

Creedy, John and D.J. Slottje (1991) 'Conspicuous Consumption in Australia', Research Paper 307 (June), University of Melbourne.

Douglas, M. and B. Isherwood (1978), *The World of Goods*, reprinted (1980), London: Penguin Books.

Duesenberry, James (1949), *Income, Saving and the Theory of Consumer Behavior*, Cambridge, Mass.: Harvard University Press.

Ewen, Stuart (1990), 'Marketing Dreams: The Political Elements of Style', in A. Tomlinson (ed.), *Consumption. Identity & Style*, London: Routledge, pp. 41–56.

Featherstone, M. (1991), *Consumer Culture and Postmodernism*, London: Sage Publications.

Frank, Robert H. (1985a), *Choosing the Right Pond: Human Behavior and the Quest for Status*, New York: Oxford University Press.

Frank, Robert H. (1985b), 'The Demand for Unobservable and Other Nonpositional Goods', *American Economic Review*, **75** (March): 101–16.

Giddens, A. (1991), *Modernity and Self-identity: Self and Society in the Late Modern Age*, Cambridge: Polity Press.

Hirsch, Fred (1976), *Social Limits to Growth*, Cambridge: Harvard University Press.

Hirschman, A.O. (1985), 'Against Parsimony: Three Easy Ways of Complicating Some Categories of Economic Discourse', *Economics and Philosophy*, vol. 1.

Hirschman, Elizabeth and Michael R. Solomon (1982), 'Competition and Cooperation among Culture Production Systems', in D. Hunt (ed.), *Marketing*, Chicago: American Marketing Association, pp. 269–72.

Houthakker, H.S. (1961), 'The Present State of Consumption Theory', *Econometrica*, **29** (October), 704–39.

Ireland, Norman J. (1992), 'On Limiting the Market for Status Signals', mimeo, University of Warwick.

James, J. (1983), *Consumer Choice in the Third World*. London: Macmillan.

James, J. (1987), 'Positional Goods, Conspicuous Consumption and the International Demonstration Effect Reconsidered', *World Development*, **15** (4), 449–62.

Jones, Stephen R.G. (1984), *The Economics of Conformism*, Oxford: Blackwell.

Kalman, Peter J. (1968), 'Theory of Consumer Behavior When Prices Enter the Utility Function', *Econometrica*, **36** (October), 497–510.

Leibenstein, Harvey (1950), 'Bandwagon, Snob and Veblen Effects in the Theory of Consumers' Demand', *Quarterly Journal of Economics*, **64** (May), 183–207.

Levy, Sidney J. (1981), 'Interpreting Consumer Mythology: A Structural Approach to Consumer Behavior', *Journal of Marketing*, **45** (Summer), 49–61.

Liebhafsky, H.H. (1980), 'Preferences as a Function of Prices and Money Income', Varta **1**, 5–6.

Mayer, Thomas (1966), 'The Propensity to Consume Permanent Income', *American Economic Review*, **56** (December), 1158–77.

McCall, G.J. and J.C. Simmons (1982), *Social Psychology: A Sociological Approach*, New York: The Free Press.

McCracken, Grant (1986), 'Culture and Consumption: A Theoretical Account of the Structure and Movement of the Cultural Meaning of Consumer Goods',

Journal of Consumer Research, **13** (June), 71–84.

Nurkse, R. (1953), *Problems of Capital Formation in Underdeveloped Countries,* New York: Basil Blackwell.

Patten, Simon N. (1893), 'Cost and Utility', *Annals of the American Academy of Political and Social Science III* (January), 409–28.

Phillips, R.J. and D.J. Slottje (1983), 'The Importance of Relative Prices in Analyzing Veblen Effects', *Journal of Economic Issues,* **17**, 197–206.

Pollak, Robert A. (1977), 'Price-Dependent Preferences', *American Economic Review,* **67** (March), 64–75.

Portes, A. (1973), 'Modernity and Development: A Critique', *Studies in Comparative International Development.*

Solomon, Michael R.and H. Assael (1987), 'The Forest or The Trees?: A Gestalt Approach to Symbolic Consumption', in J. Umiker-Sebeok (ed.), *Marketing and Semiotics: New Directions in the Study of Signs for Sale,* Berlin: Mouton de Gruyter, pp. 189–217.

Solomon, Michael R.and B.Buchanan (1991), 'A Role-Theoretic Approach to Product Symbolism: Mapping a Consumption Constellation', *Journal of Business Research,* **22**, 95–109.

Stigler, George J. and Gary S. Becker (1977), 'De Gustibus Non Est Disputandum', *American Economic Review,* **67** (March), 76–90.

Veblen, Thorstein (1899), The Theory of the Leisure Class, New York: Macmillan.

10 Perspective

In 1993, it was possible to claim that 'consumer theory within economics has remained essentially unchanged since the last century ... today's students of economics are still required to match relative marginal utilities to relative prices in a way that would be recognisable to the students of Alfred Marshall' (Fine and Leopold, 1993: 47).

The unchanging economics of demand theory owed much to traditional interpretations of consumer choice as rational sets of decisions which were optimal within any given set of economic (price and income) constraints. Consumers were still thought to make decisions independently of one another and to be concerned only with maximising a personal utility which was similarly independent of the views and actions of others. Given these central assumptions of economic behaviour, exploration of those forms of consumption which were socially motivated and which could therefore appear 'irrational' in purely economic terms, was remarkable largely by its absence from the literature. Not surprisingly, the economics of status-motivated consumption was an enduring casualty of this neglect.

While status consumption received little real attention at the theoretical level, market recognition and acceptance of such behaviour was not in question. Consumers themselves were in no doubt that consuming for status was universal, although it was always attributed to 'other people'. Similarly, business communities and government agencies clearly recognised status consumption as a market reality, and acted upon the opportunities it afforded them.

Manufacturers, retailers and their advertising agencies today commonly supply and promote goods and services to meet a continuing demand for social status and prestige. Such activity, often ignored or considered trivial by economists, can, in fact, represent a substantial part of a community's domestic and overseas trade. In 1989, for example, French manufacturers of luxury goods, bought in large part by status-seeking consumers, enjoyed a 47 per cent share of the market worldwide, their nearest competitors being Italy (14 per cent), Germany (13 per cent), the UK (12 per cent) and the US (9 per cent). The sales value was then estimated at US $52 billion annually, and of 14 identified market sectors, French products enjoyed a greater that 40 per cent market share in no less than eight.

The central importance of status-driven consumption to French business interests was recognised when, in 1954, the Groupement Colbert (named after Louis XIV's Finance Minister, and later (1957) to be renamed the Comité Colbert) was established to promote and protect the interests of

French luxury goods manufacturers. The Comité explicitly acknowledged that status-seeking consumer behaviour was a major determinant of sales. 'Clients of the luxury sector', they conceded, 'use it to express membership of a certain milieu'. At the same time, they also acknowledged that demand for status goods could be found at all levels of society and that 'it concerns the élitist facet that is in all of us'.

French business interests were not alone in realising that such a valuable market for their goods and services had to be properly managed, and the Comité Colbert was given privileged access to the French government. Between 1961 and 1976, they were invited by various government committees to contribute substantially to the fourth, fifth, sixth and seventh National Economic Plans and, by implication, to further the special interests of a key sector of the economy. The close links to government continue to this day.

Official recognition of status-driven consumption and of the special nature of the demand for status goods was evident elsewhere. In 1992, the UK Monopolies and Mergers Commission was asked to investigate the supply for retail sale of fine fragrances, defined as:

> premium-priced brands with selective distribution, expensive packaging and presentation, which are advertised and strongly promoted, and supplied by leading cosmetics and fragrance houses. The consumer appeal of these brands derives from both the characteristics of the perfume and the brand imagery (1993: 10).

This definition, in fact, explicitly recognised that consumer utility derived not only from tangible product quality in use but also from more intangible, socially-inspired perceptions of product worth. More significantly, however, the Commission was to conclude that, when consumers' purchase decisions involve products for which image, exclusivity and status are important, they are significantly influenced by their perceptions of what other consumers are buying:

> Two particular influences, in this respect, appear to be relevant to the assessment of the demand for fine fragrances. These are the' snob' effect and the 'conspicuous price' effect. For products where the snob effect is apparent a significant number of consumers may drop out of the market if price decreases lead to extra demand and, in their eyes, less exclusivity. Therefore demand responsiveness to price changes is more inelastic than it would otherwise be.

> For products where the conspicuous price effect is apparent, consumers attach at least as much importance to the product's price as to its inherent qualities. Buying the product demonstrates opulence and status, and the consumer derives psychological benefits from this conspicuous consumption. In analysing the

consequences of this it is possible to think of the product as having two prices, its real price (what the consumer actually pays for it) and its conspicuous price (what the consumer thinks other people think its price is). While actual demand is dependent on both the real and the conspicuous price, consumers attach considerable importance to the links between a product's image and its conspicuous price. In certain price ranges the demand curve may therefore be positively inclined, showing (for example) that in that price range a price cut will lead to a fall in demand rather than, as is usual, to an increase in demand (1993: 25).

The Commission's description of the nature of demand for fine fragrances mirrored the more general analysis of demand for status-linked products which had been proposed by Leibenstein in 1950. Indeed, much of Leibenstein's terminology was used, and the original paper had clearly been seen as an important point of reference. Subsequently, the Commission rejected the claims of certain UK retailers who were not members of the suppliers' authorised networks (and not therefore bound by any agreement to accept recommended resale prices), that the fine fragrance manufacturers were exercising unfair discrimination in refusing to supply them. In reaching this decision, they agreed with an earlier (1991) judgement of the European Communities Commission in favour of the French company Yves Saint Laurent Parfums, which had similarly upheld the argument that selective distribution and resale price maintenance were essential elements in securing the long-term interests of fine fragrances consumers. Most importantly, however, both Commissions had explicitly recognised the existence, importance and special circumstances of markets in which considerations of status and prestige dominate consumers' decisions to buy.

The existence of an economically significant market for status goods is perhaps best demonstrated by the thriving trade in counterfeit products which is now a worldwide phenomenon. The profitable counterfeiting of luxury goods offers particularly robust evidence of a demand for status on the part of many millions of consumers, for it highlights the distinction made by consumers between a product's tangible quality (measured in classical utilitarian terms and determined by product excellence in use) and its quite separate social and prestige value. Those who feel uneasy with concepts of status-driven consumption often assume that demand for luxury goods and services is, in fact, an expression of demand for products manufactured to the highest standards of design and performance. However, consumers of counterfeit products value only the prestige associated with a particular brand name, and are often fully aware that the goods they buy are, indeed, counterfeit and of low overall quality. Counterfeits, therefore, allow consumers to separate out the status and quality attributes of a luxury brand, and to then purchase only the status element by buying counterfeit goods of questionable quality, sold at a far lower price yet offering the status and prestige associated with the 'legitimate' high quality brands. As Grossman and Shapiro (1988) pointed out, 'the counterfeiting of a status good ... deceives not the individual who purchases the product, but rather the observer who sees the good being consumed and is duly (but mistakenly) impressed'.

The market for counterfeit products, therefore, exists to supply a worldwide demand for status expressed through the purchase and display of conspicuous goods and services whose total utility and value is measured in terms of perceived social acceptance and prestige. Further, the market now accounts for a growing fraction of world trade, and has gained a new importance in terms of commercial activity. In the 1980s, it was estimated that counterfeits accounted for approximately US $60 billion of world trade annually, and that a significant part of this business related to the demand for status goods (*Business Week*, 1985). Since then, counterfeiters and counterfeiting have become more organised, so much so that the trade has come to represent a major manufacturing activity in those countries which have been traditionally associated with the production and supply of counterfeit goods and services. As an example, it was calculated in 1995 that 'made in Italy' counterfeit designer goods enjoyed sales in Italy alone of L6000 billion (£2.2 billion), reinforcing the Comité Colbert's complaint made in 1992 that counterfeiting was so firmly rooted in Italy that it represented a 'parallel economy' providing jobs for 20,000 Italians, largely at the expense of French luxury goods manufacturers.

The social and economic consequences of product counterfeiting have now been widely recognised, and both legitimate business interests and government agencies are collaborating in attempts to coordinate policies intended to improve legal enforcement and to facilitate the confiscation of illegal items. For the purposes of this study, such activity and concern only serves to confirm that the purchase and consumption of status goods, whether real or counterfeit, represents a significant and growing element in international trade and should now feature equally significantly in modern treatments of economic theory and thought.

While both business and governments now routinely acknowledge status-motivated consumption as a significant element in overall economic activity, recognition has historically been most obvious in the area of taxation policy. As early as 1834, John Rae had argued that price increases caused by the imposition of a luxury tax on those goods which were, in reality, only being purchased to secure status and to display wealth, would have no negative effect on demand, and that these taxes were an ideal way of raising public revenues to nobody's disadvantage. John Stuart Mill had agreed, adding that, if, by some chance, demand for luxury products and services was discouraged by taxation, it could only do good by channelling expenditures into more wholesome and constructive consumption. Later, Pigou, in his *Economics of Welfare* (1920), suggested that a tax on goods which were desired 'to possess what other people do not possess' could only increase overall economic welfare. However, he did not develop this argument in his subsequent writings on excise taxes.

Given the unequal distribution of wealth and income in the later nineteenth and early twentieth centuries, discussions concerning the taxation of luxuries and 'superfluities' tended to focus on the need to rein in the excessive conspicuous consumption of the relatively few who were rich enough to indulge in ostentatious economic display. Such taxation was applauded by some for bearing mainly on an 'extravagant class of people' (McGoun, 1919), whose excesses were considered indefensible on moral and ethical grounds. At the same time, by associating such tax policies only with a small élite of very rich consumers, any tax yield would necessarily have been small in overall terms and the tax itself, however morally attractive it might appear, was, almost by definition, fiscally insignificant.

After 1950, as incomes increased, wealth redistribution gained momentum, and far greater levels of affluence were enjoyed by consumers generally, the merits and incidence of luxury taxes changed significantly. Given what was by now a universal interest in consuming for status, it was now argued, tax yields on status goods were potentially very substantial; and again, if the taxes only served to depress demand for such goods and services, tax yields would fall but the tax itself could be seen to have served a socially useful purpose by damping down wasteful expenditures which were now being made by far greater numbers of consumers at all social and economic levels.

By the 1970s, some taxation specialists within government were arguing that taxes on luxury products which could properly be described as status goods imposed no extra burden on consumers, and represented a highly desirable source of revenue (Miller, 1975). As price was an integral part of the utility of a status good, higher taxes, it was argued, added to rather than detracted from, a product's net worth. This was certainly seen to be true for those goods which were overwhelmingly bought as status symbols (Ng, 1987) but also held in the more common case of goods which derived only a part of their utility from their social status value.

The case for levying taxes on luxury goods was given added weight by the excessive levels of conspicuous consumption which were recorded in Europe, the Far East and America between 1985 and 1989. This, together with a growing concern over an increasing demand for status-linked positional goods generally, and the success achieved in the 1980s in developing a methodology to isolate and measure Veblen effects, made the case for appropriate taxes on consumption more compelling.

Arguments in favour of consumption taxation were not controversial in Europe, where such policies were well established. However, the United States had traditionally been hostile to taxes on consumption, seeing them as unnecessarily distortionary in demand terms: better to tax income, it had always been argued, than to attempt any 'management' of consumer choice. By the late 1980s, however, a few American economists were promoting a new perspective: if demand for status-linked positional goods was now so strong, then selective taxation of those products whose consumption clearly imposed negative external effects on others could only be beneficial:

> Taxing positional consumption goods instead of income would create greater private incentives to save, which would help eliminate the insufficiency in savings that arises out of other people's concerns about relative standing. Moreover, such things as clothing, condominiums and automobiles would become more costly, and such things as insurance and medical care would become less costly than they are now. A shift from income to consumption taxation would thus create incentives for people to spend less of their incomes on positional goods and more of their incomes on nonpositional goods. If concerns about position are as important to people as they appear to be, such a shift would improve the current allocation of resources (Frank, 1985: 249).

In advocating consumption taxation, Frank and others were implying that status-motivated consumers were sufficiently price-sensitive to shift resources away from expenditures on status goods and towards more utilitarian (and relatively less expensive) goods and services. This was controversial in that it assumed that concerns about relative standing could be effectively offset by price increases imposed through the tax system – a claim with which many behavioural scientists took issue. At the same time, given the high levels of ostentatious consumption which were then in evidence in the United States, consumption taxes were considered an attractive option whichever analysis was right. If concerns about relative standing were effectively resistant to increases in tax, then tax yields stood to increase substantially; conversely, if the effect of the tax was to reduce demand for status goods, then tax yields would fall pro rata, but the resulting redistribution of resources could be counted a positive benefit in overall social terms. In the event, American legislators were sufficiently persuaded of the merits of demand management in so far as status-linked consumption was concerned to introduce appropriate tax changes.

In the Omnibus Budget Reconciliation Act of 1990, a Luxury Excise Tax was introduced, with the intention of immediately increasing overall tax revenues whilst hopefully moderating excessive conspicuous expenditure in the medium term. A 10 per cent excise tax was introduced on sales of automobiles, boats, aircraft, jewellery and furs, where the retail price exceeded a given sum and the purchase could therefore (subjectively) be considered a luxury. The tax was to apply to all sales made before January 2000 but, in the event, was soon repealed with effect from January 1993.

Officially, the reason for repeal was that the industrial and commercial recession of the early 1990s had hit luxury goods manufacturers particularly hard, and the tax was, by 1993, considered to be an additional and unfair burden. In truth, it had produced other unwelcome, if predictable, side-effects which brought its integrity into question.

First, the tax on luxuries proved to be far from nondistortionary. Rather than increasing tax yields or damping down conspicuous consumption, consumers simply altered their spending patterns towards other recognised status-conferring goods and services to which the new tax did not apply. Consumers, in short, shifted expenditure within the status-driven consumption constellations identified by Solomon and others in the 1980s. The result was that sales of those items on which the tax was levied were disproportionately affected, and the resulting downturn in business was further worsened by the 1990–92 recession which severely reduced overall levels of consumer spending.

Those luxury goods manufacturers most affected by the tax responded in two ways to the new situation. Some volume producers, worried that excessive conspicuous consumption was in long-term decline, shifted design and production into more mainstream (that is, less expensive) product lines. Others stayed to fight for market share within the luxury goods sector by running promotional campaigns which offered to reimburse US customers the full amount of the tax, so guaranteeing that real post-transaction prices to consumers were unchanged while the tax-inclusive 'conspicuous price' remained impressively high in status terms.

The repeal of the luxury tax in 1993 suggested that, as a policy tool, such taxes had no enduring value and positively distorted patterns of demand and supply. The US experience, however, was far from conclusive, as the 1990–93 experiment failed for some reasons for which the tax itself could not be held to account. First, it was introduced at the worst possible point in the business cycle, at a time when the economy was entering a recession which itself was depressing the overall demand for luxury goods. Second, it was not applied widely enough across status-linked consumption constellations, so allowing consumers to be selective in their choice of conspicuous status goods, and to avoid the tax without foregoing consumption for social position and prestige. Had the tax been phased in with an upturn in the business cycle and been sufficiently comprehensive across constellations to make tax avoidance far more difficult, then the effects may have been significantly different. At the same time, others would argue that, whatever the reservations about timing and range, the tax did significantly change business attitudes and strategic planning, and was therefore unacceptably distortionary in market terms. Certainly, if luxury taxes on status goods are to be used as policy instruments in future, incidence and implementation will need to be key concerns if conspicuous consumption and the supply of status goods are to be influenced in nondistortionary ways.

The above examples serve to illustrate that, in market terms, consumer preoccupations with status and conspicuous consumption are now fully recognised; that these preoccupations are actively encouraged by consumer goods manufacturers anxious to promote their goods and services as status symbols to the widest possible audience; and that government is becoming increasingly concerned with the social and economic consequences of excessive demand for positional goods. At the same time, this recognition and activity has been paralleled by an almost total neglect of status consumption within economic theory and thought. As a consequence, a significant part of the economic activity of modern societies lacks any theoretical explanation, and the social, economic and policy implications remain largely unexplored.

It has already been noted that the emphasis on so-called rational decision making within economics has never encouraged exploration of consumer behaviour which can appear to be irrational and even perverse in purely economic terms. In more recent years, however, other changes in emphasis and direction within economics have further aggravated the situation.

A key factor which has militated against work into status consumption has been the intensive mathematisation of economic theory which has taken place over the last half century. The scale of the changes after 1945 were profound. Debreu (1991) has pointed out that, over the period, professional journals in the field of mathematical economics grew at an unsustainably rapid rate, with the index of publications doubling every nine years between 1944 and 1977. At the same time, status and prestige within the economics profession was transferred to mathematical economists and to those faculties which could demonstrate excellence in econometrics and mathematical analysis. Election as Fellow of the Econometric Society (ES) was of particular significance in the United States, and by 1990:

Of the 152 members of the economics section of the American Academy of Arts and Sciences, 87 are Fellows of the Econometric Society; and of the 40 members of the economics section of the National Academy of Sciences of the United States, 34 are ES Fellows. From 1969 to 1990, 30 economics Nobel Awards were made and 25 of the laureates are, or were, ES Fellows. Since it was first presented to Paul Samuelson in 1947, the John Bates Clark medal of the American Economic Association has been given to 21 economists of whom 20 are ES Fellows (1991: 1 – 2).

The shift towards mathematical economics in America was mirrored in Europe and elsewhere, and created an academic environment which, by common consent, produced much excellent work within the discipline. At the same time, the climate was less than conducive to research into those elements of economic activity which are heavily 'behavioural' in nature and which do not lend themselves to precise mathematical calculation and measurement. This bias against mathematical uncertainty undoubtedly worked against those who had interests in areas of consumer theory which were, by definition, grounded in the sociology and psychology of consumption and of consumer preference formation. At the same time, it often persuaded those who persevered that they had to attempt a mathematical modelling of such behaviour which was then often achieved at the cost of much market reality:

> Mathematics provides him [the economist] with a language and a method that permit an effective study of economic systems of forbidding complexity; but it is a demanding master. It ceaselessly asks for weaker assumptions, for stronger conclusions, for greater generality. In taking a mathematical form, economic theory is driven to submit to those demands (Debreu, 1991: 4).

There can be no doubt that the emphasis on mathematical economics and econometrics has, at the least, marginalised research into the causes and effects of consumption for status and display. However, in a less mathematical world, economics would still have found it difficult to respond to those patterns of consumer demand which, to economists at least, often seem to defy rational calculation. Certainly, sociologists and psychologists have been far happier to explore those forms of consumption where social considerations are to the fore, and have made a significantly greater contribution to our understanding of twentieth century material culture and its consequences. Ideally, economics needs to find a better accommodation with the other behavioural and social sciences if the economic dimensions of status consumption are not to be marginalised.

Pleas for a wider interpretation of economic motives and activity are not new, but have for the most part gone unheeded. Given the economic tradition, this is not, perhaps, surprising. Certainly, it is possible and defensible to argue that ambitions for any unified, fully integrated theory of consumer behaviour – embracing, inter alia, anthropology, sociology, psychology and economics – are not realistic; that the sum of the separate parts would not and could not make up a whole that would be of greater value than single-discipline explanations. Yet economists, in particular, have been singularly resistant even to proposals that such interdisciplinary approaches should be more formally explored.

This resistance within economics extends not only to appeals to work towards a fully integrated consumer theory, but to increased collaboration between economics and any other discipline. A review of the relationship between economics and psychology in the *Economic Journal* pointed to the differences in methodologies adopted by mainstream economists and psychologists as a significant yet understandable perceived deterrent to collaboration (Earl, 1990). More ominously, perhaps, mathematical economists have tended to see appeals to integrate psychology into their work as threatening rather than providing both new opportunities and the possibility of achieving greater insights into consumer behaviour through the use of alternative forms of mathematics. Given these reservations, future prospects for collaborative research seem to be severely restricted:

It ... seems likely that many economists will use various dissonance reduction strategies to distance themselves from the very idea of interdisciplinary research. These strategies may include appeals to the philosophy of positivism and parsimony in the construction of models, that downplay the need to understand underlying processes; or they may include attempts to define as 'outside the realm of economics' any phenomena ... that conflict with conventional axioms (Earl, 1990: 751).

These observations on the barriers to greater cooperation between economics and psychology could be applied verbatim and with equal relevance to proposals that economists collaborate more actively with sociologists, anthropologists, philosophers, or with more vocationally-minded management scientists, all of whom have legitimate and continuing interests in consumption and consumer preference formation. However, the need for some greater accommodation on the part of economics is now more urgent. In its own interests, a new, broader agenda for consumer research needs to be agreed in order to properly identify the economic fundamentals of socially-inspired, status-driven consumption, and to then move to policy issues with a greater understanding of cause and effect.

As has been shown, calls for such an agenda are not new and have not been confined to those outside economics. Within the discipline, the need for a wider, more inclusive approach to consumption has been continuously promoted throughout the twentieth century by small groups of economists often regarded in their day as 'maverick' by their mainstream colleagues. Their campaigns have met with little success: the social psychology of consumption remains 'relegated to the sidelines as a subdiscipline that is called on infrequently to handle anomalies' (Earl, 1990). While this remains the case, economics, in fact, is choosing to characterise a substantial worldwide demand for status-conferring consumer goods and services as an 'anomaly' lying outside its core interests. And as demand for such products continues to grow, economic theory will succeed, paradoxically, in marginalising itself by seeing such activity as relatively trivial and inconsequential. Economists will need to respond positively to the ongoing appeals for more inclusive, interdisciplinary research into consumption if they are to make an informed contribution to interpretations of modern-day consumer demand. Only then will status-motivated consumption, in turn, be properly regarded as an important component part of today's complex economic systems.

References

Comité Colbert (1992), *Rapport d'Activités Perspectives 1991–2.*

Debreu, Gerard (1991), 'The Mathematization of Economic Theory', *American Economic Review,* **81** (March), 1–7.

Earl, Peter E. (1990), 'Economics and Psychology: A Survey', *Economic Journal,* **100** (September), 718–55.

European Communities Commission (1991), *The EC Commission Decision on Yves Saint Laurent Parfums,* 16 December, 1991, 92/33/EEC.

Fine, Ben and Ellen Leopold (1993), *The World of Consumption,* London: Routledge.

Frank, Robert H. (1985), *Choosing the Right Pond: Human Behavior and the Quest for Status,* New York: Oxford University Press.

Grossman, G.M. and C. Shapiro (1988), 'Foreign Counterfeiting of Status Goods', *Quarterly Journal of Economics,* **102** (February), 79–100.

Leibenstein, Harvey (1950), 'Bandwagon, Snob and Veblen Effects in the Theory of Consumer's Demand', *Quarterly Journal of Economics,* **64** (May), 183–207.

McGoun, A.F. (1919), 'The Taxation of Luxuries and the Rate of Interest', *Quarterly Journal of Economics,* **33** (February), 298–320.

Miller, Edward (1975), 'Status Goods and Luxury Taxes', *American Journal of Economics and Sociology,* **34** (April), 141–54.

Monopolies and Mergers Commission (1993), *Fine Fragrances: A report on the supply in the UK for retail sales of fine fragrances,* Cm 2380, London: HMSO.

Ng, Yew- Kwang (1987), 'Diamonds are a Government's Best Friend: Burden-free Taxes on Goods Valued for their Values', *American Economic Review,* **77** (March), 186–91.

Pigou, A.C. (1920), *The Economics of Welfare,* London: Macmillan.

Rae, John (1834), *Statement of Some New Principles on the Subject of Political Economy, Exposing the Fallacies of the System of Free Trade and of Some Other Doctrines maintained in the 'Wealth of Nations',* Boston: Hilliard, Gray and Co.

Index